The Last Empires

William Allan
The Last Empires
Governing Ourselves, Our Nations, and Our World

William Allan
Melbourne, VIC
Australia

ISBN 978-3-030-10839-7   ISBN 978-3-319-59960-1   (eBook)
https://doi.org/10.1007/978-3-319-59960-1

Library of Congress Control Number: 2017949536

© The Editor(s) (if applicable) and The Author(s) 2017
This work is subject to copyright. All rights are solely and exclusively licensed by the Publisher, whether the whole or part of the material is concerned, specifically the rights of translation, reprinting, reuse of illustrations, recitation, broadcasting, reproduction on microfilms or in any other physical way, and transmission or information storage and retrieval, electronic adaptation, computer software, or by similar or dissimilar methodology now known or hereafter developed.
The use of general descriptive names, registered names, trademarks, service marks, etc. in this publication does not imply, even in the absence of a specific statement, that such names are exempt from the relevant protective laws and regulations and therefore free for general use.
The publisher, the authors and the editors are safe to assume that the advice and information in this book are believed to be true and accurate at the date of publication. Neither the publisher nor the authors or the editors give a warranty, express or implied, with respect to the material contained herein or for any errors or omissions that may have been made. The publisher remains neutral with regard to jurisdictional claims in published maps and institutional affiliations.

Cover illustration: Daniren / Alamy Stock Photo

Printed on acid-free paper

This Palgrave Macmillan imprint is published by Springer Nature
The registered company is Springer International Publishing AG
The registered company address is: Gewerbestrasse 11, 6330 Cham, Switzerland

To Sally, Georgia, and Kieran

Preface

This book was, in part, born of roughly 40-plus years' experience working on public financial management (PFM) technical assistance, aimed at strengthening government policy and decision-making in a wide range of countries. Starting with seven years in Papua New Guinea from 1972, I went on to work in several other countries in the Pacific, Africa, the Middle East and the Caribbean. Then, in Washington, DC, I continued with the Fiscal Affairs Department of the IMF, in a broader range of countries, including a number emerging from Soviet rule, and latterly in consultancies with the World Bank. The experience has been enlightening and rewarding, confirming the sense that people throughout the world, even in radically different cultures, have quite similar broad hopes and concerns for their governance and development. Ultimately though, the picture I have come away with has been deeply disappointing: governments, particularly in the less developed world, have failed—and continue to fail—nationally and globally to meet standards of equitable development and to ensure social stability. Governance in developing countries as well as development potential in them continues to be damaged in many ways by the encounters these nations have with advanced civilizations and their conflicts. But, even advanced industrialized countries now seem to be failing to cope adequately with the governance pressures emerging in the twenty-first century.

Personal reactions to the current situation, however closely held, must of course consider the broader experience of society. For many in the post-WW2 generations, the dominant themes of societal development in the previous century were those of rapid economic expansion and growing social support. But the century was also scarred by economic depression, violent ideological rivalry and brutal, massively destructive warfare. The Industrial Revolution of the eighteenth to the nineteenth centuries and the emergence of cheap energy created huge commercial and industrial wealth in the nineteenth and twentieth centuries, but it also saw parallel growth of European fiscal military states and the two World Wars. Mid-century saw the defeat of Nazism, the late 1980s the fall of Soviet communism. The so-called Washington Consensus on global macroeconomic management and of neoliberal, market-fundamentalist management of government that emerged in the West after the Cold War seemed to auger well for future world prosperity and cooperative responses to periodic crises.

That promise was not to last. The fall of the Soviet Union was briefly celebrated, triumphally as 'the end of history' by Francis Fukuyama in 1992; up to 2007 market forces, aside from demonstrating superior production and armaments potential, appeared to be providing the kind and pace of development that could raise living standards in all nations. The rapid transformation of China seemed also to bear out the power of markets (albeit controlled), but it posed a new threat of potential hegemonic conflict. The global financial crisis (GFC) of 2008 and its continuing aftermath, together with faltering European unity, continuing conflict in the Middle East, and failure of global management of the environment and natural resources, forced a fundamental rethink of many of these early conclusions.

Society's problems go well beyond economics or any other social theory's power of explanation. Economics more than rival social disciplines has vigorously peddled its capacity for 'scientific modelling' of economic reality, with some implication that economic growth provided a pathway to more general social well-being. Many prominent economists continue to contribute important ideas on causes and potential ways to revive global economic growth and stability, and indeed to contribute to greater equality. But, the profession's general reputation has been diminished by its general failure either to predict the GFC or to agree on management of recovery from it. Political decisions and public support for these decisions now seem to be driven more by populism and ideological belief than by considered professional and democratic debate. Quality policy debate continues in some sectors of the old and new media, but ideology continues to play a strong role in much of the traditional media; in the social media, volume seems to matter more than content.

Economics still of course plays an important role in addressing our current policy dilemmas, and national and global economic stability and growth remain as central aims of society. However, economics itself has some well-known weaknesses, and much more attention must be paid to these. First, the more practical strands of the profession—PFM, accounting and government finance statistics—must be strengthened. Good economic theory depends critically on accurate definition and measurement of society's main variables and targets as well as genuine accountability for achieving those targets. For too long, economic value has been measured primarily in commercial terms, and the value of government and it processes in producing social goods have lain outside the social worth equation, measured only at cost. Second, economics itself cannot define properly all aspects of social development; other socially oriented disciplines including political science, history, sociology, anthropology and neuroscience are now recognized as providing vital insights into important aspects of social and commercial relationships. The way we measure social worth must be strengthened to look beyond both commerce and narrowly focused economics.

Social science, and indeed economics, is moving in this direction. Critical weaknesses in traditional socio-economic theory are now generally acknowledged. These include: (i) structural weaknesses in economic equilibrium theory, including the need to reflect realistic behavioural assumptions; (ii) the importance of institutions (the 'rules of the game'); (iii) that GDP is neither the best measure of social welfare nor necessarily a sufficiently reliable basis for testing hypotheses of social causality; and (iv) that social policies must give greater recognition to the importance of tackling economic and social inequality. Behavioural science has become increasingly important; its evidence suggests that the 'rational economic man underlying economic theory' assumption needs to be reconsidered. Daniel Kahneman, Aaron Tversky and others have shown that 'fast thinking'—the use of rules of thumb over informed deliberative discourse—tends to dominate many individual and social decisions but often leads to faulty judgements.

Social media, public polling and plebiscites on major political issues, moreover, seem to be magnifying rather than tempering this tendency. Political developments like the election of Donald Trump to the US presidency and the UK's vote to leave the European Union raise major questions both about emerging fragmentation in national and global society and the validity of long-accepted processes in modern liberal democracies. Trends in globalization of economic activity, urbanization and increasing inequality among social groupings are posing new challenges that our legacy institutions are not well equipped to handle.

Social discourse, if it is to be constructive, cannot continue to rely on limited models of social transactions; all forces, established or emergent, that bear on political decisions—and society's consideration and acceptance of these decisions—should be subject to deep analytical and political review, and these deliberations should be communicated clearly to the public. The complexity of these processes and full engagement with all of society's issues are massive challenges, but they ones which can no longer be avoided.

Much of my analysis of the current basis of social policy formulation is based significantly on the work of the French intellectual and philosopher Michel Foucault, who died in 1984, just at the beginning of Reagan/Thatcher neoliberal-inspired political ascendancy in Western countries. Many changes have occurred in our understanding of social and political relations since then, but Foucault's work on the scientificity of social investigation and the epistemic mechanisms that determine social 'truth' remain landmark insights that should be more firmly embodied in modern social theory and political thinking. While these views have had little currency in practical economics or social policy over the last 30 or so years, their relevance to our rapidly changing modern world is becoming increasingly apparent.

Foucault aimed to explain how government of self and society must balance the basic social forces of state sovereignty, government surveillance and control of its institutions, and opportunities for free expression by individuals to state power. He traced the changing balance of these mechanisms through history: sovereignty's journey from the tyranny of antiquity to Greek city-states, through Roman and post-Roman rule, to modern sovereignty of the middle class; surveillance and control from its initial formalization in Bentham's eighteenth century panopticon design for prison surveillance to application of panoptic principles in modern institutions; and ordinary citizens' link to power, as articulated in the Athenian notion of *parrhesia*, which described the right, standing and courage of a free citizen to speak to power.

Latterly, Foucault used the term 'biopolitics' to capture the nature of interaction among these basic social forces. In the 1978–79 lecture series *The Birth of Biopolitics*, where he introduced that term into his work, he deliberated as to whether neoliberal economics, particularly as advocated by Gary Becker, may offer a mechanism to replace traditional sovereignty and guide society towards its goal of self-government. At the end of those lectures, however, he concluded quite strongly that what we now define as neoliberal economics could not by itself offer such a mechanism. The overall body of his work provides a rich though complex analysis of the way biopolitical forces have operated over the millennia and given rise to social change and competing ideological claims. While drawn initially to the application of the 'scientific' methodology of the phenomenologists to social philosophy and science, he found the approach inadequate to explain the evolution of social governance. His work remained incomplete, but his rejection of structuralist, quasi-scientific modelling of social development bears directly on the current crisis of validation in social disciplines; all dimensions, scientific, social, ethical and political, must be given due weight in recognizing social truth.

A central message from Foucault's work is that social change results from the people's assent to well-reasoned public policy; its truthfulness must be judged on the merits of the policies and forces that led to such change. Lack of challengeable and challenged reasoning, or public assent based on spurious reasoning, are fundamental failures of governance. When failure occurs at potentially catastrophic levels, recovery is both extremely difficult and highly uncertain. The fundamental Nietzschean/Foucauldian proposition is that a broad society *can* rise to these challenges and establish a will to social knowledge and power. We appear, however, once again to face the possibility of catastrophic failure in critical areas of our miraculous heritage of knowledge of the physical world and ourselves. Can we face these challenges? This book does not attempt to predict that outcome, but it offers a range of suggestions on how we can improve both our measurement of outcomes and rewrite our inherited rules to increase the chances of balanced social discourse and hence human progress to the next stage of societal development. I apply both Foucauldian theory and modern social science thinking to these questions and propose a way of thinking in a collective environment to work towards global prosperity and harmonious development. The introductory section that follows briefly describes the book's structure and major themes.

Notes

1. The time spent in PNG was a formative experience. I was part of a very solid effort by the Australian Government then administering the Territory of Papua and New Guinea (which became Papua New Guinea (PNG) in 1972 with its own Assembly under then Chief Minister Michael Somare) through its transition first to self-government (1973) and then to independence in 1975. The key initiative during that time was to establish a disciplined planning and budgeting system (termed the National Public Expenditure Plan) that required a clear macroeconomic perspective on expenditure, revenue and borrowing trends and disciplined, cabinet-controlled setting of priorities for expenditure. It worked reasonably well but was dependent on Australian budget support. However, a few years after PNG gained its independence, Australia switched to a system of project support that relied on donor oversight rather than national government discipline. A consequence of the change was that PNG no longer had responsibility for results accountability, and national oversight and control of its budget and accounting system was greatly diminished. It

became accountable to donor governments. International and bilateral agencies have continued to follow this pattern, and it has only been questioned as a basis for reform under the Paris Declaration for Aid Effectiveness (discussed later). The original PNG model seemed appropriate for its circumstances and for forging an accountable government, and much of the subsequent developments in PNG I believe are attributable to the poor fostering of national accountability for budgeting and fiscal policy. An account of that early experience was given in Allan and Hinchliffe (1982).
2. The term *neoliberal* is used frequently throughout. Like most ideological descriptions, it covers a range of views that have changed over time, but like all ideologies, presents an explanation of social development that can be used to direct a group, a nation or all of society towards objectives shared by a powerful group—or one aspiring to power. The fundamental ideas of neoliberalism (often associated with the work of Friedrich von Hayek and with the Mont Pelerin Society as discussed in Chap. 1) are that free markets, guided minimally by government, will lead to prosperity for all; and the alternative, state planning, will lead to totalitarian state control and inefficiency. These ideas have taken strong root mainly in the United States (where the term is little used because 'liberal' has become associated with socialism); there and elsewhere 'neoliberalism' is particularly associated with low-tax, small government reforms implemented by Thatcher in the UK, and, at least rhetorically, in the US under Reagan, and then, as described in Chap. 3, taken up most vigorously by the Bush–Cheney administration and the Greenspan Federal Reserve.
3. Foucault himself rejected much of the labelling of contemporary philosophical schools as 'structuralist', 'post-modern', etc. (See Schrift [2006] and Foucault/Rabinow [1997b], Vol. 2, pp. 433–458. My use of the term 'structural' throughout is more general: I apply it to all approaches that apply simple modelling of social disciplines along the lines of the physical sciences. Such approaches are not of themselves invalid, but their potential for erroneous interpretation with regard to social and political action is magnified by their limited vision. I believe this interpretation is consistent with Foucault's own description of the evolution of his approach in response to philosophy's move towards 'objectification' of the 'subject', or humankind investigating its own realities (see Foucault/Rabinow 1997b, Vol. 2, *Foucault*, pp. 459–463).

References

Allan, William, and Keith Hinchliffe. 1982. *Planning, Policy Analysis, and Public Spending: Theory and the Papua New Guinea Practice*. Aldershot: Gower.

Schrift, Alan D. 2006. *Twentieth Century French Philosophy: Key Themes and Thinkers*. Blackwell Publishing.

Introduction and Outline of the Approach

The book is organized into three parts. Part I, in two chapters, first reviews key elements of Foucault's wide-ranging work and its links to and importance for modern social and economic theory. Second, it applies a broadly Foucauldian perspective to review the major shifts in global power and resulting government and social development from the late nineteenth century to the present. This section both sets the broad analytical framework and presents the main challenges we face in this and coming centuries.

Part II describes key practical areas of governance that must be tackled individually, nationally and globally in the immediate future if society is to succeed in eventually governing the world with some assurance of reasonable prosperity and security for all. The section has four chapters covering the following topics: (i) Re-establishing global macro-economic management and social accountability; (ii) measuring social well-being more accurately and fairly in relation to all forms of capital used by enterprise and government—covering environmental and human capital as well as traditional forms of financial capital; (iii) tackling the issues of growing inequality both within countries and between the industrialized and developing economies; and (iv) managing the environment and specifically and urgently tackling global warming nationally and globally.

Part III, in two concluding chapters, looks first at the institutional framework—or the rules of the game—that ultimately determine the possibility of major governance reforms being undertaken successfully. The final chapter completes the circle by bringing all the proposals back to the Foucauldian/ Nietzschean question of whether society can acquire the will to power and knowledge to address them. It proposes a broad sociophilosophical model as a template to test progress in this direction.

Part I

Chapter 1 outlines Foucault's interpretation of the way in which philosophy and the emergence of scientific and political ideas has contributed to the evolution of government practice. He developed an analytical historical overview of the way in which power and ideas interact to establish social institutions, particularly focusing on the 'classical' period of the seventeenth and eighteenth centuries, when, he argued, recognition of major discontinuities began to replace the then-prevalent view of a continuing linear growth of knowledge. He linked his and our personal and tribal predicaments to the biological factors that shape them, arguing along Nietzschean lines that we should create the will and the mechanisms of social discourse that would allow us to govern ourselves and others. The chapter briefly describes the main elements of his methodology: (i) an 'archaeological' review of social disciplines, and (ii) 'genealogical' analyses of interactions among disciplines. Both are set within the social power and disciplinary framework of the period being analyzed.

Foucault's archaeology defined truth not simply in terms of the growth of ideas and their verification: truth must engage with power and across social disciplines, and 'truth' in this sense is a social construct. He preferred the term *veridiction* to describe the process of social acceptance and defined the emergence of social truth in terms of *epistemes*, units of social knowledge that emerged in successive eras. An episteme, however, was but a stage on the way to truth. His genealogical studies concluded that interaction between separately rational disciplines in an epistemic period often led to socially negative results. While for a time he considered that neoliberal economic theory may offer a rational framework for linking power to ideas and balancing individual aims and social goals, he ultimately rejected that idea as inadequate. Modern developments in social theory and practice are beginning to show the possibilities of an approach to social decision-making that meets some of Foucault's requirements. These are considered in Parts II and III.

Chapter 2, applying this perspective, begins by outlining the major shifts in power and prosperity that occurred over the past two millennia as measured by economic and military dominance. It stresses the complementarity of commercial and fiscal growth with military power. This cohesion eventually led in Foucault's 'classical' period to strong competitive fiscal military states in Europe that fed hegemonic and ideological competition. These developments in turn led to hubristic imperial expansion, colonization of marginal states, two World Wars and the Cold War.

Many of the imbalances we now face, the chapter argues, are a result of biopolitical imbalances that emerged in the twentieth century. The politics and power shifts of the time failed either to balance national sovereignty and global interests or to address the self-governance needs of colonial and other territories marginalized by European conflict. The consequences of these failures need to be faced soon, and the chapter identifies major areas where reform appears most urgent. Possible pathways to reform key areas are considered in detail in the four chapters of Part II.

Part II

At the beginning of the section, Chap. 3 focuses on the shift in the last part of the twentieth century towards neoliberal (or, as characterized by Kaletsky, 'market fundamentalism') ideology as the dominant political belief in Western economies, led by the United States. Neoliberalism was seen by many prominent economists as a logical development of economic theory. To be sure, it appears positive and more benign than ideologies of past centuries, most obviously last century's Nazism and Lenin–Stalinist communism. The defeat of Nazism and Stalinism by the combined productive and military capacity of liberal market economies provided persuasive evidence of the power of free market organization in democracies. In recent times, however, the argument of fundamental market superiority has been applied relentlessly to the very different post-WW2 context of the expansion of the welfare state in many Western countries.

Few, even in formerly state-planned economies, now doubt the importance of markets, and there are many genuine concerns with the nature and efficiency of much government intervention. The chapter argues, however, that neoliberal calls for small government as a secular need and fiscal austerity as the primary response to instability resulting from the GFC are simply not justified by economic theory or practice. Many of the factors ordering our present global responses have little to do with economic theory differences and much more to do with the way economics has interacted with politics, the press and public opinion. Moreover, many major weaknesses arise from the dominance of market values and private influences in government decisions. A better government rather than a smaller government is necessary to address these issues properly.

The chapter reviews the biopolitical forces that have interacted to create our present ideological and policy impasse. It discusses in turn: the politicization of popularized economic theory; development of a coalition of powerful elements of the traditional media and neoliberal and neoconservative politicians; and political and economic hubris in the so-called platinum age from 1986 to the great crash of 2008. Because of these factors, the role of economists and government policy specialists was greatly diminished while neoliberal political power massively increased in the build-up to the 2008 crash. Weaknesses in economic and social theory are being recognized, but the shift towards more direct political control and the declaration that reducing the size of government is a self-justifying goal negate efforts to improve government efficiency and effectiveness. The latter question raises the issue of the way in which our present system of valuing production treats government outputs and outcomes relative to those of commercial enterprise. Chapter 4 takes up these points and those of valuing the external benefits and costs that arise from commercial activity.

Gross domestic product (GDP) emerged in the twentieth century as the primary measure of an economy's well-being; it now dominates discussion of global progress and the relative strength of nations, regions and sub-regions; yet, its faults are widely recognized. Chapter 4 characterizes as both inaccurate and unfair GDP's exclusion of non-commercial dimensions of well-being. While the need for reform of GDP measurement is well established, actions to this end have so far been partial and inadequate; reform of such a basic and powerful measure of economic and social activity will necessarily be a very long-term process. However, some basic principles of accounting are being established that go beyond the use of traditional forms of financial accounting and reporting. The concept of *integrated reporting*, denoted throughout the book as <IR>, introduced recently by the International Integrated Reporting Council (IIRC), is based on the perception that all entities—government and private—have responsibilities for managing all forms of capital that enter their value creation (or diminution) processes. Environmental and human capital in particular, the IIRC argues, are key forms of capital that should be integrated into the business processes, accounting and reporting of all entities. This concept has far-reaching implications for reform of government and enterprise activity, particularly in relation to transparency and risk management practices. Already, as described in Chap. 4, an accounting revolution is underway in government: <IR> is a critically important new element that in the long run should transform the estimation of GDP and its incorporation into national and global policies on social development. The chapter outlines a phased program of accounting and analytical reporting that should help unify and strengthen the many strands of PFM reform now underway.

Chapter 5 addresses a second major weakness of traditional economic policy, but particularly of neoliberal influenced economics: the continuing neglect of questions of equitable economic distribution. These issues have by no means been neglected in the literature, with distinguished contributions from John Rawls and Amartya Sen, as well as Jürgen Habermas, Joseph Stiglitz, Paul Krugman and Thomas Piketty. The chapter argues that equality measures within and between countries should be given as much prominence as GDP growth rates, annual and medium-term budget presentations and global reviews by international organizations. While many agree with the necessity of addressing global and national inequality, major institutional reforms will be necessary to move forward on this goal. These institutional questions are taken up again in Chap. 7.

The second part of Chap. 5 focuses particularly on inequality among nations and the plight of deeply underprivileged countries, the effectiveness of aid, and the role of governance in ensuring sustainable improvements to government of developing countries. It argues that failure of development aid arises from too much attention being paid to universal (but underfunded and highly bureaucratic) technocratic solutions to social and economic problems, too little to establishing appropriate government institutions and governance rules at each level of government in each country. The driving aim of aid for less developed countries and regions should be to enable sustainable solutions to be developed as an integral responsibility of government at each level. Sustainable development administration depends on good government at national and local levels to ensure that available technology is applied effectively and sustainably, not on donor-led support for externally identified priorities. Continuing UN-led external technical intervention remains important, but it has had limited success, not because it is not concerned with improving development outcomes but because it has focused too little on ensuring that governments are committed to sustainable solutions for their own people. Implementation of modern technology combined with application of international standards of PFM practice (embodying modern accounting standards and practices, as advocated in Chap. 4) can do much to strengthen governance in developing and emerging market countries, and this includes better management of their natural resources.

Chapter 6 tackles the issue of global warming and the formidable political difficulties that continue to be experienced in establishing an effective global program to reduce greenhouse gas emissions. Climate science has established greenhouse gases (GHGs) and the greenhouse mechanism of global warming as the best explanation for potentially catastrophic rising global temperatures due to human activity. But national and global governance of this enormous challenge, its objective measurement, and any discussion of the potentially catastrophic effects on the environment and vulnerable peoples come up against tough political resistance driven by powerful interests vested in the fossil fuel industry. The chapter reviews experience over the past two decades both globally and nationally: Australia—and now the United States[1]—provides a case example of the way in which intensely fought political factors can derail carefully designed and publicly supported climate action programs.

Guided by the United Nations, a massive effort has been made to establish a policy framework aiming to avoid the potentially catastrophic consequences of continuing present levels of greenhouse gas emissions. These efforts illustrate the complexities of political action to address global collective action issues, but they also demonstrate the worth, indeed the necessity, of the United Nations. Because of the work at the UN and by many scientific and environmental activist groups, support for a globally organized effort to meet an existential world threat was strongly confirmed at the Paris Agreement in 2015. However, high risks remain: firm national action by influential countries based on science and acceptance of responsibility for environmental and climate change impact by all government and corporate entities will be necessary to ensure that the Paris commitments are not only fulfilled but exceeded.

Part III

In the book's final part, Chapter 7 examines the fundamental role that institutions, or 'rules of the game', play in determining the possibilities of social reform along the lines suggested in Chaps. 3, 4, 5 and 6. The way individuals and groups act in practice within these rules is a critically important sub-theme. How are these rules set, how can they be changed and by whom, and how do they work in practice? Many of the advocated institutional requirements for successful development of nations, such as pluralism, ensuring property rights, establishing state monopoly over violence and unbiased observance of the 'rule of law', are highly general. Institutionalist theorists, it is argued, need both to define the present rules and proposals more clearly and to integrate work in various fields to define the tasks of institutional and behavioural theory. Overall, much more research is needed on the dimensions of the current rules and on the processes of reviewing these rules over time.

The institution of democracy itself requires a deeper understanding and strengthening; indeed, the term 'democracy' no longer appears a sufficient description of a governance ideal. Our democratic institutions remain imperfect and themselves need to become more open to questioning and change. Democratic constitutions that have served well in the past cannot guarantee that the rules set, more than two centuries ago in the case of the US, will remain relevant to the national and global challenges of the future. The chapter covers a wide range of work that collectively is beginning to address these problems. John Keane has provided a better understanding of the evolution of democracy; he also points to major failings and pitfalls arising from its present form. Michael Coppedge and many others are undertaking a range of studies to define and measure different conceptions of democracy. These measures provide a better perspective on the nature of democratic progress and can be linked to continuing work on strengthening accountability and transparency across all types of governance regime.

Behavioural science is also playing an increasingly important role in shaping public policy in a way that is informed by empirical study rather than broad assumptions of rationality and the power of self-interest. The work of Daniel Kahneman, Aron Kversky and other neuroscientists, for instance, suggests the need to rethink the role of rational *homo economicus* as the normative standard for economic policy-making; actual individuals and social institutions tend to operate by rule of thumb (fast thinking), and their decisions are frequently at odds with those predicted by economic theory based on decision-makers' assumed careful weighing of lifetime costs and benefits (or slow thinking). More work on the dynamics of public opinion is also suggested; the contribution of John R. Zaller provides some valuable insights. These findings are congruent with a broader Foucauldian approach to social science; they also have important philosophical and social science implications, taken up in the final chapter of the book.

Achieving more coherence among social science disciplines and multilateral approaches to global governance will require fundamental change both within national borders and between nations, but such change cannot be imposed: in these modern—dangerous—times, we need to move away from the idea that a single nation can or should aim to establish a lasting imperium. The UN, however imperfect, represents the most significant existing framework for nation-states to address global issues and agree on action that benefits the global community. It has been judged harshly so far, partly because of the difficulty of establishing a well-functioning international bureaucracy without authoritative political accountability. But the United Nations functions as a forum, not as a form of world government. Under these conditions, its achievements in establishing basic cosmopolitan values in the areas of human rights, treatment of refugees, the elements of international law and multilateral progress on global issues such as climate change and tackling extreme poverty and socio-economic underdevelopment are very impressive.

The world is not yet able to govern itself politically, and there should be no rush to move in this direction; hegemonic dominance does not provide a realistic long-term solution. All nations, including those with hegemonic ambitions, should understand the great significance of the UN institution and seek ways to finance its activities and create a solid accountability framework, particularly in the fields of global security, protection of civilians and support of improved governance in developing countries. The accounting and PFM revolution that is now underway, combined with a recognition that all nations—particularly the more powerful—must accept sovereign responsibility for their impact on global well-being, should foster an advancement towards this goal

Chapter 8 concludes the book by drawing together Foucauldian insights and emerging social theory to give an overview of the philosophical and social policy implications of the governance challenge that we face as individuals, national citizens and members of the global community. The way in which we understand ourselves and our place in the cosmos has changed and will change further. The philosopher and quantum physicist David Deutsch, in *The Beginning of Infinity*, has emphasized how much more we need to know and advocates the Popperian methodology of 'conjecture and refutation' as a basic way of continuing to expand our knowledge in all fields, not just in the physical sciences. Karl Popper was a major influence on economic thinking and embedding scientific method into economic theorizing, but the way we apply the criteria of the physical sciences to investigation of our own being and the nature of social truth should not be confused with the methodology applied to investigating the external physical universe. Foucault argues that only by understanding its own evolving nature through a process of 'veridiction' can society change itself, doing so through self-aware biopolitical discourse. Social truth is not just a matter of understanding the physical evolution of our sentience, salience and sapience; it requires a coming to terms with our biological being and the ethical dimensions of social relations and development.

Deutsch and Popper are undoubtedly right in constantly seeking better explanations of phenomena through rigorous evidence-based testing of propositions and always admitting doubt and possible refutation of theories. But the physical and biological sciences themselves are insufficient to guide humanity to a just and prosperous future. Neither economics nor political 'sciences' yet provide satisfactory answers, nor should we have expected them to—any more than we expect a single religion, based on doctrinal belief, to provide a certain guide for all. The final chapter develops an illustrative model that shows the interactions among key forces that will determine our scientific, economic and socio-political futures. It combines a basic Deutschian/Popperian methodology, but applied to both physical and social epistemic problems as defined by Foucault (acknowledging Kuhnian paradigms and Dawkins' memes). Much of the direction and pace of progress, however, is determined by the relative strengths of Kahneman's 'fast', heuristic, belief-based thinking and 'slow', deliberative and critical assessment of evidence. This model provides no simple recipe to resolve the variety of problems described in the earlier chapters. It points, however, to the need to balance the demands of the Kahneman's fast-thinking populist 'social cauldron' with deliberative slow-thinking, 'ivory-tower' review mechanisms. Zaller's model of elitist and populist thinking provides a plausible explanation for this social dialogue.

Over-dependence on fast thinking either through the power of markets or populist belief seems certain to be a path to social stasis and decay. Resolution of the issues we face and cover in this book depend critically on deep analysis and critical examination of the processes of national and global governance. These depend in turn on the methods of conjecture and refutation that have worked well in the physical and biological sciences (or, for the social sciences, a more modest formulation of 'explanation and reformulation'). The methods required in the social realm differ in some respects and are more complex, but the basic principles are very similar. Much of modern neoliberal and populist thinking is to the effect that we do not need well-financed deliberative processes in government and all can be left to the market or to business-style deals. Current evidence strongly suggests otherwise. The question at the end of this book is the Foucauldian/Nietzschean one of whether society possesses or can acquire the will to power and knowledge needed to address our ever-evolving challenges. I hope the evidence will soon point to the affirmative.

Note

1. Soon after the 2017 G7 summit in Belgium, President Donald Trump announced that the U.S. would pull out of the college of participants in the Paris accord and void its commitments to curtailing global warming. The Epilogue of this book discusses this decision further.

Acknowledgements

This book has had a long gestation period, though most of the writing was done over the past two to three years. Many people contributed to the evolution of the ideas found here and in both recent and past writings. First, I owe a great deal to the many colleagues I worked with in Papua New Guinea (PNG) from 1972 to 1979. Andrew Elek, now a Research Fellow at the Crawford School of the Australian National University and expert in development and trade issues, is one of that group. Andrew and I, plus many others, worked closely on developing planning and budgeting systems for the then-recently formed PNG administration, through self-government to independence. We have kept in fairly close touch over the years. Andrew patiently responded to my communications and contributed comments and ideas to the many early drafts of this book, through to the present. Ross Garnaut, who headed the Financial and Economic Policy Division of the PNG Department of Finance in the mid-1970s and is now an eminent Professorial Research Fellow in Economics at the University of Melbourne, led much of the Australian effort to establish effective fiscal management in PNG. As a tyro economist I learned much from Ross during those early years. Because of his major and widely recognized contribution to formulating climate change policy in Australia, I consulted him on elements of the book, particularly on

Chap. 6. He drew my attention to several important details of climate policy development that I had missed. All of us have been disappointed in the way climate change policy has developed in Australia in recent years, and these views are reflected in Chap. 6.

After PNG, I worked as an IMF expert consultant in Fiji, Swaziland, Bahrain and The Bahamas for one- to two-year stints on fiscal management and budgeting issues. These assignments provided valuable experience in working closely with government officials in widely different cultures, giving me a broader appreciation of the importance of interaction between technically oriented officials and their political environment—and the need for sustained support. Our degree of success in influencing development of good fiscal management practices was, as I've noted, disappointing—none more so than Fiji, which from a well-established and functioning administration in the early 1980s has suffered a series of military coups that seriously slowed its then-promising progress.

Following these assignments, I joined the staff of the IMF Fiscal Affairs Department (FAD) at Economist level and worked there for 15 years. Working with the Fund's highly qualified staff and its effective administration taught me a great deal. FAD technical missions were then and continue to be intensive and challenging, and they involve detailed analysis and discussion with high-level national administrators and, often, finance ministers. Such missions appeared to me to be most effective when conversations with long-term resident experts were added to the planning; resource constraints and the drive for efficient use of headquarters and regional resources, however, have worked against such a scheme in recent years.

The highlight of this period for me, however, was the opportunity to work from 1998 onwards on the IMF Fiscal Transparency Code and the Manual on Fiscal Transparency and their subsequent implementation. This work was led by Richard Hemming, then an FAD Division Chief, who retired from the Fund as Deputy Director and is now a Visiting Professor at Duke University and advisor to the Bill and Melinda Gates Foundation. Under Richard's direction Murray Petrie, a New Zealand-based consultant, and I worked on developing both the Code and the Manual in consultation with other relevant organizations. George Kopits and Jon Craig, both of FAD, also provided important inputs to this work.

Subsequently, as head of a small Fiscal Transparency Unit within FAD, I coordinated efforts to promote the code and organize missions to member countries to assess performance against the Code and propose reform measures. I also led efforts to develop the IMF's initial *Guide on Resource Revenue Transparency* (2005) to help resource-rich countries apply the Code to their PFM practices. For a variety of reasons, as outlined in the book, efforts on fiscal transparency were discontinued for a time but have resumed and been strengthened in recent years.

As I emphasize in the book, accounting reforms are beginning to play an important role in establishing standards of accountability, transparency and risk management, and I've very much appreciated recent close technical discussion on these issues. Murray Petrie has continued to play a significant role in these areas through his association with GIFT, particularly on establishing common transparency norms and in promoting fiscal risk management practices. Chapter 4 of the book, which covers the area of measurement of social well-being—critical for social policy formulation as well as for transparency, accountability and risk management—has benefited greatly from inputs of key authorities involved in promoting public sector accounting standards. Comments made on earlier versions of that chapter by Ian Ball, formerly CEO of IFAC, now chair of the IFAC PSC that initiated the IPSAS program, Ian Carruthers, voluntary chair of the IIRC Working Group on <IR>, now Chair of IPSASB and CIPFA's Chair CIPFA Standards, and Murray Petrie have all been very helpful. They responded positively but gave sound, cautionary advice on the complexity of the accounting reforms underway and the limited skills available to move quickly forward in the <IR> area, particularly with respect to monetizing benefits. I've taken these comments on board while continuing to emphasize the need for a strengthened and more widely coordinated program. Jim Brumby, a former colleague in FAD, now Director, Public Sector and Institutions, Governance Global Practice in the World Bank, has also looked over this chapter, and, while considering the principles favourably, sees the need for more empirical work. I agree. As noted in the chapter, CIPFA/IIRC have undertaken several entity-level studies of <IR> implementation. Jane Baptist of the UK Crown Estate kindly provided more details of the practical issues involved in including monetary estimates of environmental impact in its total contribution report.

Lessons learned in my work on institutional aspects of GIFMIS implementation, both while in the IMF and later with Bank teams as a consultant, were also important as I developed the overall framework. Throughout this aspect of my work, I have worked closely with Ali Hashim of the World Bank, now retired, and have gained greatly from his systems expertise. We both worked on GIFMIS in Pakistan and Ghana in teams led by Ismaila Ceesay, Lead Financial Management Specialist in the World Bank. Other team members and I learned a great deal in these projects about the interaction of political and administrative factors in implementing such systems—and about the necessarily long timeframe for implementation. Long-term commitment to these projects has often become a cause for doubt by the Bank and other supporting development partners. The necessity of long-term commitment and coordinated support for PFM reform and automated modern accounting systems for developing countries is emphasized in Chap. 5.

I allow that none of my colleagues have expressed significant support for my Foucauldian-based hypotheses of the nature of social truth and measurement of social value—though no one explicitly rejected it. To me it seems clear that the present measurements and decision-making are not working well for society, and the fragility of society and the biological factors that make it so, recognized by Foucault, seem equally evident. This book aims to present a case for recognizing and addressing society's structural weaknesses so others can consider and gather evidence either to develop further or reject. Modern social science appears to be moving in that direction; political forces less so. It is important we all recognize the nature of this challenge.

Finally, I'd like to acknowledge the constructive reaction of Palgrave to my initial draft proposal. Rachel Carson, my first contact, reacted positively to initial draft material that I submitted, and since then her successor Anna Reeve has been very helpful. I'd particularly like to thank Thomas Coughlan for guiding and encouraging me through the final stages of developing the manuscript.

Contents

Part I Foucauldian Methodology, Neoliberalism and Modern Social Science … 1

1 Foucault's Biopolitics and Its Relevance to Modern Social Science … 3

2 Historical and Economic Roots of Neoliberalism … 39

Part II Constructing a Modern Episteme … 77

3 From Neoliberalism to Social Accountability … 79

4 Measuring Social Well-Being: GDP Is Neither Accurate Nor Fair … 105

5	Tackling Inequality and Social Justice: A Global Imperative	145
6	Managing Environmental Capital: The Case of Climate Change	185

Part III	Understanding Our Institutions, and Ruling Ourselves and Our World	211
7	Institutions and Behaviour: New Rules of the Game	213
8	Ideas, Power and Social Progress	245
Epilogue		263
References		277
Index		289

List of Figures

Fig. 4.1	Accounting standards and stages of reform (Source: Author)	112
Fig. 4.2	Value creation and reporting under IIR (Source: CIPFA and World Bank Group (2016)	119
Fig. 4.3	Towards gross domestic value creation and surveillance (Source: Author)	128
Fig. 4.4	Refocusing standards and practices reform (Source: Author)	135
Chart 5.1	Population pressures among the most vulnerable (Reproduced with permission. Copyright 2014, Scientific American, a division of Nature America, Inc. All rights reserved. https://www.scientificamerican.com/article/world-population-will-soar-higher-than-predicted)	170
Chart 6.1	Public support for climate action	194
Fig. 7.1	Dimensions of governance and democracy (Source: Author)	223
Fig. 8.1	Ideas, power and social progress (Source: Author)	250

Part I

Foucauldian Methodology, Neoliberalism and Modern Social Science

Part I reviews key aspects of Foucault's 'archaeological' analysis of social disciplines and 'genealogical' analyses of interactions among disciplines as presented in the first chapter of the book. Foucault's main insights are that governance of society must balance three fundamental social mechanisms: state sovereignty; surveillance and control of social institutions (including the limits of rationality and social exclusion of 'madness'); and free expression by individuals to state power. From this basis he argued that ideas of truth must engage with power and across social disciplines and that truth in this sense is a social construct which is authenticated by social acceptance in the period under review—though open to question and change as understanding develops. His concept of an 'episteme' describes the fusion of ideas and power into practice as we progress through stages of history. This approach guides much of this book's analysis. Foucault's concern with biopolitics and the emergence of neoliberal ideology are taken up in the second chapter, which links modern historical studies and technical and social science developments to the emergence of modern neoliberalism and populism and their consequences for the world order. Part I provides the frame for a more specific analysis of and recommendations on major governance issues that we face in the twenty-first century.

1

Foucault's Biopolitics and Its Relevance to Modern Social Science

Margaret Thatcher famously declared, "[T]here is no such thing as society,"[1] reflecting the Hayekian/neoliberal ideology she shared with Ronald Reagan and which has had an astonishingly powerful influence on Western economies' fiscal and social policies from the 1980s through to the present, including most Western economies' response to the global financial crisis (GFC) and its aftermath. Many, likely most, economists, but notably John Maynard Keynes and Mancur Olson, and, more recently, Paul Krugman, Joseph Stiglitz and many others have disagreed with the Hayekian view of the defining importance of individual decision-makers and the ability of unregulated markets to achieve society's goals. Nonetheless, as I develop in later chapters, influential monetarist economists like Milton Friedman, and neoliberal theorist Gary Becker, have helped instil the ideas that economic reasoning can be applied to all forms of human transaction, that market forces are the primary drivers of social advancement, and that the role of government should be limited.

Social debate over these issues, however, has not been and is not now a simple contest of rival economic ideas. The disciplines of economics, politics and journalism have interacted to produce disputes and outcomes that go well beyond the boundaries of economic or political theory;

the social impact of rival theories is determined in public and political arenas rather than those of economics or social science. Recent economic and political developments and the rise of modern media, moreover, have reduced the relative influence of academia and civil service in establishing a deliberative debate that connects with the voting public.

Michel Foucault, more than anyone else, led the way in exploring how social disciplines and power interacted—and continue to interact, into the future—to determine the way society is governed and the meaning of social truth and its emergence. He offers no theory on how society or government *will* develop in the future, but rather identifies the key forces that must be managed for society to be moved on a pathway towards truth. Three propositions from his view of the nature of truth that bear directly on political economy ideas and outcomes are these: first, ideas of truth must engage with power and across social disciplines; second, truth in this sense is a social construct; and, third, discovery of this truth is central to all aims of government. He recognized the enormity of this challenge for philosophy, social science and social order—even more, he saw that definitive answers were not within close reach. But his work was driven by his vision of the necessity to tackle systematically the nature of humanity's knowledge of itself as well as to address the multiple discontents with the human condition expressed viscerally and eloquently by Nietzsche.[2] From this starting point he charted a landscape of self- and social government and began to define government's responsibilities and society's outer boundaries in a radical way that continues to confront standard perceptions of human rationality.

Much has changed since Foucault's time. He had only begun to address the question of the future of political economy a few years before his untimely death in 1984, and his views on neoliberalism were not fully developed. But his body of work points towards more complex and constructive forms of discourse than social science and political practice had then or have yet been able to put in place. The nature of neoliberalism has changed significantly since he addressed the topic; indeed, the failure of neoliberalism to address the GFC and its aftermath has led to a much more difficult political and economic dynamic (issues I develop further in Part II). However, the fundamental questions that he raised remain of central relevance to our current problems of apparently surging nationalism, resurgent militarism and growing disparities in economic income, wealth and opportunities.

Management of the crises that are now threatening global stability and social progress is increasingly influenced by strongly entrenched political positions and uncertainly informed public opinion within powerful nations and decreasingly by balanced economic and political discourse. A Foucauldian perspective on the genesis of neoliberalism and its aftermath points to the need for a better understanding of the linkages among different socio-political disciplines and for an improvement of connections between these disciplines and stakeholders, both powerful and compliant.

As we discuss below, particularly regarding *The Birth of Biopolitics*, Foucault initially saw economics and market-exchange as establishing principles for an effective social mechanism to balance democratic government and individual freedom. But his analysis of German and American forms of neoliberalism and their potential role in building a strong basis for truthful social discourse remained incomplete and sceptical. This book's first aim is to review the impact of neoliberal ideology on U.S. and global governance over the past three decades, but Foucault's concerns and those of the book are much wider; all ideologies have dangers and Foucault's contribution does not depend on his temporary preoccupation with neoliberalism. His work, including his biopolitical thesis, provides a unique perspective and methodology to continually review and question prevalent social beliefs and practices. Let us now look at the elements of his methodology.

Foucault's Archaeology and Genealogy: Defining Social Truth

Foucault's views on political economy arose from his fundamental questioning of the role of philosophy, which itself is far from immune to deep disagreement on concepts, methodology and the nature of truth: major schisms remain, even since the beginning of this century. French (or 'continental') philosophy at the beginning of the twentieth century differed significantly from 'British' empiricism[3]; it became primarily concerned with the study of consciousness,[4] giving rise to many schools of thought from phenomenology to existentialism to structuralism to deconstruction—with many divisive disputes among the schools. This tradition became closely linked to physical and natural sciences and centrally concerned with experiential investigation of philosophical problems of consciousness and development of social institutions. Foucault's concept of social truth emerged from these contested ideas and his unique investigation of the way in which ideas developed and became accepted as part of social institutions; truth in his sense is an emerging set of social practices, beliefs and doubts that lead to revision and reverification over time—though he preferred the term 'veridiction' to emphasize the social nature of the process.[5]

Foucault looked at the broad fabric of society instead of looking through 'structuralist'[6] subdivisions. His approach involved evidence-based hypotheses with structural features, but these interpretations related to a specific era and were always presented as subject to further investigation of interplay between ideas and power. His approach thus constitutes the beginning of a radically empirical approach to social investigation and philosophy. While modelled in part on the methods of the physical, natural and economic 'sciences', the approach is very different from the narrowly defined societal models of Marxism, or indeed those of modern economic theory.

Foucault accepted the need to establish testable, or at least challengeable, explanations of social structures, but he eschewed the rigidity of structuralist philosophy and developed instead broad *archaeological* surveys of selected 'sciences' of man.[7] His studies of the development of modern institutions (particularly prisons, mental institutions, hospitals and schools), firstly, describe the evolution of society's disposition to exclude individuals and groups, and, secondly, demonstrate the complexities of engaging different professional streams in shaping the course of social awareness and development. His archaeology aimed to define development of societal knowledge at different points in time. Knowledge in this sense, however, differs from advances in metaphysical or epistemological ideas; it represents instead the acceptance of ideas by society. As discussed below, he termed such blocks of knowledge *epistemes*.

Allied to this archaeological framework his *genealogy* aimed to explain the relationship of ideas and truth to power at personal and institutional levels. Much of his work was focused on detailed examination of interaction among scientific and juridical disciplines to establish social practices from ancient to classical to modern times.[8] Drawing initially from Nietzsche's *Toward a Genealogy of Morals*, he looked at morality and social practices as being developed from experience and development of ideas over time rather than as emerging from innate original qualities.[9] His analysis of the factors and interactions leading to development of social institutions, including moral and behavioural dimensions, provides the basis of what he later termed 'biopolitics'. Three basic social mechanisms are in continuing contest: state sovereignty, surveillance and control of social institutions, and free expression of individual aspirations to power. He traces the course of their development through history: sovereignty from antiquity through post-Roman rule to modern sovereignty of the middle-class; surveillance and control links to Bentham's eighteenth century panopticon design for prison surveillance through to its application in modern institutions; the question of citizens interacting with sovereign power links, again to antiquity—particularly the Athenian notion of *parrhesia*, or the question of free citizens' right and courage to speak to power.

Foucault's approach thus points towards a radical empirical and multidisciplinary approach to truth in social science: validation of truth in society is through social change involving both evidence-based science and juridical/administrative application of scientific knowledge and is always subject to doubt and refinement. His insights on society's responses to mental illness, disease and treatment of criminals raise big and still unanswered questions on how society should deal with those at the edges of society, of the various forms of social exclusion. But, more fundamentally, he explored the complexity of socio-political explanation in a way that the limited structuralist models of philosophy and economic and political science theory had not and have not explored. His *Madness and Civilization* considered the limits of human rationality and identified fundamental areas of social understanding regarding outsiders and underprivileged for all levels of society; *Discipline and Punish* explored the role of juridical and administrative supervision of social behaviour. Both argued for the need to question the direction of sovereign authority and for the development of a political mechanism to reconcile individual and social aspirations, ideas and power.

The Archaeology of Knowledge[10] provides the most formally developed—though by no means complete—framework of his approach to analysis of knowledge disciplines. Its Chaps. 3, 4, 5 and 6 identify four main dimensions of analysis of social development to be examined in order to establish its truth qualities: (i) *knowledge objects*—the social focus of the discipline; not merely the history of development of ideas within a discipline, but their social acceptance and role—for instance, "how criminality could become the object of medical expertise" or "sexual deviation the object of psychiatric discourse"; (ii) *enunciative modalities*—who or what professional entities have the authority to make statements on the knowledge objects; (iii) *concept formation*—processes to develop and validate concepts; and (iv) *strategy formation*—processes for establishing conceptual themes and theories. Application of these principles of analysis to all knowledge domains, he postulated, would give rise to elements of social knowledge that he termed *epistemes*. And these would mark significant stages in social development.

The Episteme

His formulation of the episteme as the critical unit of social knowledge and truth represents a major break with past thinking in epistemology by defining knowledge of and by society as necessarily a social construct. But it is one that he did not develop fully, and its basic postulates have still not been absorbed in mainstream philosophy.[11] The idea flows from his rejection of 'structuralism' and consequent open approach to social investigation.[12] Social philosophy and the social sciences prior to Foucault, while they tried to employ similar techniques to the physical sciences, failed to recognize the fact and necessity of interaction between disciplines to authenticate and effect social change. They also failed to recognize that social truth must ultimately be advanced by a range of stakeholders who represent different disciplines, different convictions and different levels of power. Truth in this sense should not be dismissed as merely subjective or relativistic. Foucauldian epistemic truth is a recognition of an emblematic stage of social progress at a specific time, derived by critical analysis and record of eventual adoption of ideas and practices. It will, as he acknowledges, go through progressive cycles of criticism and reformulation, establishing veridiction over time similarly to scientific verification processes.

Foucault's archaeology is not just about the growth of ideas but about how ideas become part of the fabric of social power and how power and ideas interact to establish new formulations of social truth.[13] The relation between power and ideas operates at all levels of social relationships, not simply in the operation of repressive or aggressive state power. In *Power/Knowledge* he states that the essential political problem for the intellectual is to ascertain the possibility of constituting a new politics of truth; "not changing...what's in [people's] heads...but the political, economic, institutional regime of truth" (p. 133).

Foucault did not generally aim to advance theories of social development or promote specific socio-political programs. His analysis aimed only at contemporary objectivity, investigating the record of transformational discourse that has occurred or is underway in selected social disciplines relevant to an area of social development. His main aim was to understand the forces and ideas that have led, or are leading to, better understanding and development of social institutions. He established key structures and processes of social investigation, but invariably emphasized that his propositions were unfinished explanations.[14]

This process is comparable in many ways to David Deutsch's[15] examination of scientific and a range of other forms of critical inquiry by applying Popperian principles of conjecture and refutation. But Foucault's episteme is much more complex and focused on actual social experience than Deutsch's attempt to apply scientific methodology to the investigation of social truth. First, Foucault's analysis involves society's perception and acceptance of its own reality. Second, disputes among stakeholders must deal with evidence that crosses boundaries among a range of scientific, prescientific and juridical disciplines. Foucauldian epistemic theory, while accepting the principle of challengeable, evidence-based conjectures, requires review of interactions among disciplines and proposes evidence of advantageous social change as the main form of veridiction. Deutsch puts forth the more limited, and in some ways opposing, view that the methods of science and objective verification can simply be applied within a range of non-scientific separate disciplines. Modern social sciences have tended to follow Popperian principles and largely distanced themselves from the fundamental philosophical problem of verifying self-observation and ethical dimensions of the outcomes. But as we discuss below, and again in Part III, modern social science is becoming increasingly consistent with a Foucauldian view of epistemology as it applies to social knowledge.

The episteme concept is also sometimes compared, on the one hand, to the contemporaneous development of the concept of scientific *paradigms*[16] by Thomas Kuhn (1962) as stages in the development of accepted scientific knowledge, and, on the other, to the term *meme*, coined by Richard Dawkins and taken up by Susan Blackmoor and David Deutsch,[17] as a replicable unit of knowledge analogous to a 'gene'. Kuhnian paradigms, however, are focused narrowly on social processes involved in validation of scientific theory, which is secondary to, but not inconsistent with, Foucault's view of social truth as an emerging product of complex discursive processes. Biologist Dawkins describes memes as units of knowledge that, like genes, may replicate and be changed in social dialogue; a quasi-evolutionary process. *Memeplexes*, he suggests, are sets of memes that increase the likelihood of survival of members of the group. Even at this level, however, memes are conceived of as relatively simple, vivid statements of refutable ideas. Meme theory, as developed so far, does not expound an explanation of how the fittest ideas survive and improve social knowledge, nor does it attempt to explain the correspondence between knowledge and truth.

Deutsch does link memes with processes of social control[18]: static societies, he argues, establish rules that avoid replication of ideas that are not acceptable to the ruling elite, whereas dynamic societies are characterized by openness to new ideas and replication of memes that offer positive value, though criteria to establish positive value are not developed beyond the Popperian conjecture and evidence-based refutation and modification. He distinguishes between irrational and rational memes: the former are promoted within static societies to disable citizens' critical facilities; the latter are encouraged to help promote creative thinking and ensure replication of high value ideas. Western society, he suggests, is in a transitional phase, evolving from stasis to dynamism.

Memes like 'there is no such thing as society' and 'that government is best that governs least' can be taken as examples of replicable idea/phrases that exercise a powerful influence on public opinion and on political and social outcomes. Their replication, however, is not sufficient to demonstrate their truth convincingly—not to deny that significant groups within society may accept these beliefs. Fascist and Marxist memes were replicable and accepted by powerful social movements, but their socially disastrous consequences have definitively led to their rejection as valid elements of social truth. The political power of memes and 'dog whistle'[19] politics are discussed further in chapters that follow. Modern social media's acceptance of memes and their viral spread and influence on electoral processes and social bullying are elements of modern communication technology far removed from the deliberative discourse sought by Foucault (or indeed by World Wide Web inventor Tim Berners-Lee).[20] Their contribution to commercial profitability is a strong barrier to discursive control. But, if government aims to create a dynamic and humane society, it must ensure that mechanisms to review the factual and ethical content of electronic messages available to the broad public are actively considered and debated.

As we discuss further below, the rapid evolution of information and communications technology (ICT) in recent years raises major issues regarding public oversight and privacy. In addition, it changes the nature of social discourse and threatens the role of the traditional media.

Genealogy: Analysing Government Structure and Process

Foucault's detailed investigations of interactions among knowledge domains and their impact on social acceptance of truth complement his archaeology framework. They centre round two major themes: the emergence of discipline and control at all levels of society; and the evolution of modern sovereignty and democratic rights.[21] On the latter- he was concerned both with the historical transition from monarchy to bourgeois power and the citizens' rights to speak truth to power.

As noted above, he presented powerfully his findings regarding social exclusion and evolution of necessary discipline and control measures, first in his *Madness and Civilization*, and developing them further in *Discipline and Punish* and in his 1974–75 lecture series (*Abnormal*, Foucault 2003). *Madness and Civilization* begins with a description of the exclusion of lepers from society in the Middle Ages, a practice that resonated through to the end of the seventeenth century.[22] His investigations of the changing treatment of lepers, plague victims, the insane and criminals can be extended to all who step or have the misfortune to fall outside society's norms of behaviour. Government must continue to seek ways to create inclusion and justice for those in society's margins. He contrasted this treatment with that practiced by all religions (though not all orders) based on the teachings of Christ, which embraced all aspects of the human condition (pp. 75–76). These developments were no doubt linked to growing scientific knowledge of the nature of disease, albeit limited by then-current knowledge of its nature and of appropriate remedial measures. Scientific and cultural uncertainty regarding the nature of madness and its treatment is still very much an issue according to Andrew Scull (2015), though he offers some current evidence-based corrections to Foucault's account of earlier treatment of madness.

Foucault's treatment of imprisonment and the relation between medical knowledge and treatment of those accused of a crime illuminates the tendency for regulatory systems to base codes of justice on incomplete knowledge and extant social norms. Growth in psychiatric knowledge did not, in the times considered by Foucault—and does not yet—provide sufficient assurance that the needs of those deemed to be abnormal will be appropriately met. He goes on to describe the interaction between the law and medicine in determining just treatment of those that may suffer from mental illness as ubuesque.[23] For instance, expert medical opinion may be sought in reaching a legal judgement on the culpability of someone suffering from a mental disorder; however, the nature of evidence given at such trials is debated not in terms of scientificity but primarily in terms of legal culpability. Although the psychiatric expert is accorded scientific status in the court, this status has no scientific weight. Such interactions between the law and science tend to be accepted simply as 'the way things are', but have major ramifications both for those creating laws and those providing evidence or subject to it. We will refer to this point several times later in the text and discuss it in the context of institutional analysis, game theory and biopolitical games in Chap. 8.

Government Discipline: From the Panopticon to Modern Media

Foucault thus saw society's mechanisms of discipline and control as having a competing and more significant influence on social behaviour than 'scientific' representations of social truth. What does he mean by this? One point (which will be developed further in Part III) is that biological imperatives can lead the broad population to respond to immediate threats with convenient 'rule of thumb' remedies rather than 'scientific' explanations and formal discursive processes. The principle of subjecting inmates to a constant threat of all their activities being observed, derived from Samuel and Jeremy Bentham's panopticon design for prisons, became accepted readily by the public as an instrument of control; full consideration of the ethics and social consequences of doing so was largely subdued. Disciplinary mechanisms have been accepted as convenient and have easily been embedded in accepted practice and regulation, not as social truth emerging from discourse.

Discipline and Punish describes the evolution of punishment and the development of the prison and embodiment of panoptic oversight into prisons and other key social institutions from the Middle Ages through to the twentieth century: from the public spectacle of hanging and torture (stemming, Foucault argues, from revenge for insulting the monarchy and thus linked initially to the idea of absolute sovereignty) to the establishment of prisons. Imprisonment was seen at first as an appropriate punishment and then progressively embodied the notion of correction and training.[24] Panopticism then evolved as a general model for social control of individuals in virtually all major social organizations—military barracks, hospitals, schools and factories, as well as prisons themselves.

Behavioural norms for social institutions based on principles of organized oversight thus became established in a series of opportune steps rather than as a coordinated scientific and juridical quest for social truth. Panopticism, however, gave comfort to those of the governed who met the prescribed norms, kept those who did not at a comfortable distance from established society, and gave the governing class a practical set of disciplines to exercise and retain power.

Dobson and Fisher (2007), however, were among the first to observe that the ever-accelerating observational and communications capacity of the Internet, electronic tracking and social media has increased the threat of panopticism well beyond the scope originally described and the limits envisaged by Foucault: "[S]urveillance technology now supports myriad power relationships, some...equal...others newly unequal" (p. 321). It has become even clearer in recent years that the potentially immense power conferred on those segments of society that acquire significant control of cyberspace must now be ranked very high among the threats to socially just government, both nationally and internationally. More recently some see the development of social media as a force for democratic participation—a move from panopticism to the synopticon[25] (or the power of the many to observe the few)—its potential for public engagement in policy discourse so far seems limited (with manifest dangers of populist 'fast-thinking', as discussed further in Part III). Indeed, it seems at least as likely to be divisive; and, in the broader arena of ICT development, that rich and powerful nations, enterprises and individuals will continue to reap most of the commercial benefits and associated power and influence.

Wikipedia and the operations of the (quite unrelated) WikiLeaks appear to offer the possibilities of establishing serious platforms for engaging the broad public in investigation and debate on matters of major public concern. Though WikiLeaks is far more contentious, both offer platforms for wide public consideration of social knowledge and matters of public interest. Both are open to potential abuse, but their potential to add immense social value warrants well-directed and oversighted government support rather than reliance on voluntary contribution, and, in the case of WikiLeaks, outrage and judicial punishment.

The dangers of the nexus between ICT and national security have been highlighted by the activities of WikiLeaks in assisting publication of information from diplomatic service whistleblowers. National security classification of diplomatic documents is designed to protect premature release of information on covert operations or diplomatic communications, arguably in the national interest. Since 2006, WikiLeaks, founded by Julian Assange, has been able to release a huge number of classified documents obtained from individuals who were able to breach communications security or who had direct access to high security files and considered that release of this information was in the public interest. WikiLeaks gives access to much of the leaked material, particularly to professional journalists to publish if they deem publication of the information to be in the public interest. It claims to exercise care over the material released,[26] though that claim is hotly contested by national security agencies. These principles and practices require deeper investigation, but the information released so far certainly raises many questions about the ethical standards of the diplomatic corps and national security agencies—particularly the dominant role played by the US Department of State (the 'centre of the US Empire', according to Assange).

Control of modern panopticism/synopticism should not be left to market forces, but neither can we be assured that government control of ICT for national security can be subject to sufficient independent oversight to guarantee either national or global security. Future government structures will need to establish a much more accountable framework for social disciplinary mechanisms and open democratic institutions. Present defence and national security organizations are deliberately set up as silos that separate national security from normal social oversight. While the need for short-term secrecy must be acknowledged, some form of timely review of national security operations and their impact on broader social welfare also needs to be established. These questions need to be examined in the context of how society has viewed and should view sovereignty and the relation between individual and social truth and democracy; the spectre of Orwell's *1984* seems more than a fanciful threat. We return to these issues in Part III.

Sovereignty and Government

Foucault saw sovereign states as they emerged in the nineteenth and twentieth centuries as being both incongruent with government disciplinary mechanisms and resistant to discursive processes of change. In Europe, sovereign rule emanated from the power of the Frankish nobility established after the fall of the Western Roman Empire in the sixth century and was consolidated in 1648 through the treaties of Westphalia. Foucault argued that the emergence of disciplinary power as a product of the enlightenment "should logically have led to the complete disappearance of the great juridical edifice of the theory of sovereignty [but]... it continued to exist...as an ideology of right; it also continued to organize the juridical codes that nineteenth century Europe adopted after the Napoleonic codes" (Foucault 1997, p. 36).

It is doubtful that this evolution of modern sovereignty should be characterized as somehow 'illogical'.[27] In Foucault's own terms, many social forces, including disciplinary regulation, were at work, and so they continue. Most writing on this topic, including Foucault's, makes it clear that the path of democratization within modern states has been long and difficult. We have little evidence or reason to assume that our current evolutionary stage of democracy, or those of past eras, are either a logical necessity or optimal, a point we will develop further in Chap. 7. Foucault indeed highlighted the complexities and internal conflicts between, on the one hand, pastoral and political sovereign power relations, and, on the other, the evolution of race and class struggle, as the mode of government moved from autarchic rule to sovereignty of the state and greater power of the bourgeoisie[28] within the state. These forces continue to operate, and the challenge is to guide these forces towards a socially appropriate logic.

Foucault's Tanner lectures, (Foucault/Rabinow 2000, Vol. 3, pp. 298–325) outlined how the pastoral concept emerged most powerfully in Christian Europe after the fall of the Roman Empire and merged in a 'paradoxical' relationship with state political power in modern European and New World states. The paradox was the appropriation by kings and nobles of the time of Abrahamic/Christian values of pastoral care of the citizens under their care, a concern that was not prominent in Greek or pre-Christian Roman times. There can be little doubt, however, that the pastoral aspect of rule was less concerned with the fate of the citizens of the often complex and shifting states of Europe and much more about ensuring loyalty against whoever may become the common enemy. An interesting more recent interpretation of this topic in the pre-revolutionary period of European history between 1650 and 1750 is given by Nicholas Henshall (2010), where he contends persuasively that the nobility (who exercised power both through landholdings [estates] and the church) and kings of the time created an 'elite culture' that "deliberately distanced itself from popular culture and thereby acquired a grandeur that overawed the common people, while in some crucial respects retaining an ability to communicate with them" (p. 29). Though he adds that this 'elite culture' has little to do with current divisions between 'highbrow' and 'lowbrow' cultural characterizations, the concept resonates with modern developments of social classes and political divisions; it has epistemic qualities. In Chap. 7, we revisit the relationship between elite and popular culture as explained by John Zaller in his interpretation of public opinion formation and twenty-first century politics.

The pastoral/power nexus has certainly been used by rulers then and now. In *Society Must Be Defended*, Foucault argued that differences within and between groups makes war possible and, inverting Clausewitz, that "politics is a continuation of war by other means" (p. 48). He describes the evolution of 'race war' from its 'historico-biological' origins to nationalist movements in Europe and struggles against the 'great State apparatuses', its articulation with European policies of colonization, and then to its 'recasting' in the form of the (Hegelian/Marxist) dialectic and class struggle.[29] He does not portray racism itself as the driving force for suppression of the 'other' race—the enemy within or without. Rather leaders emerging from post-autocratic biopower and biopolitics have, in much the same way as autocrats, used society's underlying biological race/class rivalries to achieve social control and confirm power. Either as war or politics, 'racism' in Foucault's sense still provides the sovereign power with the public support needed to 'kill' the enemy. His definition of 'killing', to be clear, encompasses all forms of governmental command, from military murder to "increasing the risk of death...or quite simply political death, expulsion, rejection, and so on" (p. 256). Others, such as

Niall Ferguson (2006) or those of the Samuel P. Huntington school of thought, consider that race and cultural characteristics are so deeply embedded in national responses that conflict is an inevitable component of international affairs. There is no doubt that such elements of hostility between nations and civilizations exist (as we discuss in Chap. 2 in the context of twentieth-century conflict). Foucault's interpretation, however, is well founded in experience over the millennia, and its application should lead to a more positive, albeit still difficult, pathway to governance based on cosmopolitan values. Civilization-clash theories appear to assume intractable opposition between ethnic and religious groups—an assumption that helps to create the risk they warn against.

Foucault aimed to find the way for all social actors to govern themselves and others—the pivotal point of his biopolitics thesis.[30] The necessity to overcome both the sovereign control and social subservience that underlay much of twentieth-century political development remains the central task. By the end of the nineteenth century, absence of a discursive resolution of competing sovereign forces (no doubt aided by panoptic discipline and compliance within nation states) had allowed two world-shattering ideological influences to emerge: German fascism and eventually Nazism arose in part from the revolutionary changes in Russia and Eastern Europe, combined with the depression,[31] initially somewhat supported but demagogically magnified sentiments of post-war mistreatment through the Versailles Treaty.[32] In this environment, the Nazis could build on a myth-based belief in racial supremacy. Russian communism was created (at least nominally) round Marxist dialectic and revolutionary theory of unavoidable class struggle and the necessary triumph of the proletariat. Armed opposition of the major Western democracies and, perhaps paradoxically, the USSR was necessary to defeat Nazism. Sustained economic and military containment of the Soviet Union then contributed to the eventual collapse of the totalitarian USSR. The latter success provided a highly persuasive platform for support for liberal democracy by neoconservative political theorists.[33]

It was in the light of the perceived failure of either disciplinary mechanisms or development of more democratic sovereignty to steer society towards truth and justice through discourse[34] that Foucault deliberated on the potential of emerging neoliberal economic theory. In the US, neoliberalism was strongly motivated by the perceived need to combat the threat of Soviet-style totalitarian communism, and German ordo-liberalism was born to ensure suppression of Nazism; both favoured rule of law to ensure competition, avoid monopoly and protect individual freedom and competitive market operations.

In his *Birth of Biopolitics*, he extensively reviewed the themes taken up in the Walter Lippmann Colloque held in Paris in 1938, and which subsequently led to the establishment of the Mont Pèlerin Society (MPS) and considered the possibility of Smith's 'invisible hand' reasoning being applied to all rational conduct, including criminality along the lines advocated by Gary Becker.[35] Early in this series of lectures, he argued that in the eighteenth century, the "market—which had been the privileged object of governmental practice for a very long time...and a mercantilism which precisely made commerce one of the major instruments of the state's power—was now constituted as a site of veridiction" (p. 33). As discussed earlier, he coined the term 'veridiction' to signify "a site of verification-falsification for government practice" (p. 32). Consistently with this proposal, he explored the view that neoliberalism, of the American variety, could provide the needed principle of self-government, his 'new right,' to replace sovereignty that would also guide internal policing and disciplinary mechanisms.

But in the end he did not endorse neoliberalism as it had developed in the early 1980s. Indeed, he was clear that economics alone could not become the 'science of government': "One must govern with economics, one must govern alongside economists, one must govern by listening to the economists, but economics must not be and there is no question that it can be the governmental rationality itself" (p. 286). He promised to develop a broader theory of civil society including economic man, but, though he continued his lectures at the Collège de France until a few months before his death, his later lectures focused more on examining the basis of personal courage and his three-volume *History of Sexuality*.

This book, and much of recent development of recent social and economic theory, supports Foucault's recasting of 'economic man' as a vital contributor to social progress, but only as part of a much broader and interactive team. The weaknesses of commercial market pricing as a basis for measuring social value will be thoroughly examined in later chapters—particularly Chap. 4. Developments led by market fundamentalism in the late twentieth and early in the twenty-first provide strong evidence to the view that neither economics nor any single social discipline can provide a clear pathway to social truth in the sense that Foucault sought. Neoliberal economists, many of them senior figures in the MPS, have certainly been influential, but likely more through individual contributions rather than through direct MPS policy influence. A key aim of the MPS was to draw on a variety of disciplines to help protect market and individual freedom.[36] The MPS's overtly multidisciplinary approach resembles Foucault's epistemic method in some ways, but the MPS in practice resisted formalized cooperation and had difficulty in formulating agreed group objectives. More importantly, Foucault's overarching goal was to strengthen governance in full appreciation of the interplay between individual and sovereign rights. He rightly did not see market freedom as an over-riding virtue.

As we shall discuss, much of the problems of interdisciplinary coordination arise from complex institutional and structuralist boundaries. The social sciences (including economics) have been limited by their specialized methodologies to modelled, partial explanations of the current shape and likely future direction of specific aspects of social progress. Individual disciplines clearly can help advance these features of social understanding, but valid explanations of complex social outcomes must eventually be obliged to consider all influences that affect social change, not merely those that apply within restricted professional boundaries.

For a brief period from the end of the Cold War up to 2008, however, neoliberal economic theory (particularly as advanced by Milton Friedman and the Chicago School of Economics) appeared to represent a hope that global macro-economic management had achieved the conditions for rising common prosperity and that liberal democracy would spread by popular assent. Now, however, we face a range of major global and national governance threats, many of which have emerged from unfettered commercial operations and commerce-driven expansion across national borders. Economics, markets, competition and prices must of course continue to play prominent roles, but these must be informed increasingly by a more complete explanation of social value drawing on explicit estimation of production externalities (including environmental impact of greenhouse gas emissions) and sociological and ethical analyses. These issues, moreover, are not merely a matter of improving technical exchanges among disciplines; they must involve greatly improved communications and dialogue among governments, their technical advisors and public groups. These political and discourse relationships are emerging as the most urgent issues to be faced over the coming critical decade.

Democracy/Parrhesia: An Unresolved Relationship

The question of the relationship between the many that are ruled and the rulers remains central to concepts of government from pre-Athenian times[37] to the present. In his *The Courage of Truth* (1983–84) lectures Foucault further developed his ideas on parrhesia as it related to the evolution of democracy and its relation to truth. The right of citizens to speak frankly and publicly on matters of interest to the city or polity was a key characteristic of the Athenian assembly and its implications reverberate now in considering appropriate openness and oversight of modern government institutions, whether democratic or otherwise.

In Athens, the right to speak frankly was available only to well-born or meritorious male citizens, and could be lost through dishonour. However limited the Athenian franchise, citizens taking up their rights to speak undoubtedly contributed to the success of the assembly and government of the Athenian city state. Given the highly-contested environment of the political meetings in the Athenian *agora* (marketplace), exercising this right required presence and courage, and knowledge of the truth was necessary for speaking truth effectively. But it was not at that time a wholly effective site of veridiction. Resistance to tyranny and rival sovereign and imperial ambition through this form of democracy was relatively short-lived for the Greek states of the time.

While the Athenian city state experiment was pivotal, the most important aspect of the Athenian experience was that it led to a flowering of philosophy and literature, including a vigorous exploration of the merits of popular opinion relative to truthful discourse and sovereign power. The times were not conducive to lasting institutional development, but the basis for open philosophical debate and the application of reason to the affairs of men was clearly established in a form that has been preserved and developed (albeit uncertainly at times) through successive centuries.[38] In many ways, Foucault's work is aimed at reuniting philosophy, science and government and thus should help avoid the structural traps that competitive disciplines have created. The dangers now differ from those of the preceding two millennia or indeed those of the past two centuries, but many of the fundamental problems recognized then are yet to be fully understood or addressed.

Foucault cites two main lines of argument on our Athenian foundations, which he describes as Plato's 'reversal' and Aristotle's 'hesitation'.[39] Plato particularly emphasized the grave dangers in promoting the voice of the multitude as a driving force for government of the city, arguing in *The Republic* that rulers guided by philosophers who understood the nature of truth provided the necessary combination for governing in the city's best interest; government led by the people would be torn every way according to the self-interest of individual citizens and demagogues. Practically, he also found in his relationship with Dionysius the Younger, in Sicily,[40] the relation between ruler and philosophical advisor to be personally dangerous, but nonetheless continued to advocate the ideals of philosophical discourse and courage to speak truth to power.

Aristotle, on the other hand, looked more pragmatically at the rival forms of government, monarchy, aristocracy and the *politeia* (or government of the many); he argued reasonably that just or unjust results were possible under each form of government. Government according to Aristotle should be based on participation of all citizens but backed by constitutional laws that embodied participation by ruler, aristocrats and citizens. This formulation, with its built-in uncertainties and fallibilities, became the accepted, no doubt over-idealized, basis for implementation of forms of government from Greek states to the Roman Empire, to emerging Eurasian states and to modern times. In terms of modern relevance, however, the Aristotelian view emphasizes the relationship between philosophical understanding and scientific explanation and the public; the Platonic view does not emphasize this relationship between philosophers and autocratic rulers.

The political philosophy debate from Athens onwards thus identified key problems of establishing a realistic role for the general population to participate in government. Neither then nor now, however, have we been able to establish institutions that can be shown convincingly to allow either the people's voice to be well reflected in public decisions or to be assured that leaders' choices indeed represent the public interest. Modern democracy since the 1930s has been characterized as much by demagogues and political party machinery manipulating public opinion as by well-constructed efforts to define and respond to the public interest. Broadening public franchises and controls over electoral boundaries and processes have undoubtedly contributed to enfranchisement and the characterization of our twenty-first century Western democracy as the 'least bad' system of government. But neither democracy nor its alternatives should be immune from critical review.

The relationship between governments and different communities and sub-nationalities within countries, and the electoral processes applied to determine these, have come under intense scrutiny as a result of recent nationalist and micro-nationalist political movements, such as the British vote to exit the European Union (Brexit); surging nationalism in France, the Netherlands, Poland and Hungary; the victory of Donald Trump in the US Presidential election; and Scottish and Catalonian votes in favour of independence from their national governments. As we'll argue throughout, neither neoliberalism nor populism provide evidence that their policies can address these emerging national and global problems; indeed both threaten to make life a great deal worse for many vulnerable groups and for global well-being and security.

The second chapter in this section applies a Foucauldian epistemic approach to help explain the genesis of key socio-economic developments and challenges that have taken hold in the past three decades; these emerged from twentieth-century biopolitical conflict, including unprecedented military and armament power, increasing global interdependence, uncertain relations among economic and political disciplines, and growing influence of powerful business and media sectors. In Part II it sets the stage for more detailed analysis and suggested action in key areas.

Summary of Themes and Conclusions

The chapter has outlined the central elements of Foucault's challenge to traditional philosophy and social science. While initially embracing application of scientific methodology to the social sciences and social philosophy, he found traditional epistemology's emphasis on the growth of ideas as inadequate to explain the human condition or its predicaments. He did not reject scientific approaches to the growth of ideas, but saw the need to take the further step of explaining how ideas were then translated into social practice. His concept of the episteme, developed in his *Archaeology*, took account both of verification of scientifically testable ideas and of the processes by which ideas from different disciplines were reconciled and became part of social practice and governance. His *Genealogy*, which constituted the major part of his work, was concerned with interactions among social disciplines and between ideas and power at all levels of society from sovereign state to individuals. Truth for society emerges through these contests, but some form of imbalance is invariably present—ideally leading to a further search for truth. No one discipline has yet demonstrated a capacity to resolve such imbalances. They must be reviewed in the context of overall interaction among disciplines and power: the episteme for the period being reviewed.

For a time Foucault considered that the then-emerging neoliberal economic theories of market transactions as a common language of values may provide a mechanism for resolving these imbalances. In his 1978/79 series of lectures, however, he rejected that idea. The necessity of interdisciplinary collaboration and engagement with power mechanisms, however, remains important in considering modern challenges, including the political turn to neoliberalism and emergence of populism and nationalism. The next chapter applies Foucauldian reasoning plus developments in social theory to critical issues we now face.

Notes

1. See http://en.wikiquote.org/wiki/Margaret_Thatcher emphasizing, first, the need for government to rely on individuals and families and, second, that entitlements must be earned by fulfilling obligations.

2. Particularly *Toward a Genealogy of Morals*; see Foucault/Rabinow (1997), Vol. 2, *Nietzsche, Genealogy, History*, pp. 369–389.
3. This terminology is unsatisfactory but commonly used as a summary of a variety of differences in philosophical approaches. Anthony Kenny (2007) comprehensively covers the history of Western philosophy from classical times to the near present, but primarily from a 'British' perspective—and omits any mention of Foucault. There are many schisms within and between 'British' and 'continental' schools of philosophy; differences between them are sometimes characterized (misleadingly) as 'words' (French) versus 'things' (British). Karl Popper, an Austrian (and good friend of Friedrich Hayek), was one of the leading exponents of a rigorous empirical approach to explanation and testing of predictions in social science. Ernest Gellner (a Czech-born Briton) was furiously dismissive of what he termed 'linguistic philosophy', though his book *Words and Things* (first published in 1959), primarily directed against Wittgenstein, predated Foucault's major writings (and Foucault's *Les Mots et les Choses* [1966; translated as *The Order of Things*]). David Deutsch (2011), who cited Gellner favourably in his bibliography, has taken a similar dismissive approach to 'linguistic' philosophy in his Chap. 12 *A Physicist's History of Bad Philosophy*.
4. See Schrift (2006), particularly Chaps. 4 and 5.
5. This book is neither a piece of Foucauldian scholarship nor of professional philosophy. Nonetheless, no professionals, in particular, anyone in Karl Popper-influenced economics, can avoid engagement with key aspects of philosophy. From this perspective, I consider that in many respects Foucault bridges many long-standing philosophical schisms: he approached the sciences of man in a way that should satisfy the empiricists' need for testable (refutable or improvable) hypotheses (or Deutsch's simpler 'explanations'), but these hypotheses raise many complex questions of institutional relationships that go beyond normal scientific discipline or 'structuralist' boundaries. Somewhat late in the development of his ideas he recognized linkages between his approach and that of the Frankfurt School led by Horkheimer and Adorno, who argued that philosophy should be in a position to lead the social sciences by applying Kantian principles of reason (see Foucault's interview responses to his relationship with the Kantian approach of the Frankfurt School and Jürgen Habermas in Foucault/Rabinow 1997, Vol. 2, pp. 440–42). Mitchell Dean (1999a) compares the Kantian approaches of

Habermas in particular to that of Foucault, largely in favour of the latter, but without emphasizing the essentially empirical nature of Foucault's approach. Foucault did claim to fit in the critical tradition of Kant (Foucault/Rabinow 1997, Vol. 2, p. 459), but much of his work is richly empirical.

Broad aspects of Foucault's development of ideas are summarized in Schrift (2006), who traces the evolution of twentieth century Anglo-French philosophy and its major contributors in the context of French academic culture. Rabinow's thematic compilation of Foucault's essential writings (Foucault/Rabinow 1997) helps reveal their interconnections and linkages to central topics of philosophy and provides a comprehensive survey of the scope and importance of his writing. The essays in Burchell et al. (1991) also give a good overview of the relevance of Foucault's approach to the development of government and its linkages to knowledge, truth and power.

6. Most modern social sciences adopt an essentially structural approach to their discipline, assuming that theories within their domain of social science, generally expressed through simplified models amenable to mathematical manipulation and prediction, can explain broad shifts in society with limited reference to other variables and disciplines; Marxian dialectic, derived from Hegel, was based on an even greater overreach of theory, based on a hypothesized dialectical process of social change (dismissed by Popper as 'historicism'), albeit augmented by important observations on social injustice and industrial power relations. While in *The Order of Things* Foucault's approach can be characterized as still structuralist, his work became progressively oriented to interactions among disciplines and the relationship between ideas, power and the establishment of truth as the central issue of government of self and others.

7. *The Archaeology of Knowledge* (first published in 1969 and translated in 1972), provides an early overview of his methodology that developed ideas introduced in his *Madness and Civilization: A History of Insanity in the Age of Reason* (first published in 1961 and translated in 1965) and *The Order of Things* (first published in 1966 and translated in 1970). These ideas were further developed and applied in *Discipline and Punish: The Birth of the Prison* (first published in 1975).

8. His lectures at the Collège de France, which commenced in 1971 and ended just before his death in 1984, cover much of his development of

genealogy themes. Each lecture series consisted of a series of weekly lectures over two months at the beginning of each year.
9. Foucault uses the term 'autochthonous' (autochtone) in the *Archaeology*, which carries the meaning of 'improvement from within', tackling Nietzschean questions of individual and social free will. As we discuss in Part III, it also poses the catch-22 type dilemma that transformation needs to be initiated—or at least taken up forcefully—by those that are currently setting the rules. The rulers need to be open to persuasion; the ruled need empowerment and parrhesia.
10. Foucault compares his approach in the Archaeology to his earlier *The Order of Things*, where he says his "attention was concentrated on the networks of concepts and their rules of formation" in his earlier analysis of the development of concepts in the general grammar, natural history and the analysis of wealth. His writing became progressively more and more concerned with the discursive dynamics of knowledge development and absorption by society rather than simply with the history of ideas.
11. Foucault explained his archaeology and epistemological approach at length in response to the Paris Epistemological Circle question of how it related to the notion of epistemological rupture or periodic discontinuities in development of scientific ideas (see Foucault/Rabinow (1997), Vol. 2, pp. 297–233). The question itself may better have been better directed at Thomas Kuhn's work on scientific revolutions, which *was* concerned with development of ideas rather than social knowledge in Foucault's sense (see discussion below); Foucault was quite plainly not concerned merely with the history of scientific ideas and their discontinuities but rather with how scientific and quasi- or pre-science disciplines interacted and became engaged in social practice at different points of time.
12. Foucault's explanations at both archaeological and genealogical levels were founded on an immense range of literary and philosophical texts as well as detailed analysis of administrative and legal documents from relevant entities and administrative records. His methodology was constantly developing, but from the beginning went well beyond the limitations of previous narrow social science and philosophical analyses. In his *Prison Talk* interview (1980, Chap. 2), he emphasized the importance of detailed monographs and studies of prisons and the virtues of apparently banal detail to build a picture, not of progress, but of what had happened. He also emphasized the need to 'use' other writings (with reference to a

question on Nietzsche) "...to deform it, to make it groan and protest"; whether commentators thought he was being faithful or unfaithful to Nietzsche was of no interest. The summary statement of the relationship between power, ideas and truth is given in his interview in Foucault 1980 (Chap. 6, p. 133). A more complete overview of his writing on these topics is given in Foucault/Rabinow (1997) Vol. 3 *Power* (which also includes the *Truth and Power* interview and includes Foucault's 2 Tanner lectures under the title 'Omnes et Singulatum' pp. 298–325). A number of scholars have placed particular emphasis on Foucault's introduction of the idea of biopolitics (see Kelly 2010 and Lemke 2011); my interpretation agrees with the importance of his introduction of biopolitical ideas to his work but places more emphasis on his eventual rejection of an economic foundation for biopolitics as well as his development of the episteme concept.

13. 'Knowledge' in Foucault's sense is not merely a set of ideas detached from their social context. He illustrates the utility of the approach by reference to the emergence of a psychiatric discipline (first described in his *Madness and Civilization* but developed further in the *Archaeology*). The discipline emerged as a result of a "whole set of relations between hospitalization, internment, the conditions and procedures of social exclusion, the rules of jurisprudence, [and] the norms of industrial behaviour and bourgeois morality" (p. 197). The discursive formation of the psychiatric discipline extends well beyond the discipline of medical psychiatry; as well as its medical aspects it involved administrative regulations, philosophical texts and projects linked to assistance to the poor. Science, he argues, is localized in a field of knowledge and plays a role in it, but that role depends critically on the other influences, which vary over time. Medical knowledge in the classical period played a relatively minor role, but psychopathology in the nineteenth century became much more important. "[A]rchaeological analysis must show positively how a science functions in the element of knowledge" (p. 204).

14. Some Foucauldian scholars (Dean [1999a] and Lemke [2011]) have interpreted Foucault's episteme more narrowly and tied his work more closely to a program of governmentality closely linked to neoliberal objectives. Dean, for instance, focused on the "episteme of government...forms of thought, knowledge, expertise, strategies, means of calculation, or rationality...employed in practices of governing" (p. 31). I believe the case for much broader philosophical objectives, non-programmatic and

definitely not tied to neoliberalism, is extremely strong taken over the entire scope of his work.
15. See Deutsch's *Introduction*, where he argues that progress depends on progressive improvement in explanations "not only in scientific understanding, but also in technology, political institutions, moral values, art, and every aspect of human welfare". Though, as noted below, Deutsch, in his chapter on *Bad Philosophy*, displayed some antagonism to 'linguistic' approaches to philosophy, which, though directed mainly against Wittgenstein, could be construed as critical of continental philosophy more generally, including Foucault's.
16. Foucault's epistemes are centrally concerned with the process of developing social truth and defining the role the social sciences play in the discursive process, whereas Kuhn focused on the social process of validation of scientific truth (which incidentally led to a [in my view, overblown] disagreement with Karl Popper on truth affirmation rather than Popperian refutation). Neither Kuhn nor Foucault was arguing that the truth is *merely* a social construction; both, however, argued that determination of truth involves dialogue among stakeholders. The scientific community, however, interpreted Kuhn's work as a threat to scientific work and its funding, leading to what has been called 'the Science Wars'. (Sardar [2000] gives an overview of this debate.)
17. These points are drawn from Dawkins (2006), Blackmore (1999), including Dawkins' foreword, and Deutsch (2011).
18. See Deutsch (2011) Chap. 15, *The Evolution of Culture*.
19. Krugman (2007) describes in some detail the way political strategists in the US use the media and ply phrases and words that are coded for ideologically sympathetic groups, but blandly patriotic or religious to the general public, as the rise of dog whistle politics. This alliance between sections of the traditional media and neoliberal/neoconservative politicians has created growing power for both.
20. With the growth of social media the term *meme* has come to represent any message that goes viral on the Internet, a property that has become attractive both to those that wish to influence public opinion, such as advertising agencies and politicians, and those that wish to protect the public from such manipulation (for instance, the Adbusters movement, which has a mixed reputation, as discussed in Wikipedia). The article *The Virologist* (The New Yorker, January 5, 2015, by Andrew Marantz) reveals how this phenomenon can be and has been used entrepreneurially

and how replicability leads to public acceptance. Meme replicability and public acceptance, however, do not demonstrate social truth in either factual veracity or moral rightness of the meme.
21. Foucault (1997) argued that two 'heterogeneous' discourses dominated social behaviour from the seventeenth through to the nineteenth century: "[O]nce disciplinary constraints had to both function as mechanisms of domination and be concealed to the extent that they were in the mode in which power was actually exercised, the theory of sovereignty had to find expression in the juridical apparatus and had to be reactivated or complemented by judicial codes" (p. 37). He concluded that "we should be looking for a new right that is both anti-disciplinary and emancipated from the principle of sovereignty" (p. 40).
22. In *Abnormal*, he observes that the model of exclusion derived from the treatment of lepers was subsequently largely replaced by a 'reactivated' model, that of inclusion and control of plague victims. See also *Madness and Civilization*, Chap. 9, The Birth of the Asylum. Andrew Scull, in his encyclopaedic *Madness in Civilization* (2015), is critical of several aspects of Foucault's work in this area, suggesting among other things that he overstated the extent of mistreatment of lepers and the insane. However, his concluding statement that "[madness] remains a fundamental puzzle, a reproach to reason, inescapably part and parcel of civilization itself" (p. 411), is very consistent with Foucault's central philosophical intention in exploring these issues.
23. Foucault often referred to classical or literary formulations of biopolitical conflict. He used the anarchical *Ubu Roi* to illustrate the lack of connection between the juridical system and modern medical science. Other literary game formulations such as Heller's *Catch 22* and Orwell's *1984* offer appropriate metaphors for recent times.
24. See Foucault 1977 (*Discipline and Punish, Panopticism* pp. 218–228) which argues that panoptic disciplines (i) aim to ensure the regulation of people at lowest economic and political cost; (ii) constitute an 'infra-law' that guides people into hierarchies; and (iii) apply similar principles across all social institutional arrangements. But this development is incompatible with juridical procedures based on sovereign right. He argues (Foucault 1997, *Society Must Be Defended*, Lecture of 14th January 1976) that "the techniques of discipline and discourses born of discipline are invading [sovereign] right and ... normalizing procedures are increasingly colonizing the procedures of the law" (pp. 38–39).

25. These concepts are usefully described in https://worldwideweber2014.wordpress.com/2014/04/14/the-panopticon/ which also refers to the broader term *omniopticon*, surveillance of the many by the many, which seems most apt to our modern media experience. Gary Shteyngart's novel *Super Sad True Love Story* (2010) updates Orwell's dystopian view of a panoptic society ruled by Big Brother and newspeak to the era of modern media, where smartphones have morphed into äppäräts that let everybody know everything about all of their linked 'friends', and careful language and books are rendered superfluous. *The Economist* (Dec. 17, 2016) applied this vision to China's social credit policy—no doubt appropriate, though the implications of our social communications networks, their management and who controls them should be global concerns, and national policies on these matters considered on future UN agenda (see Chap. 7).
26. See Assange (2015) and WikiLeaks website https://wikileaks.org/About.html, "As the media organisation has grown and developed, WikiLeaks has been developing and improving a harm minimisation procedure. We do not censor our news, but from time to time we may remove or significantly delay the publication of some identifying details from original documents to protect life and limb of innocent people."
27. In his 1982 Vermont lecture *The Political Technology of Individuals* (Foucault/Rabinow [1997, pp. 401–417]), he describes the evolution of policing in France and Germany, indicating that these practices were allied to the disciplinary mechanisms of the time; order as distinct from law. He concluded that "[t]he conciliation between law and order, which has been the dream of those [utopians of the beginning of the seventeenth century…and…administrators of the eighteenth], must remain a dream" (p. 417). This appears to be consistent with his conclusion of 'illogicality.' Perhaps, however, some further investigations of the factors preventing such a union could have been fruitful in revealing a more complete analysis of the sovereignty/disciplinary 'episteme'?
28. Diminishing aristocratic sovereignty in Europe and its New World dominions eventually led to the promise that everyone would become able to exercise their rights as citizens because the sovereignty of the state and the rights of the bourgeoisie within the state had become established. European peoples after the collapse of the Western Roman Empire were caught in prolonged struggles within the coalition of the Frankish nobility (the second estate) and the (initially) Catholic Church (or first estate).

Effective policing and regulation along panoptic principles largely kept the bourgeoisie (third estate) as well as the proletariat under control, but ultimately struggles within the second estate in the seventeenth and eighteenth centuries led to severe curtailment of central sovereign powers and thus more direct power in the hands of the merchant class, much less so the proletariat.

29. See Foucault (1997), Lecture of 21 January 1976 pp. 58–61. See also discussion of his treatment of race in Lemke (2011) pp. 40–44, and Kelly (2010); both tend to focus on the limited scope of Foucault's analysis in relation to modern concerns with racism. My interpretation is that Foucault had no intention of addressing such issues, but, rather less ambitiously, he highlighted unavoidable features of biology and personal, family and tribe loyalties that made power conflicts within and between groups unavoidable. This perspective links directly to his concerns with biopower and biopolitics, but his treatment of the nexus of racism, biopower and biopolitics remained very incomplete and falls far short of Kelly's suggestion that "Foucault defines biopolitics/biopower as a *technology* of power..." (p. 3). Biopolitics has been identified only as a set of problems that must be addressed within the overall problem of governing self and others, not as a new social truth. Lemke (Chaps. 4 and 5) critically reviews approaches by Agamben, and Hardt and Negri, who aim to build alternative models of biopolitics without addressing the fundamental issues that remain to be resolved within the original Foucauldian framework.

30. On the genesis of the conflict between the two competing forces from post-Roman times, see particularly his lecture of 28 January 1976 from *Society Must Be Defended: Lectures at the Collège de France (1975–76)*. His *Security, Territory, Population: Lectures at the Collège de France (1977–78)* developed the ideas of population as the basis of state power, provided it is framed by a regulatory apparatus; the growth of statistical analysis from the eighteenth century onwards gave powerful tools for control to the state. His *The Birth of Biopolitics: Lectures at the Collège de France (1978–79)*, and *The Government of Self and Others: Lectures at the Collège de France (1982–1983)* give his most developed ideas of the task of moving beyond sovereignty and panoptic control to a self-governing society seeking to establish social truth.

31. Ferguson (2006) says of this period: "The war in the East was the war the Germans won" (p. 144). He also adds that the depression played a part

but was not itself a major factor in rising fascist sentiments in Germany. "Only in Germany [however] was fascism both revolutionary and totalitarian in deed as well as in word. Only in Germany did dictatorship ultimately lead to industrialized genocide" (p. 232).
32. Jürgen Tampke (2017) has argued strongly that the Versailles Peace Treaty was much less onerous than many—most notably, Keynes—argued. His critical review of Keynes' influence on international policy through his book *The Economic Consequences of the Peace* (pp. 203–214) includes a note (31, p. 297) citing Elizabeth Wiskemann, who had met Keynes at a gathering in London after the German Election, on 29 March 1936, and said, "'I do wish you had not written that book'. In reply, he said simply and gently, 'So do I'."
33. Including Francis Fukuyama's and Samuel Huntington's works on likely developments post-Cold War. I would argue that both the language of the analysis ('clash of civilizations' and 'end of history') and the assumption that liberal democracy is a fully developed product works against the usefulness of this line of investigation. Damagingly, it continues to lend intellectual weight to nationalist and anti-government ideology. Major articles on the 'clash', many of which appeared in *Foreign Affairs* over several years, have been included in *The Clash of Civilizations: The Debate 20th Anniversary Edition, Foreign Affairs* (2013) (e-book *The Clash at 20*). Richard Betts' review of the contributions of Fukuyama, Huntington, and John J. Mearsheimer to the debate (*Conflict or Cooperation? Three Visions Revisited*) concluded that "simple visions, however powerful, do not hold up as reliable predictors of particular developments. Visions are vital for clarifying thinking about the forces that drive international relations….but they cannot account for many specifics in the actual complexity of political life" (p. 194).
34. Discourse rather than revolutionary change is the central objective in Foucault's writing. Foucault had in practice a sympathetic but ill-defined attitude towards contemporary revolution. He was supportive of the student movements in France in May 1968, but was at that time outside France and involved in the more aggressive student revolts in Tunisia (see Foucault/Rabinow 1997, Vol. 3, pp. 278–282). Scullion (1995) was extremely critical of his original praise of the Iranian Islamic Revolution against the oppressive Pahlavi regime, but favourably considered his *Le Monde* article of May 1979, *Useless to Revolt*, in response to the Iranian revolution (see Foucault/Rabinow 2000, Vol. 3, pp. 449–453). She

concedes that in this "swan song of his Iranian adventure, the sincerity of Foucault's effort to combat tyranny and, more commendably, to engage a different kind of dialogue between East and West that might lead to greater respect for the otherness of its Oriental interlocutor, is very much in evidence" (p. 36). But she concludes by arguing strongly against his involvement in the first place.

35. Becker, who is best known for his development of the concept of human capital, gave a clear exposition of his ideas on application of economic rationality to non-commercial activity in his 1992 Nobel lecture. His ideas have been very influential in neoliberal thinking. Education has been regarded as being a good private investment and therefore something that individuals can sensibly borrow in expectation of good future returns. These concepts were taken up by government and by education providers, but with the long-term effect of making education more expensive and more easily available to the rich. The case made in this book, mainly in relation to environmental costs, is consistent with the view that the external effects of education on society are beneficial and that creation of this form of human capital should be encouraged by both government and private education providers (with a subsidy paid to the latter for this external benefit). Likewise, his ideas of rationality and responsiveness to economic incentives by criminals likely helped tough-on-crime approaches by government, but the reality is that criminals have little compunction against using intimidation and corruption as effective ways to make money and see high taxes as an opportunity for profit, through breaking the law.

36. Dieter Plehwe (2009) describes the wide-ranging nature of debate among the eminent members of the MPS, but makes it clear that political application of these ideas differed widely among countries and was influenced strongly by national and global events. The MPS provided a platform for exchange of ideas and perhaps provided a model for development of modern think tanks. It continues to operate (see https://www.montpelerin.org/wp-content/uploads/2015/12/Short-History-of-MPS-2014.pdf).

37. As Keane (2009), Sen (2009) and others make clear, the origins of democracy preceded the Athenian version, and Keane, as discussed in Chap. 7, indicates, modern democracy is far from a completed governance model.

38. Arthur Herman (2013) provides a very readable guide to the many ways in which the philosophical traditions established by Socrates, Plato, Aristotle and others of that era were developed, used, lost and regained over the past two and a half millennia. He does, however, associate Nietzsche with 'the end of reason', which seriously misrepresents modern philosophical developments.
39. See Foucault (2008) pp. 45–52 (lecture of 8 February, First Hour).
40. Ibid. p. 62 (lecture of 8 February, Second Hour).

References

Blackmore, Susan. 1999. *The Meme Machine*. Oxford: Oxford University Press.

Burchell, Graham, Colin Gordon, and Peter Miller, eds. 1991. *The Foucault Effect: Studies in Governmentality*. Chicago: University of Chicago Press.

Dawkins, Richard. 2006. *The God Delusion*. London: Bantam Press.

Dean, Mitchell. 1999a. Normalizing Democracy: Foucault and Habermas on Democracy, Liberalism, and Law, Chapter 6. In *Foucault Contra Habermas: Recasting the Dialogue Between Genealogy and Critical Theory*, ed. Samantha Ashendon and David Owen. London/Thousand Oaks/New Delhi: Sage Publications.

———. 1999b. *Governmentality: Power and Rule in Modern Society*. London Thousand Oaks/New Delhi: SAGE.

Deutsch, David. 2011. *The Beginning of Infinity: Explanations That Transform the World*. London: Penguin.

Dobson, Jerome E., and Peter E. Fisher. 2007. The Panopticon's Changing Geography. *The Geographical Review* 97 (3): 307–323.

Ferguson, Niall. 2006. *The War of the World: Twentieth-Century Conflict and the Descent of the West*. New York: Penguin Group USA, Hudson Street.

Foucault, Michel. 1966. *The Order of Things: An Archaeology of the Human Sciences*. Trans. Tavistock 1970. London/New York: Routledge Classics.

———. 1977. *Discipline and Punish: The Birth of the Prison*. Trans. A. Sheridan. London: Penguin Books 1991.

———. 1980. *Power/Knowledge:Selected Interviews and Other Writings 1972–1977*, ed. Colin Gordon. New York: Vintage.

———. 1997. *Society Must Be Defended: Lectures at the Collège de France (1975–76)*. English ed. Arnold I. Davidson; Trans. David Macey. New York: Picador

Foucault, Michel/Paul Rabinow. 1997–2000. *Essential Works of Foucault, 1954–1984*, Paul Rabinow, Series Editor: Vol. 1, *Ethics Subjectivity and Truth*, (1997), Paul Rabinow, Editor: Vol. 2, *Aesthetics, Method, and Epistemology*, (1998), James D. Faubion, Editor: Vol. 3 *Power*, (2000), James D. Faubion, Editor. New York: New Press.

Foucault, Michel. 2003. *Abnormal: Lectures at the Collège de France (1974–75)*. Trans. Graham Burchell. New York: Picador/Palgrave Macmillan.

———. 2008. *The Birth of Biopolitics: Lectures at the Collège de France (1978–79)*. Trans. Graham Burchell. New York: Picador/Palgrave Macmillan.

Henshall, Nicholas. 2010. *The Zenith of European Monarchy and Its Elites: The Politics of Culture, 1650–1750*. Houndmills, Basingstoke, Hampshire: Palgrave Macmillan.

Herman, Arthur. 2013. *The Cave and the Light: Plato Versus Aristotle, and the Struggle for the Soul of Western Civilization*. New York: Random House.

Keane, John. 2009. *The Life and Death of Democracy*. New York/London: W.W. Norton.

Kelly, Mark. 2010. International Biopolitics: Foucault, Globalisation and Imperialism. *Theoria* 57 (123): 1–26.

Kenny, Anthony. 2007. *Philosophy in the Modern World: A New History of Western Philosophy*. Vol. 4. Oxford: Clarendon Press.

Krugman, Paul. 2007. *The Conscience of a Liberal: Reclaiming America from the Right*. London: Allen Lane/Penguin.

Kuhn, Thomas. 1962. *The Structure of Scientific Revolutions*. Chicago: University of Chicago Press.

Lemke, Thomas. 2011. *Bio-politics: An Advanced Introduction*. New York/London: New York University Press.

Plehwe, Dieter. 2009. Introduction. In *The Road from Mont Pèlerin: The Making of the Neoliberal Thought Collective*, ed. Philip Mirowski and Dieter Plehw, 1–42 (http://uberty.org/wp-content/uploads/2015/10/mt-pelerin.pdf).

Sardar, Ziauddin. 2000. *Thomas Kuhn and the Science Wars*. London: Icon Books.

Schrift, Alan D. 2006. *Twentieth Century French Philosophy: Key Themes and Thinkers*. Blackwell Publishing.

Scull, Andrew. 2015. *Madness in Civilization: A Cultural History of Insanity, from the Bible to Freud, from the Madhouse to Modern Medicine*. Princeton: Princeton University Press.

Scullion, Rosemarie. 1995. Michel Foucault the Orientalist: On Revolutionary Iran and the "Spirit of Islam". *South Central Review* 12 (2): 16–40.
Sen, Amartya. 2009. *The Idea of Justice*. Cambridge, MA: The Belknap Press of HUP.
Shteyngart, Gary. 2010. *Super Sad True Love Story*. New York: Random House.
Tampke, Jürgen. 2017. *A Perfidious Distortion of History: The Versailles Peace Treaty and the Success of the Nazis*. Melbourne/London: Scribe.

2

Historical and Economic Roots of Neoliberalism

Economics has been interpreted over much of the twentieth century as providing the best available measure of social progress, and no one would deny the huge importance of commercial development in human history. But recent developments make it apparent that we need to look well beyond economics to guide government policies—even including those of managing the global economy. The latter issue, as well as the economic foundations that are taken to support neoliberalism, will be discussed in the following chapter; the dangers of continuing to base fundamental political decisions primarily on commerce-based measures of social change comprise its main topic. Together they point to the inseparability of social and economic development—and of government and markets.

Since the beginning of the twenty-first century nations have faced epochal change that includes possible imperial transition, but the processes of government that evolved over recent centuries now seem high-risk and inadequate to such immense transitions. The emergence of China as the major potential hegemonic rival to the US, faltering political and economic restructuring of Europe, the putative resurgence of Islam and increasingly violent schisms within it, lagging political and economic development in the so-called 'developing world' and management of global climate change—all point to the urgent need for government action to guide competitive market-based development and find new ways to control conflict. Many weaknesses within governments of all ideologies are evident, but many of the principles and mechanisms for establishing the relative role of government and the market are still to be fully resolved. It is even possible that the political, military and economic success of market economies has inhibited constructive analysis of broader governmental failings, including those of democratic governments. The quest to achieve outcomes that benefit the entire global society must look beyond economic prosperity as the prime measure of success; commercial success of a limited number of nations and limited numbers of individuals within nations is insufficient to guarantee the future even of these lucky few.

This chapter looks first at past epochal changes and their influences on government policies and public beliefs over the past 250 years (indeed drawing from a much longer history). Growth in economic prosperity has certainly defined much of what most see as global social development. Even clearer, however, social development and political and public views of the nature of that development have been and continue to be driven by much more than economics, as elaborated further in the following sections and subsequent chapters.

National Prosperity and Imperial Ambition

Epochal change creates lived and storied experience that becomes ingrained in public belief. No one in the current, living generations is untouched by the vast sweep of the Industrial Revolution, the impact of the American, French and Russian armed revolutions, colonial and imperial history, post-WW2 decolonization, and the Cold War confrontation between the Stalinist Soviet Union and the United States. The people of a nation absorb these values both consciously, through formal education, and subconsciously, as part of normal civic experience. National identity and pride in these events, moreover, is cultivated in all nations by careful promotion of past centuries' experience.

Since the mid-twentieth century, the metric of GDP has been used to measure national and global growth over time. Efforts have been made to apply the modern metric to earlier times, as described notably in *The Economist* (August 16, 2010, and June 20, 2012) and *The Atlantic* (June 2012); the pieces in both are based on the work of the late Angus Maddison of the University of Groningen. No purpose is served by reproducing these charts here.[1] It is now generally agreed that applying these data to times prior to the Industrial Revolution is misleading, largely because of the enormous growth in production per head, principally in Western countries from around 1820 on. Prior to that, measurement of income levels corresponded closely to population numbers. Even so, the earlier *Economist* chart, using estimated relative shares of aggregate GDP, illustrated the rise and relative decline of British economic power over the nineteenth and twentieth centuries, the dominance of the US economy in the twentieth century and today, and the steep decline of China in relative aggregate terms over the nineteenth and early twentieth centuries and its recent resurgence.

In modern times, national performance as measured in terms of GDP is accepted as a measure of relative economic importance. Representations of gross domestic product significantly mold public judgement regarding the superiority of free enterprise and trade over state-directed economic planning to develop an economy and a society. GDP has been firmly established as the primary metric of socio-economic worth.

Imperialism and Race: Prosperity for Some

History shows a much more complex picture. Commercial prosperity has been a fundamental goal for all countries and has led to prosperity for growing numbers of people as well as progress towards broader human rights. However, the trajectory of imperial competition initiated by European states and spurred by the Industrial Revolution in the eighteenth and nineteenth centuries has also established a pattern of competition among nations that has been costly for many participants, particularly those that lagged in establishing viable accountable government. Implicitly, we also assume continuation of hegemonic competition as the dominant mechanism for establishing global standards of governance.

Foucault introduces two important concepts to the debate on causal factors in national and international competitive behaviour. The first is the limits of rationality that he established in his *Madness and Civilization*, the second is his biopolitical definition of 'racism'. In the first he brought into philosophical and societal discourse the linked concepts of the limits of human reason and knowledge and the way in which a social group treats outsiders who do not correspond to acceptable 'normal' standards of behaviour. With respect to racism, he used the term in the neutral sense of biopolitical rivalry of groups with others outside family, belief tradition or regional boundaries: racism here is group fear of an external threat that is almost invariably exploited by rulers to consolidate internal power. In contrast, with respect to the latter, the historian Niall Ferguson treats racism in the more modern sense of the deep-seated ethnic hatreds that emerged virulently in late nineteenth century Europe and which he views as a major factor causing the twentieth century five-decade 'War of the World'. Both views are important, as we now discuss.

Economic differences are certainly of great significance, but for neither Ferguson nor Foucault did they provide a sufficient explanation of motivation or an adequate representation of social truth; differences arise from more fundamental causes. Innate biopolitical loyalties and rivalries play a fundamental role in creating group differences. Opportunities for adoption of new knowledge and technology are, however, critical in magnifying differences over time. Biological differences are no longer considered valid explanations for differing rates and trajectories of social development. Among recent contributions, archaeologist Ian Morris (2010) has given important evidence in his sweeping historical/anthropological overview of the past 15,000 years, speaking of how similar human civilizations are. Different rates of progress arise, he argues, not from fundamental biological and cultural qualities but primarily due to geographical and resource advantages that from time to time confer critical advantages in timeliness of technology adoption. "Biology and sociology provide universal laws, applying to all humans in all times and places; geography explains differences."[2] Morris focused primarily on the different trajectories of development of China and the Western powers, tracking social development in four dimensions: energy capture, organization/urbanization, war-making, and information technology. His data show striking similarities in these key dimensions of social development, with critical differences in timing of technological adoption and, in the broad case of China versus the West, compelling evidence of eventual catch-up.[3]

From more recent world history, however, cultural and national differences, as well as the technology of government and its fiscal management, are shown by historians to have mattered a great deal. Economic and militarily dominant civilizations have by most accounts viewed themselves as culturally superior to external 'barbarians', and conquering barbarians have usually adopted and adapted many of the customs and rules of the civilization they displaced. John Darwin's *After Tamerlane* (2006) highlights the many phases of imperial ambition, conquest and decline over the past 700 years leading to our present globalized but polarized world. Tamerlane's short empire was powerful but transitional; after his death in 1405 power shifted decisively to the settled states of West and East Eurasia rather than the previously nomad-controlled centre.[4] This transition allowed imperial ambition in the settled states to be more easily realized, albeit vulnerable to changing technology and rival powers.

The uncertainties of the past seven centuries thus have set the stage for those emerging in the twenty-first. Statehood, in a sense approaching modernity, had been more fully established in the Western European part of Eurasia and in China than in the central Asian territories. In the former case, the administrative apparatus of the former Western Roman Empire had been largely adopted by the victorious Frankish nobility. The Westphalian treaties of 1648 helped secure some degree of stability for individual states, but, of course, could not rule out either war or competition for imperial expansion among them. Darwin emphasized the emergence of the 'fiscal-military state' in Europe in the eighteenth century as being critical both to success within Western Europe and to expansion of Western power in Eurasia. Success and competition within Europe also however had a destabilizing effect on the Islamic centre as European powers vied against one another to gain trade and exert authority over central and eastern Eurasian states.

John Brewer, whose classic *The Sinews of Power* (1989) established the phrase 'fiscal-military state', had earlier argued that Britain's fiscal processes were more developed than its rivals in Europe, and its fiscal effectiveness gave it an initial advantage in geopolitical expansion. Britain's development of effective fiscal management practice was inextricably entangled with its growing need to finance military action associated with mercantilist and imperial expansion during the seventeenth and eighteenth centuries. Britain's edge over its rivals arose from several factors[5]:

- Earlier than other European countries, it established an effective, well-organized tax collection system, moving progressively from 'tax farming' (selling the right to collect various taxes—a practice continued in other European states such as France and Prussia well into the eighteenth century) to control of tax collection by centrally appointed government officials.
- Effective control and parliamentary accountability of taxation, combined with the establishment in the late seventeenth century of centralized expenditure management through the Treasury Board, provided in turn the necessary basis to secure credit on good terms and establish a market in government securities.
- The Bank of England, founded in 1694 as a privately held corporation (nationalized only in 1946) to raise finances for the government, progressively took over the functions of public debt management and established basic principles and practices for national central banks.

These fiscal administration developments contributed crucially to Britain's emergence as a leader of the Industrial Revolution and its dominant position in European colonial expansion; their success established a foundation for the powerful role that fiscal management and economics allied to national security has come to play in all economically advanced countries. These practices were progressively taken up by competing European states and their powerful successor, the United States.[6]

Darwin's subsequent treatment of the British imperial experience, *Unfinished Empire* (2012), focused on the dominant British role up to 1914 and decline thereafter. Continuing imperial ambition and competition among the European states, combined with a breakdown of the post-1815 Concert of Europe, created an environment at the beginning of the twentieth century that led to the First World War and all that followed. While he emphasizes that imperial ambitions incorporated an element of civilizational responsibilities, these were mingled inextricably with a multitude of competing interests and proved to be a lesser priority in the face of continuing military and economic battles for survival.[7] In the end, the British Empire, like others before it, found that the expenses of maintaining a command structure in the face of endless and powerful competition could not be sustained. The United States, a product of British-initiated ruthless colonization of native-held lands, emerged from the European imperial struggles as both ruler of a resource-rich and technologically-advanced continent and leading member of the victorious allies after the Second World War defeat of Germany.

Niall Ferguson's treatment of the culmination of European imperial conflict in the twentieth century, the ascent of American power and what he claims is the inexorable decline of the West in favour of a resurgent East adds interesting and important dimensions to the debate over the causes and consequences of imperialist-driven conflict. As a historian, he was concerned with providing better record-based explanations of what caused the calamitous worldwide conflicts of the first half of the twentieth century and not at all with analysis of the Foucauldian forces that could lead to social progress and truth. His analysis in many ways, however, can be seen to be complementary rather than opposed to Foucault's epistemic approach to social struggle and change; it helps us to understand more of the social factors that ignited the conflict but not necessarily what institutional change is needed to improve government of ourselves in the future. But he also runs some risks of hypothesizing historicist theories of inevitable repeating conflict and decline among human tribes. Foucault, in contrast, seeks ways to analyze the underlying biopolitics of group conflict and promote resolution through recognition of these forces and public discourse.

Ferguson's invocation of Richard Dawkins' concept of memes (outlined in Chap. 1) constitutes a significant difference between his and Foucault's analytical perspective. He proposes that racism "in the sense of a strongly articulated sense of racial differentiation" (p. li) is a stable replicable idea identity—a meme, comparable to a biological gene which survives through generations. He does establish a body of clear evidence of the genesis and visceral reality of ethnic, religious and racial hatred throughout Europe in the late nineteenth century. His research gives a convincing picture of the deep-seated prejudices of the time, and these would have provided a fertile ground both for hostile actions among groups and for engaging popular support for continuing and escalating conflict. The reality of this form of racism, which continues in present times, cannot be denied, and its portrayal is of value in understanding the ease with which small conflicts escalated into WW1 and its continuation in WW2.

Foucault's contrasting thesis, to which I subscribe, is that racism is not a fundamental feature of human nature in the same way as is the instinct for protection of self, family and group. Racism exists, of course, but it becomes effective through manipulation of basic group instincts by mechanisms of sovereign (and religious) discipline that had been well established by the early twentieth century. The power of the fiscal-military state (though Ferguson does not use the term), competition among the hegemonic competitors in Europe and growing competition elsewhere, which he describes, provide much more compelling explanations for the genesis of the War of the World than the prevalence of the racism meme. He cites twelve European-based empires that controlled roughly half the world's territory and population by 2013, as well as nascent Japan, and declining China, which controlled around a further 3 and 24 percent, respectively, of the global population (pp. 16–17). He adds that "[w]hen these [European] empires acted in concert, as they did in Africa from the 1870s and in China from the 1890s, they brooked no opposition" (p. 16).

European imperialism massively damaged both the countries that it colonized and ultimately the prospects of Europe. Imperialists presented a cloak of civilizational intentions with respect to its multitude of colonies, as described by Darwin regarding Britain. But all imperialists, including Britain, were primarily motivated by the interests of the parent state. From the late eighteenth century onwards, moreover, a major shift in sovereign power from the monarchy and aristocracy to the fiscal-military apparatus of the state had occurred as a consequence of revolution in North America and France and democratic reform in these states and Britain. Jürgen Tampke (2017) adds an important rider to the interpretation of German militarism, which from Bismarck onwards (see his Chap. 1, *Imperial Germany*) became a driving force of Germany's foreign policy and was a major factor both in WW1 as well as military build-up leading eventually to WW2.

Thus, quite critically for their relations with each other, European nations were driven by the internal power of their national fiscal-military bureaucracies. In describing the genesis of WW1, Ferguson puts the case clearly: the war did not, as many had represented, arise because of rifts within the linked European monarchies and the ambitions of Kaiser Wilhelm II. On the contrary, "...the Kaiser, like his Saxe-Coburg relatives, lacked the power to override the military and political professionals if they were resolved to go to war" (p. 100). Ferguson refers to WW1 as a 'general's war'. Military mobilization by any European state that appeared to threaten another state necessitated, first, diplomatic overtures, but equally a show of opposing military strength would almost always be necessary. The complexity of these interactions prior to the outbreak of war is well described by Ferguson (here too, however, Tampke's observations need to be taken into account). Normal diplomacy required Austria to demand redress from Serbia for the assassination of Archduke Ferdinand; Soviet support of Serbia was equally predictable. When diplomacy failed, war seemed a 'pressing necessity' to the generals. British involvement in the war made globalization of the conflict inevitable because of its control over around a quarter of the globe's land surface and a higher proportion of its sea lanes (Ferguson p. 109). It could be added that the close connection between Britain and the US made this outcome and its global consequences, including American military and economic dominance, even more certain.

Ferguson's analysis of the genesis of the twentieth century's disastrous conflicts is remarkably consistent with Foucault's view of the consequences that flow from poorly articulated governmental processes. In many ways, Foucault's 'ubu' metaphor (referred to in Chap. 1) is more tellingly applied to the horrific outcomes of WW1 and WW2 that Ferguson describes than to Foucault's examples of routine miscarriage of justice. The latter undoubtedly do arise from disciplinary disconnection in application of criminal codes and are significant at many levels of society, but international conflicts and their resultant injustice represent much more significant failures of government. Both types of miscarriage demand attention, but the potential for international conflict should be more urgently addressed.

Neither grave international nor ongoing national issues can be resolved by market forces or by small, weak governments. We need stronger and better governments that can recognize and react to such threats and consequences, which in turn will require multilateral institutional change to address them. Imperial history up to this point gives little indication that hegemonic dominance by a single power will allow, far less lead to, strong support for multilateralism. Evidence so far seems to point to the contrary, and though the US should be given credit for initiating moves towards creation of the UN—it deserves less for its subsequent record of support.

It is worth reflecting at this point that economics has contributed somewhat ambiguously to this national/international defence and security debate. Defence has long been seen as *the* classical collective good that clearly requires government control and investment, a position that is all very fine when considered from the point of view of an individual national government. From a multinational perspective, however, a national collective good becomes a local product whose production threatens its neighbours, creates competitive pressures to improve military technology, and increases the threat threshold and potentially reduces non-military growth for all nations. Competition for nuclear supremacy has hugely raised these stakes. Even in relatively peaceful times it is necessary for our current hegemon as well as its rivals to maintain capacity to counter potential nuclear armed enemy states.[8] Privatization of the non-nuclear weapons supply by modern military-industrial complexes[9] adds a profit motive—and consequently limits economic and/or ethical examination of the consequences of commercial arms (or critical components) sales to all potential combatants; as Bhojani (2016) has noted, the availability of components with military potential throughout the world has greatly increased the potential for effective non-state terrorism (and effectively nullified the often-quoted institutionalists requirement of 'state monopoly of violence', discussed further in Chap. 7). I will return to the political dynamics of collective choice in Chaps. 4 and 6 and the problems of global security in Chap. 7.

Changing Biopolitical and Ideological Balances

As outlined above, though Foucauldian biopolitics explains the driving forces of neoliberalism, the balances among these forces have been transformed, particularly in the last three decades. First, *ideology*: neoliberalism, which espouses market sovereignty as the basis for national and global government and pushes strongly for strict limits on the size of government, has established a strong ideological influence on Western economic policies, particularly in the US.[10] Planned economies, in contrast, combine Leninist central direction of government with controlled market freedom. Anatole Kaletsky appears to regard both as variants of modern evolving capitalism; each version could be driven by what he sees as an inherent capacity of capitalism to renew itself. However, the marked difference in approach to capitalism by the main hegemonic contenders and their views of the relative roles of government and aspirations of citizens pose risks of conflict that go well beyond economic governance relationships.

Various forms of conservatism have also been renascent, most prominently through the emergence of the neoconservative Bush–Cheney 2001–2008 US administration, which sought to reshape the theocracies of the Middle East in anticipation of public and ultimately political acceptance of US-style liberal democracy. Such an approach was seen to be justified in large part by the military and economic triumph of Western capitalism over the totalitarian ideologies of Leninist communism and Nazism. This resolve was buttressed by the support of neoconservative academic literature led by Samuel Huntington's thesis regarding the 'clash of civilizations' and Francis Fukuyama's 'end of history'. The continuing combination of neoliberalism and the military and security implications of neoconservative policy and 'clash' theory challenge world prosperity and security in a way that is becoming comparable to what was seen in the early twentieth century. The constellation of protagonists has changed and their fiscal-military power has increased, but all forms of government seem slow to absorb recent lessons or to tackle more purposefully the biopolitical forces they faced from antiquity.

The term 'ideology', moreover, cannot ignore competing theistic explanations for humanity's existence, growth of knowledge and standards of behaviour. Scientific explanations cannot refute the possibility of the existence of a supreme being, but no one set of theistic beliefs has provided enough evidence to justify its claim to be a better explanation of God's existence and the human condition than any other. Religion has nonetheless proved a powerful ideological ally to various forms of sovereignty, and it continues to be so, most evidently in theocratic states. It also exercises a profound influence in the United States, despite the explicit separation of the state and religion in its Constitution. Established religion remains influential in most modern states.

All ideologies are equivalent in this respect, and all need very careful and critical examination. Religion, as Marx declared, can serve as the opium of the people—but so too, for a time, did Marxism! Both sovereignty and religion, even predating Bentham's panopticon, established forms of social discipline. Pure sovereignty exercised control by militaristic surveillance, religion more subtly (at least pre-Reformation and Inquisition) by requiring public display of religious observance. When combined, sovereignty and religion merged these techniques, at the frequently brutal expense of individual liberty and parrhesia. The weakness of both traditional sovereignty and ideology is that they resist critical examination and develop self-protecting social surveillance mechanisms to preserve power and avoid exploring alternative ways to establish social truth.

A second defining feature of twenty-first century social and political development is the exponential expansion of *information and communications technology* (ICT), intertwined with ever-advancing military technology. These twin factors, as described in Chap. 1, have created an enveloping apparatus of social surveillance in both liberal democracies and centrally directed economies, far beyond anything envisaged in Foucault's panopticism—indeed with potential shades of Orwell's *1984* or Shteyngart's collapsing US and global society. Together, these ideological and technological trends present an existential challenge for government of the world in this and future centuries. An ordered society demands and needs wide-ranging information and communication on its citizens, their activities and issues. But overly secretive and unaccountable panoptic control of information and communication, or its synoptic misuse, pose huge dangers for the ruled and relatively powerless masses. Better and timelier information is needed on the ways authorities are handling these technical and ethical challenges.

Continuing *heavily militarized hegemonic rivalry for world sovereignty* seems likely to pose the most extreme threat for the future and should demand the most attention by national governments and global governance institutions. The utility of market forces is not now a major point of difference among nations; but continuing to divert resources toward military rather than civil production should be recognized as both wasteful and high risk for global security. We have moved violently from proto-democratic Athenian city-states to the imperial states of Macedonia and Rome to European fiscal-military states dominated in the nineteenth century by Britain; then, following two World Wars, to the present democratic American leadership of world affairs and domination of international institutions. It is not yet clear that the democratic credentials of US leadership will avoid or reduce the brutality and waste of past quests for dominance and resulting conflict.

Julian Assange has declared the United States to be the world's last empire, on grounds of its present technological and economic predominance, and particularly through its surveillance and security links with close allies. A central point made by Assange, particularly regarding the United States but with general application, is that national security concerns among hegemonic rivals should not be allowed to determine international outcomes without effective oversight by independent representatives of the public. Not least, given the threat of terrorism arising from the fractured states of the Middle East and South Asia and the tension between legitimate oversight of potential terror threats and legitimate privacy rights, it is becoming increasingly necessary to establish a structure for surveillance that meets both national and international goals of peaceful cooperation and just treatment of citizens of conflict countries.

Understanding and controlling the modern panopticon/synopticon is therefore critical. The continuing contest between the US-dominated alliance and directed capitalism rivals, once dominated by Russia and now by China, makes continuing security-linked surveillance operations necessary for all. WikiLeaks has amply demonstrated both the remarkable extent of official surveillance and the US security-based cover-ups for unethical, indeed murderous, diplomatic and military behaviour; though equivalent or worse cover-ups doubtless occur in other jurisdictions. While WikiLeaks and Assange need to be open to and answer questions regarding their own transparency, revelations from available WikiLeaks documents do highlight the need to strengthen controls over national security operations relative to citizen and civil society rights in *all* jurisdictions. They also point to the urgent need for formal and timely oversight of national security by organizations that are independent of it and answerable to the public in a form that meets 'rule of law' standards (of which more will be said in Chap. 7).

The current US national security reaction, by mandating extreme punishment on whistle-blowers and on WikiLeaks operations, runs counter to these objectives. The reactions are quite consistent with the ethos of national security worldwide, but not with the higher ethos of global security. In an ideal future, more aligned with global interest, national security should be subject to a higher ethical oversight, looking beyond hegemonic contest and towards least-cost/high-global-security outcomes. The difficulties of tackling entrenched national and international security practices must not be underestimated, but if democracy is to be preserved, enhanced and promoted among all nations, the US should take steps towards reconciling its diplomatic and security procedures with its own avowed standards. Clearly reciprocal measures from hegemonic rivals would be essential for the process to take root and challenge the presently entrenched realpolitik of the UN Security Council. The new realpolitik being framed by the Trump administration, however, shows no signs of these kinds of calculations. We return to these issues below and again in Chap. 7.

Now, however, we look more closely at three aspects of national and imperial contest in the modern era: first, the ambitious but now crumbling integration of Europe; second, the marginalization of developing countries; and third, the changed environment for balancing hegemonic competition. All three demonstrate the continuing fact of competition among and within sovereign states. But these concerns highlight the necessity and hope of improving and directing national and local government away from commercial and military competition and towards building multilateral policies aimed at the common good. Key reform areas that are emerging to help move economic and social policy in this direction are examined in more detail in Part II, but first we need to review the key biopolitical issues that demand these reforms.

European Integration: Renewing the Vision?

Europe after the Cold War seemed to show promise of a friendly but powerful counterbalance to US hegemony. Now it is demonstrating an apparent inability of its democratic states with a shared inheritance to work towards bigger regional and global roles. The EU, the Commission, and the eurozone all appear to have lost momentum, certainly in terms of the original and seemingly eminently worthy aims. Much of Europe's current problems have been attributed to the introduction of the euro as a common currency.[11] As Timothy Garton Ash (2012) records, the continuing EU economic crisis was already foretold prior to the establishment of the European Monetary Union (EMU) in 1999, including in an earlier article by him in 1998.

In 1996 Rudiger Dornbusch had warned of the dangers of creating the eurozone:

> "At the outset, European integration was a historic move to bring Germany and France together and thus avoid the recurrent wars that have plagued this century. Then European integrationists developed bigger ambitions—the creation of a common market with no obstacles to trade in goods and services or the movement of people. Monetary union was to be the next step on the way to full union. Even as that agenda is being implemented, the circle of candidates for inclusion in the European Union (EU) widens, public disenchantment grows, and the contradictions between enlarging the circle and deepening the integration of members become more apparent." (p. 111)

This critique was widely held—and seemed prophetic: the EMU seemed doomed to fail because of the disparities in fiscal competence among its member states and the very limited political authority of either the European Parliament or the Commission. While European nations were very willing to integrate in the interests of avoiding future wars and improving trade, sovereignty of European national states appeared too deeply established to expect fiscal decisions to be subject to a strong higher authority. Certainly too little was done to support development of fiscal management standards among the weaker members.

Given the wide range of governance and fiscal management experience among the countries eventually included in the EMU, more attention given to long-term institutional strengthening of prospective (and even existing) members could have paid dividends and provided insurance against the collective failure that instead emerged. Greece—the focus of continuing efforts to save the euro—perhaps more than most member states, lacked the fiscal and political infrastructure to ensure it could become a viable member of a common currency zone. "Greece was admitted as the 12th member of monetary union in 2001 although all governments knew that Greek financial statistics were unreliable." (Majone, p. 3) The fundamental weakness of its fiscal administration undoubtedly contributed more to the Greek debt crisis and the continuing impasse over Greece's future in the EMU than any lack of higher level understanding of appropriate fiscal and monetary policies. The other side of this picture, however, is the failure of EU creditor nations and the institutional framework to foresee the risks and accept some responsibility for the outcome. A failure of detailed implementation appears to be at least part of the problem, but there now looms a potential abandonment of the overall concept of a unified European contribution to regional and global government: Brexit rather than Grexit!

Concerns with the weaker nations have now been overshadowed by the decision of the UK to leave the EU, and populist reactions are causing concern elsewhere. At the time of writing, the processes of departure and future relations between the EU and Britain are being determined. Anti-immigration sentiments are strong in France and the Netherlands and in several other EU member countries. As one of the stronger economic and military powers of Europe, however, the nature of its departure and its continuing relationships with the EU will have enormous implications for the future direction of European integration and its weight in global policy and development. The decline of Europe as a significant force for global progress will diminish both the prospects of all European countries and the impact of Europe as a power to promote global integration consistent with liberal democracy.

A stronger and more integrated Europe remains vital for effective and balanced global development, but it will be necessary to rethink the institutional changes needed to achieve this goal—so far, too much has relied on the broad aspirations of European politicians, too little on assessment of national differences and ways to create sustainable institutions in this given environment. The notion of a federal or quasi-federated EU entity was perhaps never feasible. Federation for Europe was strongly advocated by Hayek in 1944[12] as the best way to limit sovereign power and avoid what he saw as the twin dangers of 'master race' domination by hegemonic power and the impossibility of government-led economic planning. The damaging effects of these forms of social development, he argued—doubtless persuasively at the time—were demonstrated, on the one hand, by the rise of Nazi Germany and communist USSR and, on the other, by hegemonic power exercised by imperial powers over their colonies in the nineteenth and early twentieth centuries. While these issues loomed large then, it was not evident that a federal governance structure was the appropriate solution. Hayek's real issues arose from his reaction to Marxist–Leninist ideology, imperial overreach and overestimation of hegemonic virtues. He did raise an important point, however, regarding the need to limit the hegemon's ability to set rules of government for the disparate peoples under its protection.

Federation as practiced since the American and French revolutions remains an intensely difficult form of government; variations in form and implementation of federal institutions should prohibit a general endorsement of this being the most favoured for democratic government. The strategy for doing so in Europe was never defined and now seems out of practical reach. The need to address growing economic and political crises in Europe, however, should make finding a new way forward a matter of urgency. Potential Grexit, likely Brexit, continuing threats to the EMU and the rise of nationalist, micro-nationalist and anti-immigrant sentiments in many parts of Europe present a set of problems that simply must be addressed in the interests of the region and for the contribution that a coherent European voice and power can make to global governance.

Constitutional federalism does not seem promising in this environment. The EU's 'hybrid constitution' and complex institutional structure seem to have contributed signally to the results we are now experiencing; a root and branch review appears necessary. The quasi-federal nature of negotiating between EU law and sovereign laws has long been recognized as problematic, perhaps particularly by the UK, but increasingly by others.[13] A much more detailed analysis of the problems and possibilities for Europe post-Brexit and with a substantially remodelled EMU arrangement is urgently required.

It may be helpful to examine some alternative views of how national and cosmopolitan values can be reconciled, not necessarily through formal federal structures. Jürgen Habermas (2012) has advanced some general principles of how the crisis of the European Union should be addressed. He suggests (both for the EU and the UN) that responsibility for political decisions should rest with the *established nation-states*, but a *supranational association of peoples and states* should be responsible for setting moral standards for human rights and the use of force. Member states of both supranational organizations would "retain control over the means for legitimate use of force, though not the right to use them as they please" (p. 58). Habermas' methodology is to establish sound ethical and veridical principles and expect these to be taken up by political and administrative leaders. His view could accommodate a variety of mechanisms that could promote cosmopolitan values and their gradual adoption within national laws. These principles have not, as far as I'm aware, been explored as basis for political action, but conventional attempts to establish a new order for either Europe or the world are not only not working, they are degenerating into tribal rejection of cross-border migration. Consistent with Habermas' proposal—and not far out of line with the UK view—the EU could be reconstituted as the 'United European Nations', a formal grouping of nations under the UN, with a mandate to deliberate on matters of international law and relations, but with individual nations responsible for its national rules; these rules would aim to become progressively more consistent with regional and global aims for justice and security.

Jakub Grygiel (2016) has also recently written optimistically about a return to a grouping of nation-states as a possible upside to its continuing crisis. He writes critically of the ineffectuality of present policies in response to crises, and concludes: "It's time for U.S. leaders and Europe's political class to recognize that a return to nation-states in Europe does not have to end in tragedy...Europe will be able to meet its most pressing security challenges only when it abandons the fantasy of continental unity and embraces its geopolitical pluralism" (p. 101).

Foucault's biopolitical approach in this field is somewhat complementary to that of Habermas (though they are sometimes presented as polar opposites).[14] Foucault simply requires us to explore much more deeply why proposed adoption of cosmopolitan values are unlikely to be taken up spontaneously and what factors may help persuade those in power to change. We are still far from understanding what levers can be pulled to establish international standards of behaviour that will lead nation-states to observe universal standards for human dignity and human rights, but governments and supranational organizations should begin devoting resources to find workable answers to these problems. Give their deep-seated political and social problems, European leaders should consider a less juridically driven process.

The UN is often criticized by national governments as being inefficient and ineffective. Its role like that of its predecessor the League of Nations has been contentious over the past century. Nonetheless, despite these difficulties its achievements have been impressive, as we discuss further below. Deliberative discourse via UN or related multinational channels will—or should—become increasingly important over the coming century.

Such solutions, however, are not immediately in reach. As with any major institutional change much depends on the past trajectory ('path dependency', as institutionalists remind us is an ever-present barrier to radical institutional reform). Any disentanglement of Europe's future from its past mistakes must admit the problem of revising the vast legal infrastructure member nations already agreed to. As many commentators on the future of Brexit have observed, Britain faces huge legal and administrative problems in renegotiating the trade, immigration and budget commitments it acceded to while a member of the EU. A huge step in administrative and diplomatic practice would be required to reimagine and renegotiate the notion of the EU as if the failed concepts of the past had never happened. In the meantime, other players such as Russia and the US are urged by some to take opportunities to diminish the importance of the EU as a global player. We will revisit these issues in chapters ahead, particularly in Chap. 7, in the context of global security.

Developing Countries: Governance by Others

The task of spreading economic and social growth to developing countries is a challenge that was only fully acknowledged after WW2. While some elements of developing countries that did not participate fully in the British and European Industrial Revolution began during colonialization of Africa, Asia and the Americas, the task of spreading governance and the rule of law was very much secondary to that of establishing national power and prestige by the competing colonial powers.

The institutional framework for transnational policy-making that developed post WW1 is heir to the past and still remains work in progress, as well-described in Mark Mazower's *No Enchanted Palace* (2009) and subsequent *Governing the World* (2012). In these books he traces the tortuous path of multilateralism and something of its impact on countries outside the European imperial expansion. He describes first the role of the colonial powers in shaping both the League of Nations post-WW1 and the UN at the end of WW2, and subsequently the starts and shifts under US-led policies through the Cold War and beyond.

In *Enchanted Palace*, Mazower emphasizes the role of British imperial thinking, which had an underlying aim of maintaining domination of the subordinated countries, and which, rather than Wilsonian internationalism, formed the basis for establishing the structure of the League of Nations. The influence of Jan Smuts both in setting up the ill-fated League and his contribution to drafting the charter of the UN was extraordinary, more particularly in the latter case because so little had changed in the imperialists' perspective of their colonies and the necessity for paternalist oversight of (their) developing world. "Smuts and other theorists of the British Empire had turned to the concept of commonwealth to imagine a way of unifying nations in a common cause for the sake of democracy."[15]

In *Governing the World*, Mazower examined the ways in which post-WW2 US/USSR ideological and military rivalry replaced multilateralism with bilateral, ideologically driven competition. He observed that the ideological diversity of member states and the 'relaxed' criteria for membership[16] *could* have prevented the UN merely being used as a tool of superpower policy. However, its structure, and the emergence of USSR-led competition and the Cold War, effectively meant that the US ignored the UN as a means for achieving multilateral policy agreement.

The initial phase of Truman internationalism from 1949 embodied a large element of American technological confidence, which, combined with emerging development economic theory, led to the belief that US, as the most technologically advanced and powerful nation in the world, could lead the delivery of economic growth to the less developed nations.[17] Western nations in general supported delivery of investment and aid to the 'third world' to drive growth guided by economic modelling, one which identified the twin gaps of investment/savings and foreign exchange that could be closed by foreign investment and aid. This approach also helped initiate national development planning commissions or departments throughout much of the developing world as well as a rapid growth in international development bureaucracy. Though the term 'planning' brought to mind Soviet-style planning to command and control national production and likely added an edge to US ideological opposition to development aid, in Western-influenced developing countries it mainly reflected the need to set up mechanisms through which foreign aid needs to promote economic growth could be estimated and channelled to identified programs.

These technocratic solutions to fundamental geopolitical problems, however, were unsustainable for several reasons: (i) funding was never adequate to meet the required investment; (ii) political support for continued aid to developing countries was driven more by Cold War rivalry than a solidly agreed-to need to rebalance the world order in favour of the developing world; and (iii) the models on which aid and investment needs were calculated underestimated the grave institutional/governance and delivery weaknesses. Promised results were unsurprisingly not delivered.

As Mazower points out, on the first and second of these points, US (and advanced country, generally) support for developing countries has waxed and waned depending to an extent on the political party in power in the US. Republicans have generally been less supportive, but even under the Kennedy/Johnson administrations political concern has been highly influenced by the political necessity of being seen to combat the advance of communism in the developing world. Because of these pressures as well as extreme doubts about the direction of UN thinking on aid financing and ambitious proposals for expansion of the UN, the US strongly supported the International Bank for Reconstruction and Development (IBRD) as the key agency to channel finance to developing countries in preference to such UN organizations as the United Nations Development Program (UNDP) and the United Nations Commission for Trade and Development (UNCTAD). The IBRD and the IMF thus became (and have continued as) the favoured instruments of US international development policy.[18]

Sustainable growth objectives for newly independent countries also suffered from US- and UN-led decolonization and rapid establishment of new independent states among the former colonies throughout the 1960s and 70s (signalled by UK Prime Minister Harold Macmillan's 'Winds of Change' speech in Ghana and South Africa in 1960). Rapid departure of colonial administrative staff and inadequate resources gave little time to set up the institutional strength needed to establish effective self-government in the new nations. Aid dependency and technocratic solutions to development from multiple aid donors, including regional development banks and bilateral support particularly from former colonial powers, became features of international development policy that continue to the present day. Reflecting on my own early experience in Papua New Guinea, I believe that Australia's departure from support through building a strong national planning and budget administration in the 1970s towards project-by-project supervision from the 1990s onward was over hasty.

Thus, rather than a more inclusive world governance structure, the colonial era legacy and decolonization after WW2 under US hegemony combined with Cold War rivalry ensured that development policy thereafter, while under broad US political direction, enjoyed only piecemeal support. The alternative, proposed by the UN halfway through the 1960s 'development decade', notably including Dutch Nobel laureate Jan

Tinbergen, however, was unwieldy in many respects, particularly in the proposed expansion of the UN,[19] and would most certainly have been ineffective, possibly even with US support. The failure of the proposed technocratic solutions to give priority to reform of national government in developing countries and to establish effective coordination among competing donors was then, and continues to be, a crucial weakness in moving towards a balanced participation by least advantaged countries in the world order. The subsequent unwieldiness, expense and inefficiencies of many major UN initiatives continue to raise fundamental questions about the merits and feasibility of defining global objectives that are not built from national objectives and strategies. Grand strategies to implement global programs without fully engaging national governance reform seem impractical, as I will discuss in Chap. 5 and revisit in Chap. 7.

Reform of internal governance in developing countries is increasingly being seen in the twenty-first century as critical to sustainable implementation of global goals. However, national sovereignty arguments are used in most countries to resist adoption of global values and norms. Some progress has indeed been made on establishing international legal frameworks, but resources to ensure that these broadly agreed upon global standards can be met are clearly inadequate. Limited progress has been made on advancing human rights in general terms—mainly, however, in the industrialized countries—but far too little on protecting minorities within national borders. Internal reforms continue to be problematic, and, while mentioned, are rarely core elements of project or policy assistance from development partners (DPs). Development assistance aims mainly to strengthen bureaucratic procedures but cannot properly address their institutional and political context and constraints.

The epochal change emerging in the early twenty-first century will certainly deliver new challenges for a more cooperative world order. Mazower's conclusion that "[t]he idea of governing the world is becoming yesterday's dream" (p. 427) seems too pessimistic—at least prior to the advent of the Trump administration. Chapter 7 revisits this question in light of the changing nature of hegemonic competition; while some aspects give little cause for optimism, our recent economic and political shocks should—once administrations settle—lead all sides to lean more towards calculation and advancement of global benefits and costs rather than the potential calamity of global conflict. Indeed, the UN continues to play a vital role in broadening discussion and awareness of human rights and environmental issues and steady progress is being made towards acceptance of human rights, albeit in the face of continuing resistance in many areas. As briefly discussed below, the nature of the challenges between the US and China seemed in some respects objectively capable of being managed in a much less confrontational way than those of the Cold War. But the dangers of a more unpredictable stance by the US under President Trump and counteraction by China and Russia cannot be discounted.

The case that market and trade (particularly through predominantly bilateral negotiations and deals) by themselves will lead to international cooperation is simply untenable. Government must be improved at all levels of domestic and international order to address the problems and inequalities that are emerging, much through unfettered cross-border corporate activity. Judgements on the needed size of government should be based on a much better-defined and measured assessment of the value of collective services it provides and its capacity to ensure effectiveness of delivery. Nation states and our present structure of international organization are unavoidably the starting points for building this new international order. The eventual structure of international cooperation will undoubtedly differ from the vision of Mazower's nineteenth century internationalists, but some grouping of nations, international forums, and discursive processes must surely be maintained and strengthened to enable the community of nations to agree and implement global goals and norms. As we will revisit in Chap. 7, the world community must use multilateral forums and new forms of regional cooperation to establish respect for and protect minority rights and to avoid ideological hegemony. This objective will not be achieved soon, but it should not be prematurely ruled out of reach.

Balancing Superpower Relations

The United States, well before the end of the Cold War, had achieved its status as the most powerful nation on earth in both military and economic terms. But by sheer force of population and adoption of market-based (albeit directed) principles of economic management, China is close to surpassing the US in aggregate GDP terms and is fast acquiring competitive military capacity. Militarily, Russia, and several other states not allied to the US have sufficient nuclear arms capacity to pose a threat of significant damage to America or its allies, and Russia, in particular, is showing signs of ruthlessly pursuing the goal of 'making Russia great again' through strategic deployment of force in areas of weak governance and resource riches or strategic importance.[20] The case for boosting multilateral action to reduce these threats and help move resources globally from military to socially and economically productive activities seems undeniably strong. But points that seem rational from a global perspective are, in present practice, outweighed by realist national security pressures, and many of the rules are set by the major hegemonic contestants. Is this a game that is blessed by history with inescapable rules? Or can we at last learn to seek alternatives to military build-up and economic aggression? Multilateral institutions are in place; can we use them better to avoid the worst features of hegemonic competition?

A defining feature of hegemony is that less powerful groups and nations have limited scope to speak truth to power—parrhesia written large! This limitation is true both of minorities within the powerful nations and of relations between the hegemon and its less powerful allies. Australia, for instance, has long been the representative of British imperial power in the Asia-Pacific region and has played its role in many wars of the British Empire, importantly in the Boer War and the two World Wars. With the post-Cold War shift in hegemonic competition from the countries of the Atlantic to those of the Pacific, the Australian alliance has unavoidably become much more linked to US interests in preserving, or establishing a new, Pacific, balance of power. As Martin Parkinson (2016) has observed, perhaps somewhat optimistically, "the [new] diffusion of power, both among nation states and from nations to non-state actors, means that the US will need to operate differently...if it is to achieve success... [meaning it] needs a 'smart power strategy,'... [A] change to global economic governance arrangements is not only necessary, but inevitable." (pp. 160–1)

As an Australian, he was reluctant to criticize US diplomacy in the region because of past benefits flowing from US leadership. US leadership in the

Asia-Pacific region will undoubtedly become more disputable, but it also provides an opportunity for Australia to play a role in establishing multilateral approaches to regional problems—as it has done through engagement in G20 initiatives and did in playing an important role in setting up the Asia-Pacific Economic Cooperation (APEC) initiative in 1989. Only through such groupings and promoting their successful operations can countries with limited economic or military weight hope to influence the major players. This task now appears much more difficult for Australia with the new US administration.

So-called 'G-summitry' and regional political arrangements have arisen in part with the aim of giving greater voice and consideration to smaller countries within the UN system. The G20 grouping of 19 high- and middle-income countries plus the EU was formed following the Asian financial crisis.[21] In terms of global issues this grouping can easily be (and has been) criticized for its continuing domination by North America and Europe, and its minimal inclusion of the sub-Saharan African region (only South Africa), and North African and Middle East (Saudi Arabian) representation. The G20 could potentially play a critical role however in addressing the current Asia-Pacific-centred global issues and emerging hegemonic rivalry, but much will be determined by the approach taken by the US vis-à-vis China, and the relatively restricted mandate of the group may limit its impact on regional cooperation.

What of the major hegemonic contenders? Domestic politics in the US is entering its own, seemingly radically nationalist, regime change following the two-term Obama administration. The successful Trump campaign has seemingly brought an almost unparalleled power to the Republican Party and its business-friendly, small-government policies. As president, Trump has continued to signal 'America first' and business-like and business-friendly policies to virtually all aspects of US national and international policies. The extent to which these policies are supported by Congress and the bureaucracy remains to be seen, but it seems likely that policies will veer sharply away from the pattern of engagement with the rest of the world taking shape under the Obama and most earlier administrations. Far less are they likely to take up the challenges of political and administrative dysfunctionality identified by Jacob Hacker and Paul Pierson (2016) by adopting more features of the mixed economy. Many predict that Trump's putative policies will likely not deliver benefits to his supporters, may inflict great damage to the global economy, and may even initiate a new Cold War. Almost certainly, progress towards multilateral solutions to global issues will be impeded by the unpredictability of US rhetoric and practical responses. That may change in response to the range of influential policy advice and increasing experience of the realities of global negotiations and their consequences.

Little is to be gained by assuming the worst, but experienced policy-makers, academics, progressive think tanks and civil society in general must continue to fight for objective review of policies and strengthening of institutions to ensure open discussion and review of these policies. Should events prove threatening to global wealth and security, it is reasonable to assume that the US system will respond vigorously, but, as Fukuyama (2014a, b) and others before him have observed, constitutional constraints in the US system do not allow for rapid response to dubious policy competence or conflict between administration and legislature, and the same constraints have frequently led to gridlock. The Constitution very deliberately aimed at controlling executive powers in contrast to the strong centralized executive powers of the Westminster system—a primary reason for the American Revolution. Though US constitutional checks and balances are intended to avoid policy extremes, they have not always proved successful. On national security, the executive has often veered toward a strong military position; constitutionally, it must command congressional and ultimately popular support. In practice (Viet Nam and Iraq) these processes have often been subject to considerable manipulation by the executive.

On the other hand, economic policies of the executive are frequently constrained and redirected by Congress, which can directly modify the President's budget proposal (presented to Congress in January; detailed appropriations are modified and approved by Congress in October). These decisions have, particularly in recent years, been subject to widely divergent political ideologies; and local 'pork-barrelling' has long been a feature of the congressional budget process. The relative strength of Democrats and Republicans in the presidency and in Congress is thus of crucial significance to policy outcomes. Now, with Republican dominance of the presidency and both houses, plus the Supreme Court and judicial appointments, measured debate on the relative merits of policies seems unlikely. Either a major political turnaround or, preferably, very significant long-term institutional change will be necessary to achieve a solid basis for more constructive dialogue in the future. We discuss some aspects further in Chap. 7.

In this milieu it is impossible to predict policy outcomes, and perhaps too many analysts start from an over-rationalized model of ideal political behaviour. Blackwill and Harris (2016), for instance, lament the US's decreasing use of economic instruments to achieve geopolitical objectives (which they term geoeconomics); the US "too often reaches for the gun instead of the purse in its foreign policy." They suggest that adversaries such as China and Russia, in contrast, are embracing geoeconomics. Perhaps so, but the realities of United States' present and likely future military superiority may leave the other powers little choice. Part of the geoeconomic calculation that the US must come to terms with, they contend, I believe rightly, is that military power is yielding diminishing geopolitical returns. There appears to be room in the present hegemonic contest, therefore, for all sides to look towards an optimal geoeconomic solution—vitally, while also establishing broader global control over the availability of massive military power. Small government and dominance of commercial enterprise cannot resolve these fundamental national and global dilemmas. Establishing a clever government capable of balancing global and national goals, which should surely not be beyond the long-term capacity of the United States, is essential to tackle these existentially important tasks.

Analyzing and envisioning the perspective of the main hegemonic rival is also essential to establishing a balanced global policy. Nathan and Scobell (2012) provide a valuable overview of how China perceives itself and how it may see America. The world seen from Beijing is "a terrain of hazards," which they describe in terms of four concentric rings: The first comprises the territories China controls directly or claims, which includes dissident groups in Tibet and Xinjiang, Taiwan, which has its own government, and a wide range of business and civil society organizations within its borders. The second ring comprises the 14 adjacent countries, many of which have been bitter enemies over the past 70 years. The third and related ring is the regional geopolitical relations that have been established within the surrounding countries, some aimed particularly at developing mutually supportive policies against potential Chinese intrusion. Finally, there is the challenge of China's emergence as a global force, which involves new ventures in securing critical resource supplies, increasing trade and building global diplomatic links.

In all four areas the United States plays a commanding role. It serves everybody's interests for China to continue to grow and play its role in global economic and social management. Nathan and Scobell argued that the US should "continue to upgrade its military capabilities, maintain its regional defence alliances, and respond confidently to challenges... [in the western Pacific] ... and continue to push back against Chinese efforts to remake global legal regimes in ways that do not serve the interests of the West." (p. 47) But this position seems to run somewhat counter to their general theme of making efforts on both sides to understand each other's position. US–Chinese relations should not become either a two-person or zero-sum game. There are enormous benefits to all nations in the region from cooperative economic arrangements and hosing down of military competition. Intensive military and economic competition between the US and Russia following WW2 was likely unavoidable, given the huge territorial gains made by the Eastern bloc and the beginning of nuclear armament. This is not the situation that the US and China face; each should have the capacity to learn from the recent lessons of history and to calculate both the enormous risks of confrontation and the great benefits of cooperation. The initial moves towards America first deal-making by the Trump administration, however, do not auger well for the future management of the global economy—and stand in marked contrast to Chinese President Xi's speech at Davos in January 2017.[22]

Institutionalizing a continuing dialogue on harmonizing both economic and military relations through a G20 Asian subgroup may help, though, as noted above, its set-up would be complex. As Singaporean Bilahari Kausikan (2017) writes, a great deal depends on the way in which diplomatic dialogue between the Trump administration and China develops. He reviews three new books, one by Kurt Campbell, formerly in the Obama administration, concerning the US pivot to Asia, a second, by Michael Green, who worked in the George W. Bush administration.

Both represent strong views on the necessity for continuing US leadership. But a third book, by Michael Auslin, who also from a US-centred policy perspective, describes a series of threats emerging from Asia, which Kausikan considers misrepresent the real dangers that are emerging. He draws from President Xi's speech at Davos the conclusion that China recognizes it is in no position to lead the global order. However, even the Obama pivot was interpreted as threatening; highlighting a new (but actually long-recognized) set of dangers may severely limit the possibility of constructive cooperation in a quite disparate region and has depended so far on US-led order.

A particular danger emanating from the US and Europe identified by Kausikan is that of Islamophobia, which could alienate Muslim communities across Southeast Asia. Beyond that, however, the Trump administration's early moves have been aggressive in both trade relations and militarily. Kausikan concludes that "[u]nder Trump, as under any US president, East Asia will remain an arena of great-power competition. Ultimately the region will deal with the Trump administration the same way it has always dealt with change: by adapting." In one sense, that is inevitably true, but we should have reached a stage in arranging the world order that seeks a more cooperative international dialogue and, above all, tries to minimize aggressive impositions by any hegemon. The G20 grouping could help, but only if the leaders of the new world order allow it to do so.

A great deal, possibly the entire future of global governance and security, thus hinges on the next developments among the two main superpowers and their relatively advanced allies. But billions of people have not had access to the fruits of the Industrial Revolution. Chinese development in the latter part of the twentieth century certainly brought economic security to many within China, but development success still eludes many in Africa, South America and Asia; sub-Saharan Africa, in particular, faces huge demographic and governance challenges. Rebalancing the economic and social order in favour of those marginalized by imperial progress is one of the major tasks of modern governance, as discussed further in Chap. 5.

Summary of Themes and Conclusions

The chapter has looked at the sweep of economic development over the past two millennia using both the twentieth century metric of GDP and historical analysis applied in recent years. Conflict and competition among tribes and nations has been a feature throughout, culminating in what we had hoped was the ultimate 'War of the World' in the twentieth century. Commercial and social development was a major achievement following the Industrial Revolution, but it was associated with the development of powerful fiscal-military states and then emergence of military-industrial complexes combining military power with the armaments industry, the latter extending beyond national boundaries. The present world order cannot yet rule out the possibility of global conflicts comparable or worse than those of the twentieth century. The biopolitical forces identified by Foucault remain in play, but their nature has changed dramatically through both political and technological changes.

Politically, neoliberal belief in the power of markets and the need to reduce the size of governments has held sway in much of the Western world, particularly the US, for much of the last three decades. ICT has developed exponentially over the same period, bringing great opportunities to many, changing both business models and job opportunities. These changes have not been beneficial for all: many in the developing and emerging-market world, particularly in China and much of Asia, have gained, but multinational companies have moved production to lower wage-cost countries and reduced opportunities for less skilled workers. ICT also presents major issues of personal, commercial and national and global information security. Emerging populism, either in the Trumpian or European nationalism varieties, has exhibited no concerns with these problems—indeed, these nascent ideologies appear willing merely to exploit ICT weaknesses for personal or commercial advantage.

The need to return to global calculations and multilateral processes for both national and global progress is supported by much evidence and theory that suggests any alternative will lead to destruction of much of humanity. Basic economics suggests that some form of cost-effective criteria should be applied to these choices. The chapter argues to the effect that neither Adam Smith nor John Maynard Keynes nor Arthur Pigou would approve of the choices for humanity that are being made in their names. It focuses mainly on three areas that appear critical to ensure continuing global security and integration: continuing integration of Europe, balancing hegemonic competition, and addressing developing country issues.

No easy way forward is apparent for Europe; the overall EU concept and strategy has been poorly conceived, planned and executed. Brexit, and the continuing tensions of a potential Grexit and development of nationalist and anti-immigrant sentiment, pose major threats to the notion of a united Europe as a major global force. Its failure under present direction seems unavoidable—and may be furthered by the populist, deal-making strategies being developed by the new US administration and its potential deals with Russia. A move to less federalist and more coalition of nation-states picture in Europe may provide a much-needed fresh start; though it is recognized that such a strategy would be difficult to put in place given the weight of current legal commitments to the present EU by member states.

The need to rebalance superpower relations is almost certainly the major problem faced by humanity in the twenty-first century. All hegemonic contenders need to take account of the global impact of their actions and the need to avoid a retreat to mercantilism and protectionist bilateral deals. Mercantilist deal-making, being advocated initially by the Trump administration, is almost universally seen as a retrograde step, one which should be vigorously opposed in all multilateral forums.

Notes

1. Both *The Economist* and *The Atlantic* charts based on Maddison's work are worth viewing, but the task of graphically illustrating these data over the sweep of two millennia proved very challenging as described in http://www.economist.com/blogs/graphicdetail/2012/06/mis-charting-economic-history and https://www.theatlantic.com/business/archive/2012/06/the-economic-history-of-the-last-2000-years-part-ii/258762/. Reference to TEDTalk by Hans Rosling in *The Economist* 2012 article is also

of interest in terms of a graphic illustration of the power of demography using Maddison's data.
2. Morris (2010, Kindle Locations 9120–9121). Consistent with Foucault's structuralist criticisms, I would say, "Biology and sociology [*aim to*] provide universal laws. . . ."
3. See Morris (2010) Table 2.1, Kindle Locations 2290.
4. Darwin (2006, p. 6) writes: "His empire was the last real attempt to challenge the partition of Eurasia between the states of the Far West, Islamic Middle Eurasia and Confucian East Asia. Secondly, his political experiments and ultimate failure revealed that power had begun to shift back decisively from the nomad empires to the settled states. Thirdly, the collateral damage that Tamerlane inflicted on Middle Eurasia, and the disproportionate influence that tribal societies continued to wield there, helped (if only gradually) to tilt the Old World's balance in favour of the Far East and Far West, at the expense of the centre. Lastly, his passing coincided with the first signs of a change in the existing pattern of long-distance trade, the East–West route that he had fought to control."
5. See Brewer (1989), Chap. 4, particularly pp. 91–5 and 138–9. The Commissions of Public Account established after 1691 played a significant role in establishing basic oversight and rules of public accountability—despite the reputation of that decade for financial scandal (pp. 150–2). McPhee (2016) adds more detail on the failings of French fiscal administration in the years leading up to the French Revolution in 1789 and its aftermath (see his opening chapter, Patchworks of Power and Privilege: France in the 1780s, pp. 1–22).
6. On this theme, Darwin (2006, p. 165) made the following points: "The expansion of trade thus contributed directly to war-making power, and financial resources became the ultimate arbiter of military fortune. 'A financial system. . . constantly improved, can change a government's position,' remarked Frederick the Great, who knew a thing or two about both. 'From being originally poor it can make a government so rich that it can throw its grain into the scales of the balance between the great European powers.' By 1815, governments in London had ten times the revenue enjoyed by their predecessors a hundred years earlier. The 'fiscal-military state' did not by itself create conflicts and crises. But, by changing the rules that governed success, it opened the way for a new pattern of power."

7. He writes: "'Empire' is a grand word. But behind its façade (in every place and time) stood a mass of individuals, a network of lobbies, a mountain of hopes: for careers, fortunes, religious salvation or just physical safety. Empires were not made by faceless committees making grand calculations, nor by the 'irresistible' pressures of economics or ideology. They had to be made by men (and women) whose actions were shaped by motives and morals no less confused and demanding than those that govern us now." (p. xi)
    On civilizational aspects of colonialization, he says: "[C]olonial peoples and their leaders were rarely without some friends and supporters in Britain to encourage their hopes of eventual release into a free 'British world'. And far from imposing a common culture on their colonies, the British could neither agree on what it should be, nor on whether to risk the political fall-out that might follow any attempt to enforce it" (p. 279), emphasizing the internal conflicts within the civilizational responsibilities of Empire. Darwin (2012), p. 279. Penguin UK. Kindle Edition.
8. Lieber and Press (2009) argue that preserving the American deterrent will be far more difficult than it has been in the past, but the US, which has the responsibility of protecting its global network of allies, may find itself "embroiled in conventional wars with nuclear-armed adversaries." And "Unless the United States maintains potent counterforce capabilities, US adversaries may conclude—perhaps correctly—that the United States' strategic position abroad rests largely on a bluff."
9. A term coined by President Dwight Eisenhower in his 1961 farewell address, in which he said: "This conjunction of an immense military establishment and a large arms industry is new in the American experience. The total influence—economic, political, even spiritual—is felt in every city, every State house, every office of the Federal government. We recognize the imperative need for this development. Yet we must not fail to comprehend its grave implications. Our toil, resources and livelihood are all involved; so is the very structure of our society." See http://coursesa.matrix.msu.edu/~hst306/documents/indust.html
10. Ideological labelling becomes particularly confusing in the US, where the term 'liberal' has become synonymous with 'left-wing' or even 'communist'. Paul Krugman (2007) traces the evolution of 'market fundamentalism' in the Republican Party from initial opposition to Roosevelt's New Deal, to bipartisanship in the Eisenhower era, to the new conservative policies, articulated by William F. Buckley and his *National Review*,

through to the emergence of Ronald Reagan and eventually, the 2001–2008 Bush–Cheney administration. While labelled 'neoconservative' and broadly sympathetic to a conservative nationalist and militaristic agenda, its policies wholly endorsed goals that are elsewhere labelled as neoliberal to minimize the role of government and give as much freedom from regulation as possible to private enterprise. According to Kaletsky (2010) ideology was central to economic policy; market-fundamentalist overreach in the eight Bush–Greenspan years prior to the GFC—and indeed, even prior to that under Clinton—gave close-to unbridled powers to market and financial risk-taking in the US and globally.

11. John Lanchester (2016), writing in the *New Yorker* of October 2016, provides a good, broader overview of the politics of the foundation and trajectory of the EU, based on work of Joseph Stiglitz, Markus Brunnermeier, Harold James and Jean-Pierre Landau. He emphasizes the driving role of Jean Monnet (the 'fixer'), the continuing dominance of France and Germany, particularly the latter's 'ordoliberal' traditions and economic and political strength. He agrees with the Stiglitz (and general) view of the damaging effect of the introduction of the Euro, but suggests "[t]he lack of pragmatism, the willingness to go on doing something that visibly doesn't work, would have appalled that old fixer Jean Monnet" (p. 76).
12. See Hayek (1944), Chap. 15, pp. 225–244.
13. See, for instance, http://www.europarl.europa.eu/RegData/etudes/STUD/2016/556938/IPOL_STU(2016)556938_EN.pdf, which describes negotiations with the UK on sovereignty issues just prior to the Brexit vote. It cites, among other things, the UK preference for a "Europe of States" rather than an "ever closer union" (pp. 5–6). The institutions and legal framework of the EU are overviewed critically by Penelope Corfield in her blog (http://www.penelopejcorfield.com/whats-wrong-with-the-european-unions-hybrid-constitution/ and well summarized in Wikipedia (https://en.wikipedia.org/wiki/Institutions_of_the_European_Union).
14. As described and somewhat redressed in Ashendon and Owen (1999).
15. Mazower (2009, Kindle Locations 196–197).
16. "Its relaxed criteria for entry were designed to encourage universality of membership precisely in order to avoid the creation of international factions and rival alliances outside the world body. Thus the sole criterion

for membership was deliberately established as an external one—the fact of a state's "peace-loving nature" (Kindle Locations 1785–1787).
17. See Mazower (2012) Chap. 10, Development as World-Making, 1949–73.
18. In both cases the US has a huge influence on policies; as the major shareholder, and by convention that still continues, the World Bank President has been nominated by the US, and the IMF Managing Director by Europe, but always with a US-nominated First Deputy Managing Director.
19. See Mazower (2012), p. 315 and Tinbergen (1966).
20. As Stephen Kotkin (2016) observes, "Russia has almost always been a relatively weak great power," citing the major losses in terms of military and influence from the Crimean War through to the Cold War. "But the impetus behind Russian grand strategy had not changed. And over the last decade, Russian President Vladimir Putin has returned to the trend of relying on the state to manage the gulf between Russia and the more powerful West." (pp. 2–3) The possibility of a sustained improvement between the US under President Trump and Putin's Russia on the basis of commercial and geopolitical deals seems wildly improbable, and, if successful, at great cost to the poor and vulnerable.
21. See Gordon Smith (2011) Asia's representation in the new global grouping was expanded from Japan, as the sole representative of the G7/8, to six countries from the region (Japan, China, and South Korea–East Asia; Indonesia–Southeast Asia; India–South Asia; and Australia–Oceania). He emphasizes that to be sustainable it must be both effective and demonstrably more representative than the G8, but concludes that it remains the best option for working through such complex challenges. Since that time, the G8 has become the G7 and it is fair to say that the G20 role is still to be fully defined.
22. See https://www.weforum.org/agenda/2017/01/full-text-of-xi-jinping-keynote-at-the-world-economic-forum

References

Ashendon, Samantha, and David Owen. 1999. *Foucault Contra Habermas*. London/California/New Delhi: Sage Publications.

Bhojani, Fatima. 2016. How ISIS Makes IEDs: The Supply Chain of Terrorism. *Foreign Affairs*, Web March 2.

Blackwill, Robert D., and Jennifer M. Harris. 2016. The Lost Art of Economic Statecraft: Restoring an Economic Tradition. *Foreign Affairs* 95 (2): 99–110.

Brewer, John. 1989. *The Sinews of Power: War Money and the English State*. New York: Alfred A Knopf.

Darwin, John. 2006. *After Tamerlane: The Global History of Empire*. New York: Bloomsbury Press.

———. 2012. *Unfinished Empire: The Global Expansion of Britain*. Kindle ed, xiv. London: Penguin.

Fukuyama, Francis. 2014a. America in Decay: The Sources of Political Dysfunction. *Foreign Affairs* 93 (5): 5–26.

———. 2014b. *Political Order and Political Decay: From the Industrial Revolution to the Globalization of Democracy*. New York: Farrar, Strauss, and Giroux.

Garton Ash, Timothy. 2012. The Crisis of Europe: How the Union Came Together and Why It's Falling Apart. *Foreign Affairs* 91 (5): 2–15.

Grygiel, Jakub. 2016. The Return of Europe's Nation States: The Upside to the EU's Crisis. *Foreign Affairs* 95 (5): 94–101.

Habermas, Jürgen. 2012. *The Crisis of the European Union: A Response*. Trans. Ciaran Cronin. Cambridge : Polity Press.

Hacker, Jacob S., and Paul Pierson. 2016. Making America Great Again: The Case for the Mixed Economy. *Foreign Affairs* 95 (3): 69–90.

Hayek, Friedrich August. 1944. *The Road to Serfdom*. London/New York: Routledge.

Kaletsky, Anatole. 2010. *Capitalism 4.0: The Birth of a New Economy*. London/New York/Berlin/Sydney: Bloomsbury.

Kausikan, Bilahari. 2017. Asia in the Trump Era: From Pivot to Peril? *Foreign Affairs*, Review Essay, May/June (online version).

Kotkin, Stephen. 2016. Russia's Perpetual Geopolitics: Putin Returns to the Historical Pattern. *Foreign Affairs* 95 (3): 2–9.

Krugman, Paul. 2007. *The Conscience of a Liberal: Reclaiming America from the Right*. London: Allen Lane/Penguin.

Lanchester, John. 2016. Money Trap: Can Europe Survive the Euro. *The New Yorker*, October 24, pp. 73–76.

Lieber, Keir E., and Daryl G. Press. 2009. The Nukes We Need. *Foreign Affairs* 88 (6): 39–51.

Mazower, Mark. 2009. *No Enchanted Palace: The End of Empire and the Ideological Origins of the United Nations*. Kindle ed. Princeton: Princeton University Press.

———. 2012. *Governing the World: the History of an Idea*. London/New York/Melbourne: Allen Lane/Penguin.

McPhee, Peter. 2016. *Liberty or Death: The French Revolution*. New Haven/London: Yale University Press.

Morris, Ian. 2010. *Why the West Rules – For Now: The Patterns of History, and What They Reveal About the Future*. Kindle ed. London: Profile Books.

Nathan, Andrew J., and Andrew Scobell. 2012. How China Sees America. *Foreign Affairs* 91 (5): 32–47.

Parkinson, Martin. 2016. Economics of Power: Stepping Towards a New Global Order. *Griffith Review* 51: 59–173, South Bank Campus, Griffith University, Queensland.

Smith, Gordon S. 2011. *G7 to G8 to G20: Evolution in Global Governance*, Centre for International Government Innovation (CIGI) G20 Papers, No 6, May.

Tampke, Jürgen. 2017. *A Perfidious Distortion of History: The Versailles Peace Treaty and the Success of the Nazis*. Melbourne/London: Scribe.

Tinbergen, Jan. 1966. International Economic Planning. *Daedalus* 95 (2), Conditions of World Order (Spring): 530–557 (http://www.jstor.org/stable/20026983).

Part II

Constructing a Modern Episteme

Part II offers a Foucauldian treatment of historical and economic developments that led to the dominance of neoliberalism at the beginning of the twenty-first century. Economics is an important element of this story, but development of fiscal military states and the resulting contests of power dominated twentieth-century development, and the questions of the resulting imbalances of power and wealth have yet to be fully addressed. The victory of free market liberal democracies in the two World Wars and the Cold War helped set the stage for neoliberal dominance of economic policies from the 1980s onwards; it also helped set the stage for the 2008 GFC and its aftermath. It is critically important that we look to rebalancing the biopolitical forces identified by Foucault and apply modern social science advances to help policy-makers achieve this end.

This part analyses issues and describes measures needed in the areas of global and national governance identified broadly in Part I. These key issues are: First, to establish a balanced view of macroeconomic management subject to well-organized professional debate and communicated clearly to the public. Second, to develop a socially valid measurement of well-being and a strategy for implementing mechanisms of accountability for social value management in all private and public entities. Third, fundamental issues of social justice and inequality must be recognized by all levels of government, and programs to maintain progress in reducing inequality must be put in place subject to regular national and international review. Fourth, national and global mechanisms must be put in place to manage the environment responsibly while maintaining welfare growth and stability. These issues are closely linked, though not set in order of relative importance: all demand sustained global and national attention.

3

From Neoliberalism to Social Accountability

Neoliberal Economics and Neoliberal Ideology

Neoliberal ideology as it has developed in the early twenty-first century embodies a range of beliefs linked loosely to elements of economic theory:

- Market operations with minimal government regulation will maximize economic production and growth over the long run;
- Government is by its nature inefficient, and much of its operations, even in production of collective goods, can be performed more efficiently by private enterprise; and
- Austere fiscal policy (cutting public spending and taxes) and post-2008 reliance on monetary policy controls by independent central banks make the correct policy mix to boost private sector confidence and recover from the GFC.

Many of these proposals are contested theoretically and empirically by eminent economists and are steadily losing credibility within the economics discipline. However, the notion of 'small government' as a stand-alone concept retains a high degree of traction in the arena of public opinion.

Without either theoretical or empirical standing, it is very much a product of conservative politics that took root during the heyday of Thatcher/Reagan policies curated by a powerful traditional media. Perhaps even more than under these conservatives, neoliberalism flourished in the Clinton and Blair 'third way' era and reached its likely apogee under the market fundamentalist era of the Bush–Cheney administration in the US. Establishing a clear societal understanding of neoliberalism's contradictions and the range of alternatives is essential to social, economic and political progress in this century.[1]

Small-government policies have limited the capacity of government to respond to collective needs, and they most directly threaten the underprivileged. They are closely linked to neoconservative demands to 'get tough' on crime and to protect national borders, both of which have substantially increased demands on the public purse at the expense of other needs. They have cut back social safety nets and reduced foreign aid. Despite these well-known effects, public support to limit the power of government appears to have grown over the period from the 1980s to 2008 and beyond, at least judging from election results in the US, Canada, Europe and Australia. The simple proposition that reducing taxes will increase investment and put money back in productive private hands rather than being wasted by the government has had enormous and easy appeal to many voters, despite the negative effects that globalization, corporate tax reduction and offshoring investment to even lower tax regimes have had on many of these voters. The power of dog whistle politics, introduced in Chap. 1 and discussed further here, is well understood by politicians—and indeed has been taken to an extreme by Donald Trump's successful US presidential campaign. While market fundamentalism is now widely contested academically, these discussions have not yet had a sufficiently persuasive public impact on neoliberal politics; countering Trumpian populism may present an even greater challenge.

Not all these difficulties, however, can be attributed to politics. Some have arisen from within economics itself, and require a close review of the nature of the discipline and its policy perspectives. Fortunately, much current analysis points towards emerging professional agreement, particularly on the relative roles of monetary and fiscal tools, and use of active fiscal policy to encourage private investment in times of stagnant growth.

The first parts of this chapter examine recent economic thinking on how the macroeconomy should be managed, including realignment of monetary and fiscal tools and more active use of fiscal policy to achieve economic recovery and stabilization. Governments, it argues, must go beyond aggregate economic management concerns and re-establish their mandates to deal with the broader threats to social welfare and global security described in the previous chapter. Government authority in these areas has been significantly weakened by continuing loss of government tax and spending powers and encroachment of corporations in delivery of public interest goods, as well as by the sheer power of multi-national corporations and by low-tax competing jurisdictions in the globalized economy.

Beyond these concerns, which amount mainly to resetting government to practical, liberal and just standards, many theorists are re-examining the way in which economic activity is measured and used for policy both within government and by corporations. This work raises fundamental questions about economics' claims that it is a 'science'; such claims depend heavily on the validity of the data used to develop and test theoretical economic propositions. A key conclusion of this chapter is that accounting measurement needs to be recalibrated for both corporations and government. Accountability frameworks need to be strengthened to meet these demands, and they need to be more clearly linked to political decision-making and public information forums and media commentary. First we shall examine the changing landscape of interactions among the main professional disciplines.

Macroeconomic Theory, Politics and the Media

Economic theory as it developed over the twentieth century, particularly in the contest between the ideas of Friedrich Hayek and John Maynard Keynes, was pivotal to the debate regarding the role of the state in stabilizing economic cycles and growth of national economies—or, alternatively, being seen as a source of inefficiency and a barrier to growth.[2] While some aspects of that debate are now fairly settled, modern economic theory remains some way from reaching either a theoretical explanation for economic instability on which all agree or a consensus on the most appropriate mix of policy levers to stimulate continuing global economic growth at different stages of the economic cycle.

Hayek's position on macroeconomics drew from the Austrian School's belief in the power of individuals and free markets to adjust to periodic instability without government intervention. His views were strongly influenced also by his (and many others') strong reaction to the excesses of Soviet and Nazi state control.[3] At the same time, Keynes was revolutionizing economic thinking by focusing on the differences between individual reactions to economic downturn and the reaction of the state. His development of the 'paradox of thrift' showed that individual response to hard times by spending less and saving more did not work for the state as a whole: more individual saving meant less aggregate spending and less profit, less incentive for investment, and hence less investment and savings for the economy as a whole. Government, therefore, played a crucial role in balancing the economy—not but not by balancing the government budget (except over the long term). Government was to control aggregate demand by borrowing and spending more in times of economic downturn and restraining spending in boom times. Keynes won that part of the debate at that time, and his views and further developments of his ideas dominated political views on macroeconomic stabilization policy, including in the US through to the 1970s.

But neither Keynes nor his followers took sufficient account of the impact of fiscal spending on inflation and on the quality of public spending in terms of outcomes achieved or questions of distribution, as discussed further in Chap. 5. The main assault on Keynesian macroeconomic theory and practice came in the 1980s from Milton Friedman and the Chicago School, who earlier had identified monetary expansion as the primary cause of inflation and argued that monetary rather than fiscal failure was the major cause of the Great Depression following the 1929 US stock market crash.[4] While some aspects remain in contention, as we discuss below, there is little disagreement that monetary control is a critical element of macroeconomic management. The idea that government itself was a major part of the problem of maintaining stable economic growth, however, gained significant political traction over that period. As Harold James (2010) pointed out, both Keynesian and Friedmanite prescriptions have been applied quite successfully to deal with major economic crises in recent years, even up to the 2007–8 GFC. But the aftermath of the GFC shifted political opinion and public support decisively in favour of monetary policy instruments both for control of inflation and recovery from economic downturn. This shift is not supported by fundamental changes in macroeconomic theory; its backing comes from neoliberal political dominance and supportive commercial media. The lack of success in using interest rates to stimulate economic activity in a very low or deflationary environment, however, lends support to many economists' (and some central bankers') continuing calls for fiscal stimulus to be applied in the current environment.[5]

The ascendancy of Margaret Thatcher in the UK and Ronald Reagan in the US in the 1980s gave enormous momentum in much of the advanced economies in favor of reducing the size of government.[6] Both subscribed strongly (at least rhetorically) to Hayek's small government philosophy and to Milton Friedman's advocacy of monetary control combined with tax-cutting as the new basis for macroeconomic management. For a while it appeared as if macroeconomic controls were effectively in place, with the main emphasis placed on encouraging enterprise, limiting government and relying primarily on monetary controls to steer the economy. Alan Greenspan, President of the Federal Reserve from 1987–2006, was given much credit for guiding US and world economies to prosperity and growth and responding appropriately to a series of economic crises up to the GFC of 2007–8. In a 2013 *Foreign Affairs* article, however, Greenspan made the case that economists, he included, had collectively failed.[7]

The failure to consider the impact of housing inflation and the potential housing market bubble on the Fed's banking oversight responsibilities has been generally recognized. According to *The Economist*,[8] however, since the GFC much of the risk associated with housing loan securitization has been transferred to government (the Federal Housing Administration, Veterans Affairs and Ginnie Mae) and thus more directly to the taxpayer.[9] There is general agreement on the necessity of strong Fed control of consumer price inflation in boom times, but the issue of the relative roles of fiscal and monetary policy with respect to assets or in times of recovery from recession remains contentious. Control of the derivative-driven inflation of home prices prior to the GFC should have been on the radar screens of both commercial bank managers and the Fed. The current threat of a housing bubble in the US, however, stems directly from fiscal incentives to increase home ownership. A somewhat similar fiscal policy pressure on housing prices has operated for some time in Australia through allowance of tax offsets against rental losses and reduced capital gains taxes on house investment; foreign investment in the housing market has also added greatly to the pressure on prices there. As well as adding significant macroeconomic risks, the housing market raises important equity concerns; these are discussed further in Chap. 5.

The immediate response to the GFC, however, was influenced not so much by competing theories but by political perceptions of the need to act decisively. The decisions made then are now widely seen to have compounded the problem and allowed political and public opinion-driven instincts to prevail over measured policy. Anatole Kaletsky (2010) was particularly critical of US Treasury Secretary Henry Paulsen's "unpredictable and reckless handling first of Fannie and Freddie, then of Lehman, and finally of AIG". Martin Wolf (2014), noting Kaletsky's points but putting aside the question of culpability,[10] focused on the magnitude of the crisis and its global significance in terms of basic confidence in the financial sector throughout the world, particularly because it emanated "from the core of the world's most advanced financial system and from transactions entered into by the most sophisticated financial institutions, which use the cleverest tools of securitization and rely on the most sophisticated risk management" (pp. 18–19). As he describes, once its potential magnitude was realized initial reactions to the crisis among the high-income countries involved fiscal, monetary and regulatory responses. In part, the strong initial fiscal response arose from the crisis itself; lower private investment and spending triggered automatic stabilization mechanisms through increased unemployment benefits and government revenues, which meant higher fiscal deficits (which were, however, widely regarded positively at the time).[11]

The position against continuing active Keynesian fiscal policy was driven by politics not theory. Opposition came particularly from the Republican Party, dominant in the Congress in the US,[12] by conservative politicians in Germany, the powerhouse of Europe, and by the conservative-dominated coalition government in the UK. Conservative politicians, influenced by neoliberalism, were dismissive of the need for the state to address social goals, particularly those extending beyond national boundaries, and were instinctively supportive of free enterprise direction of production. Wolf suggests that in the US the Republicans had more blatant political motives, while ideologically they were "irrevocably opposed to the idea that government could do anything useful about the economy except by leaving it alone, and so could not tolerate the possibility that the Obama administration might prove the opposite" (p. 43).

In Europe the inability of the EU to manage the impact of the crisis on weaker states within the eurozone, particularly Greece, continues to be particularly damaging both for recovery and for the future of the eurozone itself. Because of these disparate and unopposed forces, fiscal austerity combined with monetary easing became the cornerstone policy for the most powerful and influential countries in the world. These ideas have been accepted by the ruling politicians in Europe, the United States and Australia, *not* because they are empirically tested and supported by a majority of economists but because they still enjoy public support from a media-led understanding of the nature of economics. Ironically, some politicians have appeared to be aware of the nature of this bargain but found it increasingly necessary to espouse ideological 'austerity' positions to retain power.[13]

Powerful elements of the media have played and continue to play a very significant role in establishing public acceptance of neoliberal policies in the both the UK and the US—and extending this acceptance elsewhere. In the UK the British tabloid press developed techniques that heavily influenced public opinion towards streamlining government and favouring business. Rupert Murdoch's News Corporation was itself taking on the print unions and strongly supported Margaret Thatcher's small-government, anti-union reforms. Murdoch played initially a lesser but similar role in supporting Reagan in the US. A brilliant journalist and businessman, he quickly grasped the opportunities to enhance the power—and profitability—of the media by a close engagement with the emerging UK/US neoliberal coalition.[14] Indeed, from that point, and well past the Reagan/Thatcher era, he was able to nurture an agenda, increasingly centred in the US, that squared with his business interests and supported business-oriented aspirants to government in Britain, the US and Australia. Krugman (2007) describes in some detail the rise of dog whistle politics: a practice in which political strategists in the US use media and ply phrases and words that are coded for ideologically sympathetic groups, but that sound blandly patriotic or religious to the general public. This alliance between traditional media groups and neoliberal/neoconservative politicians has created growing power for both.

This phenomenon is not new and its evolution continues in the Internet era. In 1922 the distinguished journalist and political commentator Walter Lippmann argued that democracy was fatally flawed, first, by the limited capacity of the average citizen to understand the complex issues on which they cast their votes, and, second, by the inability of the press to provide balanced and coherent explanations to help with these decisions.[15] The press of the time, he argued, was not in any case in the business of providing the truth to the public; it focused on timely delivery of *news*, describing current events of interest, often with limited distinction between fact and opinion. Moreover, the contract between the press and the public was to provide the news free of charge; revenue came from advertising. Circulation and profit rather than the search for truth had become the main objective of the press. In the tabloid press, drama and entertainment linked to unveiling of scandal remain more likely to interest the public and raise circulation or go viral than does sober and continuing analysis of public policy.

The Internet now certainly provides many options to access academic studies, examine interdisciplinary linkages and communicate with a variety of views, but commercial competition for short-span public attention continues to dominate modern media activity. The near universal use of public opinion polls in western democracies builds a tight feedback loop which helps ensure that both government and the public focus on a simple set of policy labels centring on commercial and wage prospects, costs of welfare and external threats. These notions are time-honoured but strengthened by technique and technology; most politicians, their strategists and the media now use Twitter, Facebook, or other fast-evolving means of social communication. Donald Trump, aided by ex-Murdoch senior executive Roger Ailes, ruthlessly exploited the weaknesses of social media to muster support for his campaign without regard to verifiable truth of his Facebook or Twitter claims.

Modern media have thus altered the environment dramatically, but the basic contracts identified by Lippmann and exploited by Murdoch and his peers remain unchanged in many important respects.[16] Pursuit of advertising revenue still dominates all media forms, and it remains to be seen if the exponential increase in access to information can be harnessed to govern self and society in the way advocated by Foucault. Governance of the polity encompassing the Internet has yet to address properly the questions of establishing effective modes of discourse between political representatives and the public they purport to serve or of financing such platforms. Wikipedia, for instance, has clear and admirable objectives of providing high quality, verifiable information to the entire population, but it is non-commercial, relying on voluntary support to control factual and ethical standards of entries. It remains vulnerable to mischievous editing and insufficient resources to maintain high editing standards—but I believe it offers a very useful first overview of most topics. Measures to address these issues, including pricing and accountability, will be considered again in later chapters of Part II, and institutional reform and the continuing struggle between academic, 'ivory tower' search for truth and the cauldron of impulse-driven public discourse will be revisited in Part III.

As I describe in relation to tackling inequality (Chap. 5), corporate media, whether old or new, has not been alone in applying the techniques of media manipulation—extensively so. A range of corporate interests and allied think tanks, particularly in the US during the Obama era, spent many billions to build support for market fundamentalist ideas and to impede government fiscal measures intended to promote growth and assist lower income and disadvantaged segments of the population. Such corporations have been and remain the high priests of neoliberalism, and, albeit with initial hesitation, they continue as prominent supporters of the Trump regime. Indeed, as research by Jane Mayer (2016, 2017) indicates, the Koch brothers and the formidable Robert Mercer played a critical role in guiding the Trump campaign to victory. Mercer, she suggests, was driven not towards a Republican victory but rather by a mission to reduce trust in government overall and diminish government's role in running the country; from that point of view Trump was seen as an ideal candidate because of his presence and confidence rather than political competence. Mercer invested in Breitbart News and played a key role in re-establishing Trump's campaign after its uncertain start; he had considerable experience and skills in digital technology, which he saw as a weakness in past Republican campaigns. As Mayer describes, Mercer invested heavily in computer research on people's reactions to surveys and the possibility of predicting political responses based on these data. While no firm conclusions can be drawn, there seems little doubt that these efforts had a significant impact on the election results.[17]

Economic and Political Rebalancing: Some Technical Issues

Several interlocking factors beyond those outlined above have contributed to the diminution of influence of professional economic voices. The widely acknowledged failure of oversight mechanisms leading up to the GFC punctured both professional and public confidence in government macroeconomic policy competence. Economic policy hubris operating prior to the global financial crisis, continuing disputes over the most appropriate economic policy remedies, the global scale of the crisis, and US political reactions all contributed a heavy emotional basis for public dissatisfaction in most countries. Power over public policy has thus shifted significantly away from the professional policy analysts of academia and the civil service mandarins towards politicians because of the psychological impacts of the GFC. The political power of neoliberalism may be diminishing, but it is still quite vital that technical issues within economics be resolved. Some, however, raise significant questions on the future direction of economic theory.

Debates among rival contemporary economic theorists have not offered a convincing theoretical basis for driving a policy turnaround—not in the way Keynes and Friedman did in their day. The best theorists, like Krugman, Stiglitz and Wolf, acknowledge the contest of political and public opinion, but political manipulation considerations generally take second place to formal modelling or theoretical conjectures within an economic model structure. Kaletsky, in his 2011 epilogue (pp. 349–353), suggested four distinct schools of thought among economists on the possibility of recovery—or rather the probability of recession or stagnation following the GFC: 'ultra-Keynesians', arguing that recession was inevitable because of a lack of sustained fiscal stimulus; 'orthodox monetarists', countering that "fiscal stimulus, far from supporting the economy, was damaging employment and growth...[and] the best way to revive economic activity was to slash public spending"; 'conservative commentators', who predicted hyperinflation would result from US Treasury and Federal Reserve policies; and finally, a fourth group held that "the world economy would suffer for years, or even decades, from the damage caused by the financial crisis". These categories represented some of the strong views held at the time, but something approaching a pragmatic consensus may be emerging.

Several economists, including many cited by Kaletsky as members of the various groups, have moved towards establishing a firmer theoretical explanation for the sustained failure of the world economy to grow out of the post-GFC recession. Lawrence Summers (2016) has supported the idea that failure of the recovery is caused by secular stagnation driven by mature industrialized economies' tendency to generate more savings, reducing demand, lowering investment incentives and thus lowering growth and inflation and reducing real interest rates. He adds that the new, technologically driven economy tends to conserve capital and acknowledges that other factors also have an impact, including Kenneth Rogoff's theory of the effects of a debt overhang[18] and Paul Krugman's support for the Keynesian theory of a liquidity trap. Much of the theoretical debate centres round the question of influencing the 'natural' (or neutral) interest rate (supposedly the rate consistent with the natural rate of unemployment and the targeted inflation rate), particularly at its lower bounds. Such a focus gives a central emphasis to monetary control and the necessity for independent authority of the central bank over interest rates. Most economists regard the argument as being particularly weak when interest rates and inflation risks are extremely low—intuitively, investors seem unlikely to respond to low interest rates unless they foresee an increase in demand for products.

Many of the factors cited by Summers and others are plausible causes of the continuation of the global crisis, but these do not constitute a sufficient basis for an economic equilibrium theory centred on the role of interest rates that can be applied to establish growth and stability in the future. In practical terms, however, Summers does argue that all the theorists mentioned give broad support to the case that it is time to 'get fiscal'. He argues that quantitative easing and the independence of central banks to target inflation were appropriate in the circumstances, but that "primary responsibility for addressing secular stagnation should rest with fiscal policy". Monetary policy is critical in boom times, but he suggests (perhaps too carefully) that "[w]hen the challenge is to accelerate rather than brake economies, more cooperation with domestic fiscal authorities and foreign counterparts is necessary". Many central bank governors appear to be moving to this position.[19]

In one sense, the proposal for cooperation returns to the demand management scenarios of earlier decades, as cited by Harold James earlier. However, we have apparently not yet learned the lessons of Herman Minsky, highlighted in many recent books on the GFC and its aftermath, perhaps most clearly by Martin Wolf. Booms and busts are an unavoidable phenomenon of unregulated markets. The conclusion from recent experience should be that governments must have the capacity to monitor and evaluate trends and the authority to respond appropriately to each phase of the cycle—not neglecting untoward increases in asset prices. The terms in which governments ensure cooperation between their fiscal and monetary instruments have yet to be defined clearly. In part, however, as we develop in later chapters, these difficulties arise because neither fiscal nor monetary instruments are clearly measured nor are their social impacts valued or understood adequately.

Keynes' view that in downturns even non-productive spending, such as digging ditches and filling them in again, would boost the economy is no longer taken seriously; setting rigorous priorities for public spending is supported by all sides of the debate—though, as I discuss further in Chap. 4, practical accountability for such practices is less than rigorous. The 'small government' mantra, however, promotes the view that all government spending (except defence) is inefficient, which tends to be accepted by large sectors of the voting public. Summers and many others point out that the present environment of low interest rates, low prices and high construction unemployment is an ideal time for a large public investment program. Yet, not only in the US but also in the UK, Australia and many other OECD countries, public infrastructure is falling into disrepair because of secular budget cutbacks and failure to use active fiscal policy in response to cyclical downturn or to ensure adequate modernization and repair of decaying infrastructure.

Monetary control practice is little more settled. Kaletsky points out that Friedman's finding that rapid monetary growth always precedes a bout of high inflation "in no way implies...that a period of high inflation always follows a burst of monetary growth" (p. 217). In other words, while control of the money supply is a vital tool to control high inflation, monetary growth on its own does not create sufficient conditions for high inflation—or, more pertinent to the GFC aftermath, recovery from recession. He adds that, because 'money' cannot be precisely defined, its supply cannot be defined precisely enough to establish clear, causally persuasive links between money supply, inflation and economic recovery.

No theory seems capable of identifying the road to capitalism's recovery or even showing that a further variant of capitalism (which he defines broadly to include directed capitalism) is the necessary way forward. Kaletsky uses his analysis of past failures and projected recovery as a foundation for his central thesis that capitalism is an organic evolving system and that each stage rectifies the errors of the past. We are, he argues, just entering 'Capitalism 4.0', in which the contradictory forces arising from neoliberalism (as described broadly above) will be resolved. But he suggests little more than the belief that capitalism will somehow 'muddle through' to reinvent itself. His reservations about economics' limitations as a science, and economists' use of the Pareto principle "to relegate all questions of justice, social solidarity, and so on to what they considered the junior league of unscientific academic disciplines" (p. 160), suggest deeper restructuring is needed. Absent elaboration on these reservations, his concept of capitalist self-correction is unconvincing.[20]

Theses now being advanced, and reviewed in this part of the book, support more radical steps. A critical point is to redefine what the 'capital' in capitalism really means. Below, and in chapters that follow, I develop the argument from strong recent contributions, first, that both economic theory and democratic processes have major flaws that need to be addressed firmly and soon; and, second, that analytical collaboration among the developing social disciplines is essential for genuinely remedial social governance. Capitalism has been far too narrowly defined in the past century, although alternatives are now much better recognized in economic theory. We should not start with the assumption that yet another variant of commercial capitalism will emerge; such a theory has not yet been elaborated by Kaletsky or anyone else. Rather we must explore broader alternatives and better explanations of the nature of capital and measurement of output value. New building blocks are being proposed, appear feasible, and seem essential to allowing us to comprehend more clearly what changes are needed to make society work for the common good.

Measurement and Accountability in Economic Theory and Political Practice

Our understanding of the implications and indeed the validity of economic theory depends critically on how economic activity is measured and how effectively national and international entities use this information for policy-setting and for public communication and accountability. Some advances have been made in recent years, but these are not yet sufficient to establish validity or ensure accountability on all key dimensions of economic and broader social development.

Over the last two decades modern accounting standards, including accrual basis recognition, have been established for government accounting and fiscal statistics, and many countries have benefited from the introduction of a longer-term risk management and 'balance-sheet' approach to fiscal policy. As Peter Heller (2003) of the IMF described them, these changes have helped persuade governments to use the annual budget to begin facing predictable short- and long-term risks that fall beyond the annual span of the budget. Single-year cash basis budgeting, which was the norm for most governments up to the 1980s, simply did not identify or track the full range of liabilities and assets, far less so the potential risks from unfunded liabilities and policy commitments to finance the pension and health needs of aging populations. Accrual accounting and a balance sheet approach are now recognized as essential to modern government management, as is fiscal sustainability analysis that looks not only at 10-year but also 40–50 year horizons. As Heller pointed out, from major gains should emerge "a policy that aims at addressing long-term imbalances in the present [which] may involve a much smaller sustained increase in the fiscal burden than would be necessary if the adjustment were deferred" (p. 154). We have only begun, however, to chart the real nature of enterprise and government responsibilities and how they and their interactions should be measured.

The changes to government accounting, analysis and reporting identified by Heller, while important, have so far, had limited impact even in industrialized countries. The adoption of accrual basis standards by government is much more complex than for a public enterprise. The difference between a commercial balance sheet and that of government is vast: the latter extends beyond financial assets and liabilities of government to its sovereign rights and obligations. Longer-term fiscal sustainability analysis is open to political spin and difficult to convey to the public; the media in general have not taken up this challenge and continue with a traditional news-oriented focus on program costs, the budget deficit and debt, and wasteful spending by politicians and officials. The introduction of accrual basis accounting is actually seen positively by small government proponents as a step towards government efficiency and awareness of debt; its broader potential for management of the range of government and private sector responsibilities to society has yet to be accepted and realized.

More radical and comprehensive changes have been and are being proposed to recognize governments' broader liabilities and assets as well as to require enterprises to take explicit account of their outputs of non-market costs and benefits. These changes go far beyond the important but partial technical improvements that have been introduced so far: they raise basic issues about the foundations of economic theory and government practice and accountability to the public, and would have a significant impact on macroeconomic and microeconomic theory and policies.

A fundamental issue for both economic theory and government practice is that current theories of social progress are based predominantly on measurement of commercial value. Placing commerce at the pinnacle of social aspiration towards truth poses major verification/veridiction challenges for theories aiming at broader social explanation. Even though economics has recognized for a long time, certainly in the ideas of Adam Smith, that moral values were of central importance to the human condition, and commerce and exchange of goods for a promise of a material claim of equivalent value have been the inspiration of both commercial growth and national wealth and power. While these foundations have often been questioned in past centuries, more recent concerns with the management of the environment and the need for individuals and corporations to recognize broader social responsibilities have given some urgency to addressing the task of establishing a more representative social and global balance sheet.

Economists have, of course long recognized the social impacts of private enterprise activity, formalized as 'externalities' or costs and benefits to society that result from commercial activities but which cannot easily be charged or paid to the enterprise. Following Arthur C. Pigou's formalization of these non-pecuniary externalities in 1920, debate has continued regarding the virtues of internalizing such effects by way of state-imposed taxes or subsidies. The debate has become more intense in recent years because of mounting scientific evidence of possibly catastrophic changes in the global climate, predicted as the result of CO_2 and other GHG emissions through burning fossil fuel to power industry, transport and domestic heating/cooling. More generally, Mancur Olson's (1965) theory of collective choice helps explain why individuals are unlikely to support collective action to ensure control of non-pecuniary activities unless their personal benefits exceed the costs of doing so. Game theoretical approaches, particularly the 'prisoners' dilemma' formulation, have been applied by many economists to help persuade national politicians to accept responsibility for undertaking joint action to ensure sufficient response by all nations to meet collective challenges such as mitigation of climate change or managing international fisheries resources.[21] In the case of climate change, while economists generally believe that setting a price on carbon emissions is the most efficient way to persuade producers and consumers to change their behaviour and choose clean energy sources, the task of gaining political and industry support for global action has proved formidable. We return to the specific issue of climate change policy and the application of game theory in Chap. 6.

The more general problem, however, arises directly and simply from the narrow commercial basis of both corporate and government accounting. That, combined with the increasing financial and political power of multinational corporations in a globalized world, presents huge barriers to introducing a different set of prices to those established for centuries in the corporate and personal exchange world. Both the nature of accounting measurement and reporting and the mechanisms of corporate and government accountability need to be strengthened. Many eminent economists have advocated changes to the way that national accounts are calculated and used.

More recently, the International Integrated Reporting Council (IIRC), has advocated a practical way forward using Integrated Reporting (<IR>), which provides guidelines that help both private and public entities to report on value creation from uses of all forms of entity capital, including environmental and human capital as well as traditional forms of financial capital. In line with the IIRC, Jane Gleeson-White's *Six Capitals* (2014) argues that the <IR> extended definition of capital will play a critical role in meeting the challenges of social responsibility that government and corporations must address in this century.

Chapter 4 develops this case further and advocates a strong international effort to strengthen government and private sector accounting and accountability linked to established broader programs to establish and monitor country standards of governance and accountability. Existing international programs such as the Standards and Codes (S&C) initiative fostered by the IMF and World Bank,[22] which were initiated following economic crises in the 1990s, could benefit greatly by being anchored in a much broader recognition of capital and the responsibilities of all entities to be accountable for all of their value creating/diminution activities, not just commercial activities. The chapter emphasizes that implementing such a program will be a considerably long-term venture and require coordinated efforts from all major international and bilateral agencies and standard setting bodies involved in promoting good standards of transparency and accountability. Ultimately, these efforts should allow a greatly strengthened measure of 'well-being' to replace the current GDP metric. Strengthening our measurement of well-being beyond commercial growth is vital to improving our understanding of critical causal relationships within society, or modern biopolitics.

The issue of inequality within and between countries is taken up in Chap. 5, whose central point is the necessity to improve governance at all levels of national and global government to achieve sustainable improvements in the UN's sustainable development goals (SDGs). Chapter 6 takes up the issue of global and national efforts to tackle climate change; here both measurement and valuation of the impact of human activity on the environment are critical. Reconsideration of our standards of measurement of human productive activity is thus central to our understanding of society's real problems and our will and power to change them.

Summary of Themes and Conclusions

This chapter has outlined the evolution of economics as the key pillar of social science helping to shape modern industrialized society. While in its origins economic theory took some account of both the moral and ethical dimensions of commercial transactions and the social impacts that took place 'externally' to monetary transactions, it was the primarily the monetary aspect that informed social development: the 'invisible hand'. In practice, narrowly interpreted economics became the main intellectual support for the commercial world and fiscal-military states that determine its direction. This direction of development provided a strong platform for the emergence of 'market fundamentalist' neoliberalism in the US and, to a lesser extent, many leading OECD countries. This ideology, curated by powerful media and corporate sectors, created an environment that allowed the GFC to occur, and from it was born the political failure to address the continuing market weaknesses and impacts of globalization. The subsequent widespread rise of populist political contenders, feeding on the fears of established but low-income groups of citizens, should not be surprising. Market fundamentalism offered no basis on which the needs of either established or incoming underprivileged communities could be addressed; it is now critical that open liberal debate re-emerge as the basis for democratic governance.

Economics will play a leading role in revitalizing well-informed debate on the future of governance, but it, too, must face up to its dependence on the commercial transaction as the essential measure of social well-being. The importance of government fiscal activities in recovering from recession as well as in promoting growth in human and environmental capital should be recognized more plainly in economic theory and policy advice—and the notion that either markets alone or with the support of populist deal-makers can solve the complex problems we face in the twenty-first century debunked with rigorous evidence and reason. This chapter, drawing on many eminent economists, suggests a way forward regarding macroeconomic policy-making. Issues of measuring social well-being are taken up in the following chapters of Part II.

Notes

1. As noted earlier, the rise of neoconservative academic views, notably Francis Fukuyama's declaration of the 'end of history', also had an important influence in cementing neoliberal influence on economic policy, at least temporarily. (Fukuyama's own views have changed somewhat since then as discussed in Chap. 7.) Though distinct from economic neoliberalism, the idea of self-evident superiority of Western democratic capitalism appeared to have a strong influence on the neoconservative administration of George W. Bush, which seemed wholly persuaded that liberal democracy could be transferred easily to other countries, and in particular would be welcomed in the Middle East. At that time, after the collapse of the USSR, US-style governance and policies were generally seen by formerly planned economies as offering the best model for reform. The case in the theocratic Middle East was much less evident, as is now evident.
2. Nicholas Wapshott's *The Clash that Defined Modern Economics* gives an overview of the twists and turns in this debate. His account makes it clear, however, that political factors weighed at least as heavily as the resolution of differences in economic theory.

3. Hayek's classic contribution to the debate, The *Road to Serfdom*, was written during the Second World War and explicitly directed against state dominance of capital and production under Nazism and Communism. The economic elements of Hayek's argument were anti-Keynesian and based on a firm belief that free competitive markets could deliver most of what society wanted. Though the book was well received, it was of little influence in terms of macroeconomic policy until the Reagan/Thatcher political ascendancy. He did, however, clearly eschew "dogmatic laissez-faire", favouring "making the best possible use of the forces of competition as a means of coordinating human efforts" (p. 37). His arguments were to the effect that terms like the "common good" and "general welfare" had no clear meaning, and that "it would be impossible for any mind to comprehend the infinite variety of different needs of different people which compete for the available resources and to attach a definite weight to each" (p. 62). Nowadays practical planning can be defined more constructively (albeit with no immunity to criticism) and seen as a necessary though difficult task of government—not as a road to serfdom.
4. See Friedman (1962, revised edition 2002).
5. The Trump administration's calls for greatly increased infrastructure investment in the US appears welcome in this context (as of March 2017), but it is quite unclear what fiscal outcome will eventually be determined in November through the fiscally conservative Republican legislature.
6. The aggressive reforms of government implemented by Margaret Thatcher and Ronald Reagan conferred an enormous impetus to anti-government sentiment in many Western countries. An initial intellectual impetus came directly from Hayek—though technically probably more influentially from Milton Friedman. Broader public support for cutting the size and scope of government arose from a number of sources. Particularly in Britain there was widespread and justified frustration with the inefficiencies of public administration, growth of a complex array of regulatory bodies and frustration with the power of unions. Reagan/Thatcher policies did not definitively establish neoliberalism nor wholly reject Keynesian macroeconomic demand management, and they did address a number of real problems. But their initial success set a solid base for subsequent popularizing and consolidating the 'small government' ideological stance. Wapshott (2011) argues that Reagan's

economic successes came from a combination of Keynesian spending (on defence) as much as his supply-side lowering of tax rates, deregulation and Volcker's tight (Friedman-inspired) monetary policies. (pp. 262–5). Much political weight during this time, however, was given to the need to reduce big government.

7. See "Never Saw It Coming: Why the Financial Crisis Took Economists by Surprise," *Foreign Affairs*, 92(6), pp. 88–96 November/December 2013. He cites IMF as late as spring of 2007, declaring that "global economic risks [had] declined" (p. 89). He looked to avoiding future collective failure through a more complete analysis of 'homo economicus' and Keynes' 'animal spirits' via behavioural economics and more effective incorporation of such findings in forecasting models. Sebastian Mallaby (2016) in a compendious biography and exposition of the development of the financial system and policies extols the virtues of Greenspan as Fed Chairman relative to his predecessors Burns and Volcker by controlling inflation and moderating volatility (see Appendix 1). His failure to control the shadow-banking sector and the housing crisis of course shattered that reputation. Mallaby suggests that failure was partly due his upbringing and non-assertive personality. Ben Bernanke in a Brookings post of November 3, 2016, however did not find this explanation plausible.

8. *The Economist* article, Nightmare on Main Street, August 20, 2016, highlights the continuing problems being encountered in the United States; this time not because of the operations of private sub-prime lenders, but because of the continuing subsidized operations of Freddy Mac and Fanny Mae (who were part of the sub-prime crash) and direct federal subsidization. See http://www.economist.com/news/briefing/21705316-how-america-accidentally-nationalised-its-mortgage-market-comradely-capitalism. See also Stiglitz (2016) p. 162.

9. In this context, the *Economist* (Comradely capitalism, August 20, 2016) noted that new concerns are emerging with respect to a potential bubble vis-à-vis US housing stock, which at $26 trillion is the largest asset class in the world and, with $11 trillion of debt is "probably the biggest concentration of financial risk to be found anywhere". But this time the risk-takers are not the big banks and their shadow-banking subsidiaries: "Some 65–80% of all home loans are [now] repackaged by organs of the state."

10. He notes later, however (p. 23), comments by Thomas Ferguson and Robert Johnson that "the evidence that the Lehman bankruptcy sundered

world markets is overwhelming". If blame is to be attributed, however, likely it started earlier and more broadly. Ross Garnaut (2009) makes the point that the 1998 bailout of hedge fund Long-Term Capital Management, organized by then-Fed Chairman, Greenspan, had established the 'too big to fail' principle that shadow banking would be protected by the implicit government guarantee (the Greenspan put). Gillian Tett (2015) describes the almost complete lack of knowledge and information on risks being taken by the shadow banking sector by the banks or the Federal Reserve, which she attributes to 'the silo effect', which should be studied and countered both within government and any large enterprise. Michael Lewis' book, *The Big Short* (2010) and the 2015 film of the same name, dramatically illustrate the nature of operations and misunderstanding of risks at all levels of mortgage-based lending and the derivatives market.

11. The need for and virtue of fiscal stimulus was widely supported by G20 participants and the IMF, and was seen initially to be successful in halting and reversing the economic downturn by end-2009. But by mid-2010, the political mood shifted dramatically toward fiscal austerity primarily by reducing spending and aiming for a balanced budget or budget surplus, quite contrary to the Keynesian approach that had been used with some success up to that point. As Wolf points out, research by prominent economists argued for the need to limit debt and to promote what was termed as 'expansionary contraction' of government, but this view was not widely supported by leading economists.

12. As described by Krugman (2007), conservative anti-government views were becoming strongly entrenched in the Republican Party, which became increasingly dominant in Congress from the 1990s onwards, particularly from the first mid-term election of the Clinton presidency, and then in Obama's final mid-term election.

13. Athanasios Orphanides, in his article What Caused the Crash? The Political Roots of the Financial Crisis, *Foreign Affairs*, June 16, 2015, cites Jean-Claude Juncker, the President of the European Commission, as saying: "We all know what to do, we just don't know how to get reelected after we've done it." This quote is also included in John Lanchester's *New Yorker* review of 2016.

14. Murdoch almost invariably in recent years takes a strong and broadly neoliberal position on government or opposition policies with an explicit intention of shaping public opinion in a business-friendly direction. His

effectiveness in this regard has been well documented by David McKnight (2012).
15. See *Public Opinion* (1922). Lippmann in contrast to Murdoch was mainly concerned with the development of social institutions and education as a path towards resolving the problems of easy manipulation of public opinion rather than taking advantage of them for commercial and political advantage. He knew Hayek and shared his scorn of state planning and became associated with the early stages of development of American neoliberalism, through the Walter Lippmann Colloquy that initiated the Mont Pelérin Society, but in the end he was not a supporter of Hayekian neoliberalism.
16. Edward Herman and Noam Chomsky (1988/2002), however, have put forward what they call a "propaganda theory" to explain the power and focus of the media to advance its commercial interests. While they compile an impressive range of data to show the enormous power and reach of media groups and case studies demonstrating media reach and bias, I think Lippmann's thesis provides a simpler explanation of recent media history and the likely trajectory of modern media; the build-up of commercial and media power is part of the story of neoliberal emergence. Herman and Chomsky focus on the virtues of democratization and conclude: "The organization and self-education of groups in the community and workplace, and their networking and activism, continue to be the fundamental elements in steps towards the democratization of our social life and any meaningful social change. Only to the extent that such developments succeed can we hope to see media that are free and independent." (p. 307) Foucault, in contrast, saw democracy as a part of the whole biopolitical process which itself had to be explained. Foucault and Chomsky debated some of these issues somewhat inconclusively in 1971 (https://chomsky.info/1971xxxx/).
17. In many respects these efforts are comparable to the work described later of Kahneman and Tversky and John Zaller (Part III). Information on behaviour can be used to understand voting behaviour, to 'nudge' people in a socially appropriate direction—or simply to achieve political power.
18. See Stephanie Lo and Kenneth Rogoff (2015).
19. On August 5, 2016, for instance, the *Financial Times* said this: "The arguments for active fiscal policy at the moment are clear. Central banks have been contorting themselves into positions of ever-greater complexity—inducements to bank lending, QE, zero or negative interest rates—

to try to loosen monetary conditions...the BoE's policy rate is now down to 0.25 per cent. Yet there are a few welcome signs that fiscal rather than monetary policy may finally be taking some of the strain of stimulating a sluggish global economy." Summers, in his FT blog, August 18, 2016, also notes the comments from San Francisco Fed President, John Williams, suggesting that the "currently chronically very low neutral rate has important [fiscal] policy implications". Summers, however, doubts the effect of increased spending on education as having any impact through effects on the interest rate; rather, he advocates the more direct benefits of infrastructure investment. In her speech at Jackson Hole, Wyoming, in August 2016, Janet Yellen, Chair of the Federal Reserve, in explaining the modern monetary toolkit, cited as among the headwinds faced by the economy and limiting the speed of recovery "a period of contractionary fiscal policy".

20. Other theorists also advance diverse explanations and predictions on the present crisis and future of capitalism. Mark Blyth (2016) in his *Foreign Affairs* review, Capitalism in Crisis, reviews three recent books: historian Jürgen Kocka, largely blames modern banking and financialization; sociologist Wolfgang Streek sees the crisis as arising from conflict between capitalism and democracy and growth in reliance on debt rather than taxation for public finance; and journalist Paul Mason looks to Kondratieff's long-term cycles and neoliberalism's capacity to avoid necessary correction through financialization—he also sees neoliberal and global failure to address climate change as offering a challenge that capitalism may not be able to meet unless there is a fundamental change in the 'structure of property rights'. Most of these arguments, as presented by Blyth, are covered in other analyses, but none appear to provide a clear justification for an organic theory of the evolution of capitalism.

21. See further discussion of this issue in Chap. 6, including Todd Sandler's (2004) highlighting the limitation of this approach in the highly complex issue of addressing climate change. See also more general discussion of mathematical formulation of games and actual games in Chap. 8.

22. A continuing program covering twelve policy areas covering three broad groups: (1) Policy Transparency, covered by the IMF; (2) Financial Sector Regulation and Supervision, developed by specialized standard setting bodies; and (3) Institutional and Market Infrastructure, developed by specialized standard-setting bodies with input from the IMF and World Bank. See http://www.imf.org/external/np/exr/facts/sc.htm. The

Fiscal Transparency Initiative component of Policy Transparency was developed from principles outlined in the Kopits and Craig (1998) IMF Occasional Paper.

References

Blyth, Mark. 2016. Capitalism in Crisis: What Went Wrong and What Comes Next. *Foreign Affairs* 95 (4): 172–179.
Friedman, Milton. 1962. *Capitalism and Freedom*, 40th Anniversary ed., 2002. Chicago/London: University of Chicago Press.
Garnaut, Ross. 2009. *The Great Crash of 2008*. Victoria: Melbourne University Press.
Gleeson-White, Jane. 2014. *Six Capitals: The Revolution Capitalism Has to Have – Or Can Accountants Save the Planet*. Sydney/Melbourne/Auckland/London: Allen & Unwin.
Heller, Peter S. 2003. *Who Will Pay: Coping with Aging Societies, Climate Change, and Other Long-Term Fiscal Challenges*. International Monetary Fund: Washington DC.
Herman, Edward S., and Noam Chomsky. 1988. *Manufacturing Consent: The Political Economy of the Mass Media*. New York/Toronto: Pantheon Books of Random House. (reprinted with a new Introduction, 2002).
Kaletsky, Anatole. 2010. *Capitalism 4.0: The Birth of a New Economy*. London/New York/Berlin/Sydney: Bloomsbury.
Kopits, George, and Jon Craig. 1998. *Transparency in Government Operations*, IMF Occasional Paper No. 158. Washington, DC: International Monetary Fund.
Krugman, Paul. 2007. *The Conscience of a Liberal: Reclaiming America from the Right*. London: Allen Lane/Penguin.
Lewis, Michael. 2010. *The Big Short: Inside the Doomsday Machine*. New York: W.W. Norton & Co.
Lippman, Walter. 1922. *Public Opinion*. New York: Free Press Paperbacks; published 1997.
Lo, Stephanie, and Kenneth Rogoff. 2015. *Secular Stagnation, Debt Overhang and Other Rationales for Sluggish Growth, Six Years On*, BIS Working Papers No 482.
Mallaby, Sebastian. 2016. *The Man Who Knew: The Life and Times of Alan Greenspan*. London/New York: Bloomsbury Publishing.

Mayer, Jane. 2016. *Dark Money: The Hidden History of the Billionaires Behind the Rise of the Radical Right*. New York/Toronto: Doubleday/Random House.

———. 2017. The Reclusive Hedge-Fund Tycoon Behind the Trump Presidency: How Robert Mercer Exploited America's Populist Insurgency. *New Yorker*, March 27.

McKnight, David. 2012. *Rupert Murdoch: An Investigation of Political Power*. Sydney/Melbourne/Auckland/London: Allen & Unwin.

Sandler, T. 2004. *Global Collective Action*. Cambridge: Cambridge University Press.

Stiglitz, Joseph E. 2016. *Rewriting the Rules of the American Economy: An Agenda for Growth and Shared Prosperity*. New York/London: W.W. Norton.

Summers, Laurence H. 2016. The Age of Secular Stagnation: What It Is and What to Do About It. *Foreign Affairs* 95 (2): 2–9.

Tett, Gillian. 2015. *The Silo Effect: Why Putting Everything in Its Place Isn't Such a Bright Idea*. Kindle ed. Little, Brown Book Group

Wapshott, Nicholas. 2011. *Keynes/Hayek: The Clash that Defined Modern Economics*. Brunswick: Scribe Publications.

Wolf, Martin. 2014. *The Shifts and the Shocks: What We've Learned – And Have Still to Learn from the Financial Crisis*. New York: Penguin Press.

4

Measuring Social Well-Being: GDP Is Neither Accurate Nor Fair

The production data underlying most economic and social decisions embodied in GDP are derived from commercial accounts transactions[1] plus government consumption and investment spending valued at cost. The need for better measurement of social well-being has long been recognized, as have the inadequacies of the GDP metric. The 2009 Stiglitz, Sen, Fitoussi Commission report on measurement of economic progress and social progress gives a comprehensive set of suggestions on improving measurement of the various dimensions of well-being and tackling the weaknesses of our present GDP measure. We'll return to consider some aspects of these proposals for long-term reform of the GDP measure later in this chapter. Our main focus, however, is to highlight improvements in government accounting that are already underway and to suggest ways in which these technical improvements can best be incorporated in current fiscal reporting and PFM practices. In the longer run, such improvements should also contribute to broader GDP reform; we should start now, however, to develop a more inclusive set of production and wealth metrics to guide our rapidly changing global society.

This chapter examines the governance problems that arise from GDP's inaccurate representation of social value and the need to build on the steps that have been taken by governments over the past three decades towards better accounting for social well-being. It advances elements of a long-term strategy to measure all elements of social well-being and to coordinate public and private efforts to ensure a better political focus on that metric and goal. The question of *unfairness* in this context is largely one of addressing the continuing valuation imbalance between marketed private goods and the production of needed collective goods valued mainly at cost. Estimating value at cost assumes no added social value and gives no signals regarding future public investment needs. These fundamental accounting and statistical issues have a major impact on government economic and social policies. Good economics is much more dependent on accounting and statistical reform than is commonly appreciated.

The following two chapters in Part II deal with other aspects of measurement and social policy. Chapter 5 tackles distributional unfairness. Economic policy has been dominated by questions of economic growth, as measured by changes in GDP, and commercial efficiency, at the expense of serious efforts to reduce personal inequality within national boundaries, or the even greater income gap between income levels of advanced and emerging market economies and those of the developing world. Whereas this chapter is concerned with accurate measurement of social well-being, Chap. 5 looks at its distribution. Evidence is emerging that reducing inequality is likely to promote rather than hinder national and global growth (particularly if a broader measure of well-being is adopted); these issues require as much attention as growth, stability, and efficiency of well-being outcomes. Chapter 6 returns to the theme of measuring the value of collective action—specifically the importance of continuing to strengthen our scientific understanding and estimation of the costs of climate change. The global program to counter the effects of fossil fuel energy production on global warming has established near-universal recognition of the tangible costs of unregulated private production. These principles are beginning to be recognized as an essential element of the System of National Accounts (SNA), which sets the rules for measurement of GDP.

Together, the three chapters argue for a sustained and substantial increase in efforts to revise our systems of measuring well-being and to coordinate global action to generate growth for all. Each, however, recognizes the existence of substantial barriers to reform arising from established entities and organizations and legacy practices. The proposed reforms can only be fully established over the long term; implementation will become easier, however, once the basic principles are articulated and accepted professionally and by the public. Chapter 7, in Part III of the book, deals with broader questions of institutional frameworks and power structures that set the rules for current policy and thus often pose significant barriers to introducing new social reform programs. While some aspects of the 'rules of the game' are being addressed by institutional economics, the chapter incorporates developments in behavioural and political disciplines and discusses steps towards a framework that can deeply review existing rules.

A Framework for Improving Well-Being Measurement and Fiscal Management

Measurement of government activity contribution to production is an important element of GDP and thus of the measurement of economic growth. But, if government activity is measured only by the amount spent on government functions in the annual budget, its policies are not soundly based. Professionals, and indeed most of us, are aware that monies spent on, say, education, health and scientific research bring tangible economic and broader social benefits to the recipients of these services. While many of these benefits are in principle measurable, their measurement through commercial monetary exchange is not immediately practicable—and bureaucratic assessment in non-monetary terms is complicated, costly and often ineffective.

Appraisal of relative values of government and corporate activity is made separately through political process, often aided by cost-benefit analysis (CBA) techniques. CBA assessments, however, are generally done only ex ante, no record of estimated gains is kept, and political decisions are not assessed transparently by the media. More often, the impact of spending on specific electorates seems to provide the main justification for general spending and is accepted without too many questions from the media or the public.[2] Program/performance-based budgeting (PBB) techniques, using CBA, are now widely used by most governments, and performance indicators and higher-level key performance indicators (KPIs) are claimed to be used to determine budget priorities and assess long-term performance. Evidence for the effectiveness of these techniques is slight, however. CBA assessments are rarely made public, examined by the financial press, or discussed in public debate. Public performance data has not yet captured the interest of the media or the public. The technical difficulties of implementing a more sophisticated valuation system may have inhibited politicians and the media from promoting such a debate; no doubt the costs of investing in improved budget decision-making and valuing government outputs and outcomes will be seen to have played a role in the prevailing 'small-government' political environment.

Yet, in the background a revolution in public accounting is underway. The question of 'Who will pay?' for political promises to support the chronically ill or the elderly, referred to in Chap. 3, has now been well recognized. The solution has increasingly been pushed back by neoliberal governments and agencies to the choice of individuals to make provision for their own future through defined contribution pension schemes. In many ways recognition of personal responsibilities in this respect is appropriate. But such policies are much less acceptable when the global economy and technological progress are at the same time shifting or reducing opportunities for many to keep jobs and make adequate provision for their own future. (No simple answers can be provided; the issues of equality and impact of globalization are taken up further in the next chapter.) But ways of strengthening accounting systems to more accurately record all transactions and their impact on assets, liabilities and risks are now emerging. It is vital to establish a deeper professional and public understanding of these initiatives and their potential to establish a clearer sense of personal and collective responsibilities for collective goods investment and production.

From the 1990s onward, governments in advanced countries, as well as some emerging market economies and developing countries, began to grapple with these issues and make fundamental changes to their accounting and reporting to strengthen analysis and control of government fiscal accounts and policies. The progressive adoption of accrual basis accounting by many governments has shifted the focus of fiscal policy from one of short-term concern with the balance of payment and receipts flows to a long-term concern with the balance of stocks of assets and liabilities and the potential risks associated not only with long-term debt but also with risks on the asset side of the balance sheet. Conceptually, a balance sheet approach (BSA) to government accounting and management of fiscal risks is widely accepted.

Progress, however, is uneven: Many advanced countries have adopted accrual basis accounting, and some have adopted aspects of so-called accrual budgeting, which in principle requires BSA to be applied across the whole public sector and estimated for future years. Few, however, even among the OECD countries, have fully embraced the range of international accounting and reporting principles and standards that are being developed. Acceleration of reform should be a global priority, but neither national nor international agencies have been able to take up the challenge adequately. Technically, a range of initiatives have been proposed and are described below. The continuing revolution in accounting and measurement of value and risks must be developed into a coordinated program that sets standards of value measurement for all entities, nations and the global community.

The introduction of accrual basis accounting to the public sector is now widely recognized as a critical step for public sector accountability. Beyond these fundamental public sector reforms the development of Integrated Reporting proposed by the International Integrated Reporting Council, aims to apply much broader social accountability principles to all private and public entities. The <IR> reform is aimed at no less than accounting for all forms of capital and value creation in government and private sector entities; practical application of the concept of non-traditional forms of capital (particularly environmental and social) is being actively promoted by the IIRC. The same concept implicitly underlies the development of environmental accounts in the SNA, though general application within SNA requires careful review of all its national and international implications. Thus, <IR> should initially aim to transform entity decision-making; in the longer run, it should help lead to governmental and international adoption of a much more inclusive measure of social progress and well-being than GDP. A more detailed discussion of <IR> is given later in the chapter; the immediate priority is to consolidate the move to adopt accrual basis accounting across the public sector.

Progress towards these goals, though relatively modest to date in terms of social change, has been significant. Long-term and broader social impact will require coordinated efforts among many professional disciplines—economics, accounting, statistics and political science—and multiple international entities with distinct and well-established mandates. These challenges can only be met over the long term, but the potential improvement in measuring national and global well-being promises to transform policy-making at all levels. Adoption of <IR> should therefore become more firmly established as a clear long-term objective within the broad framework of accounting and governance reform.

Such a program is complex, and requires an overarching strategy and roadmap to guide the variety of stakeholders towards a collectively beneficial solution. Key elements to continue and consolidate this accounting revolution are these: First, a high-level agreement on the importance of common accounting standards covering financial transactions by government and commercial enterprise. Second, promotion of risk management should be encouraged at all levels, particularly emphasizing that adoption of risk management techniques needs to be recognized as being dependent on comprehensive reporting by all public sector entities and by strengthened government transparency and accountability practice. Third, a strong communications effort should be mounted to ensure that all agencies, public and private, are made more aware of their responsibilities for managing all forms of capital and value creation.

The first two of these elements are already being established in commercial accounting through adoption of International Financial Reporting Standards (IFRS) and are becoming so in the public sector through adoption of International Public Sector Accounting Standards (IPSAS).[3] The challenges for the public sector, which has been dominated by macroeconomic rather than accounting professionals, are much greater. Cash-basis recognition of payments and receipts and limited recognition of assets and liabilities have, as noted earlier, been the general practice of government in most countries. Continuing progress will require greatly enhanced cooperation among the professions involved, which is in itself a challenge. The key entities that promote global standards and practices will need to agree on common guidelines and a roadmap to help countries at different levels to advance in stages to meet their entity and national reporting needs.

For individual countries, the overall program would encompass three broad phases: first, full adoption of accrual basis accounting across the public sector; second, and broadly in parallel, establishing fiscal risk analysis and management that covers the whole of government; and finally, implementing legal standards for integrated reporting on the use of all forms of capital, with an initial focus on the public sector. The program will require very substantial investment in automated accounting systems and development of Government Integrated Financial Management Information System (GIFMIS) for all levels of government (this aspect is developed further particularly in relation to developing economies, in Chap. 5). Each stage of the program is considered in more detail below.

Establishing a Strategic Vision and Goals

Each country must start from its current situation. For the most part, public financial management (PFM) reform in emerging market countries under the World Bank, multilateral development banks, IMF technical guidance, or bilateral programs all involve investment in automated systems and a commitment to eventual adoption of IPSAS for accounting and reporting. Importantly, IMF standards for Government Finance Statistics (GFS), though broadly compatible, differ from those of IPSAS regarding accounts consolidation. IMF GFS defines primary[4] (generally non-commercial) activities of government under the GFSM 2014 'General Government' classification (often subdivided into central and subnational levels); state-owned financial and non-financial enterprises are treated separately as subsectors more allied to the corporate sector. IPSAS, on the other hand requires consolidation of the entire government-operated sector as the 'Public Sector' reporting entity. As developed below, I argue that application of the IPSAS consolidation is critical to ensure adequate reporting, analysis and management of government fiscal risks. For many

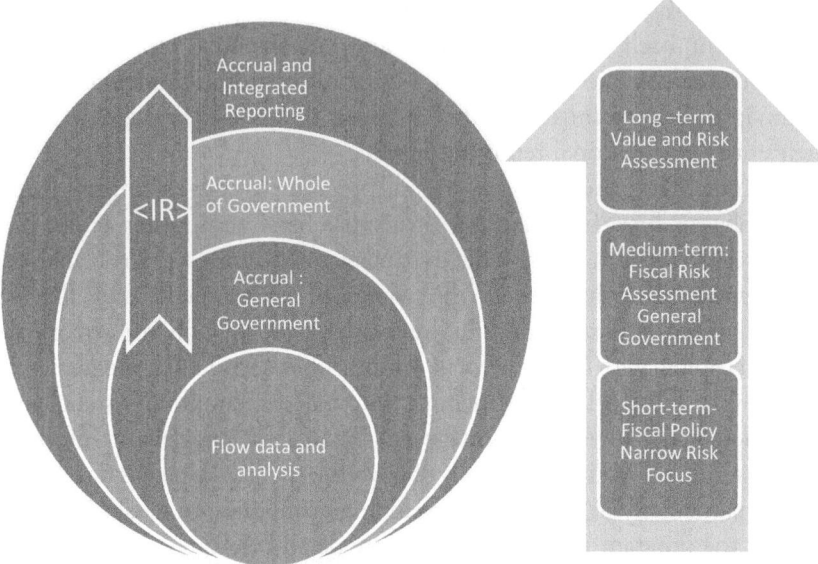

Fig. 4.1 Accounting standards and stages of reform (Source: Author)

countries, however, the distinction between general government and state-owned enterprises remains important. Consolidating accounting processes to meet IPSAS standards is thus necessarily a design-intensive and long-term program for each country, but it needs a well-coordinated international effort based on a common and widely understood process.

Whatever the starting point, each country should be expected to commit to a process of reform that will establish both full 'whole of government' accrual and <IR>, as illustrated in Fig. 4.1. In each phase, steps should be taken to establish the needed technology and standards for the next phase. As discussed in more detail later, the introduction of <IR> is challenging and unlikely to be very successful unless reasonable progress has been made with the implementation of accrual basis accounting and reporting, at least at the central government level, but aiming to encompass general government.[5] Thus, in moving from a traditional focus on flows and short-term policy analysis to accrual basis accounting, all units of general government should be party to plans to adopt the key

IPSAS standards and publish a general government balance sheet. Only when these standards are broadly met can the total set of risks from flows and balance sheet changes be reasonably inferred from the available data. It is well-recognized, however, that many risks emanate not just from the liability and asset risks of general government; significant vulnerabilities arise from the operations of other elements of the public sector. In practice, risk analysis is highly dependent on available government accounts and balance sheet data, very often with limited data on public enterprise operations. Development of risk analysis and management capacity is thus dependent on the quality and availability of accounting data from all public sector entities seeing improvement.

Moving to the broadest stage of public sector accounting coverage is thus fundamental to the whole process of improving PFM and risk management. A comprehensive 'whole of government' set of accounts on IPSAS/IFRS standards is the aspirational and ultimately necessary goal for providing the full range of data needed to assess public enterprise and government fiscal risks. To attain the ultimate objective of reporting on value creation/diminution for all national and global socio-economic activity, the principles and practices of <IR> across all public and private value-creating activities should be initiated in key entities as soon as is practicable. This full set of goals and the long timespan to achieve them should be understood by all policy-makers and practitioners. Ideally, strong principles along these lines should be enshrined in national PFM acts that commit governments, ministers and departmental secretaries to observe the basic principles of fiscal management, accounting, reporting and public transparency and accountability.

This proposed process would invert the prevailing mode of PFM reform strategy. The current emphasis is that improving PFM practice will promote the adoption of international standards. Under the proposed approach, progressive adoption of the relevant standards becomes the prerequisite for improving PFM practice. Fundamentally, policy analysis and review can only be as strong as the data used to guide it. Such a standards-led reform strategy is obviously very long term, but no more so than our current approaches, some aspects of which are now seen to be faltering, as we discuss below. Measures to improve PFM practice should, of course, be continued, but linked more closely to the suggested baseline program to improve accounting and reporting standards. In the final part of this chapter, I argue that a survey of the extent to which international standards for measuring value creation and attendant risks are being adopted and used in social policy would give an objectively measurable indicator of the status of government reform. A program along the lines illustrated in Fig. 4.1 would provide a strong foundation that should help coordinate the variety of 'good practice' assessments now being used to promote PFM reform.

Risk Management

Over the past three decades, fiscal policy-making among some of the advanced countries has increasingly emphasized the need for explicit assessment of fiscal risks and publication of these estimates. As Murray Petrie (2013a) describes, *fiscal risk* can be defined as exposure to the consequences of potential deviations from the planned and legislated flows and stocks in the annual budget, and declared as policy in medium-term or long-term budget projections. Fiscal risk, he notes, covers: *calculable risk*—variations in outturn that can be estimated by standard probability analysis; *uncertainties*—where possible outcomes can be identified but insufficient information is available to estimate probability; and *ignorance*—where policy-makers are unaware of potential risks. The last of these is to an extent unavoidable and can only be overcome as knowledge of the scope of PFM systems and potential threats to the systems grows; likely the narrower the focus of government fiscal policy (and associated standards) the greater will be the impact of ignorance.[6] The suggested broad program of accounting reform leading to complete coverage of whole-of-government accounts should thus do much to reduce the impact of the 'ignorance' component of risk analysis.

Risk management as conducted in a BSA and whole-of-government environment, it should be emphasized, will enable more attention to be paid to asset risks as well as liabilities and debt sustainability. This aspect is particularly important for countries that are well endowed with natural assets. Such countries are faced with the issue of replacing an invariably risky stream of earnings from the non-renewable resource with an equivalent stream of income from economic development or investment in alternative assets. Norway provides the standard model for managing this situation through its sovereign wealth fund, which invests mainly in offshore financial assets to avoid undue impact on the non-resource economy. It has proved difficult, however, to apply the Norwegian model to many developing countries because of limited financial and risk management capacity and lack of assurance of accountability on all aspects of the operation. Asset valuation will certainly pose problems, since much of the knowledge of asset values is held by mining or oil companies that have gained exploration rights and in production-sharing agreements for ongoing operations. Nonetheless, all governments should aim to establish a full balance sheet approach covering all aspects of the production, revenue and revenue fund asset holdings to provide the essential basis for oversight and risk management of all aspects of its fiscal policies and operations.

At any level of government and any stage of development of the PFM system, however, steps should be taken to incorporate formal risk management as an integral part of the fiscal management and reporting processes. As Petrie outlines, the IMF has, since the late 1990s been a strong proponent of action to assess, disclose and mitigate fiscal risks. Its 1998 Code of Good Practices on Fiscal Transparency (Fiscal Transparency Code) called for comprehensive disclosure of fiscal risks in government budget and accounts documents, and since then a considerable amount of work has been done by the IMF and other organizations to elaborate the requirements for establishing effective fiscal risk management as part of PFM operations.

Progress to date on methods to improve fiscal risk management is well covered in the IMF (2016), which aims to show best country practices in analyzing and managing fiscal risks. The paper catalogues the main fiscal risks faced by countries and their relative magnitude, and proposes a toolkit for their management. Some risks are directly related to operations of government entities either within general government or as part of the public sector, others are external. For those that are part of general government or the broader public sector (including issuance of guarantees, operations of state-owned enterprises, subnational government, and public-private partnership risks), the analysis and management of risks would benefit greatly by extending accrual accounting and reporting to general government and eventually to whole of government. Each entity within government should then be subject to similar standards of audit and become increasingly aware of its contribution to risk, as well as its responsibility for risk mitigation.

Much of the difficulty of present country-level fiscal risk analysis, however, arises from the lack of data and authority over the operations of entities outside the scope of central government reporting; setting up a separate independent review authority has generally proved difficult for that reason. Establishing whole-of-government accounting and reporting standards would greatly assist this task. Assessing risks from external macroeconomic shocks, such as exchange rate, interest rate and commodity prices, is less dependent on accounting data coverage, but requires a strong macrofiscal forecasting and management unit with good linkages to the central bank.

Some risks are largely external to government fiscal management operations—the chief of these are risks arising from the financial sector, risks which have been relatively infrequent but of major magnitude, as evidenced by the 2008 GFC. The IMF paper indicates that government rescues of troubled financial institutions happen about once every 24 years and have an average cost of about 10 percent of GDP, though in one case producing a fiscal cost of 57 percent of GDP. Financial sector risks require special attention and fall under the jurisdiction of the central bank; most aspects of financial risk management policy seem still to rely on central bank regulation and controls. Because of the magnitude of risk and the potential fiscal cost, close consultation between the central bank and fiscal management agencies seems increasingly necessary. As discussed in Chap. 3, this view of balanced macroeconomic coordination of fiscal and monetary policy, however, runs somewhat contrary to much immediate post-GFC practice.

The fiscal risk management toolkit (see IMF [2016] summary table, p. 14) covers each of these risk categories and the process that a risk management unit should go through with each category of risk: identifying and quantifying; mitigating through direct or indirect controls, or through risk transfer instruments; and, finally, ensuring provision of resources to cover the realization of risks. Decisions regarding mitigation or provisioning would be subject to cost-benefit analysis as part of the budget decision-making process. Ultimately, they see the maintenance of a safe debt level, informed by risk analysis, as being the desired management outcome. Application of the toolkit would vary substantially among countries, and the paper suggests that low-income countries would benefit more from direct controls; emerging markets could make use of risk mitigation and transfer tools, while "countries that already have sophisticated risk management systems could more explicitly recognize their residual exposure in their fiscal plans" (p. 34).

This picture suggests a program of progressively improving practice from developing and emerging market economies up to the level of more advanced countries, some of which already include fiscal risk statements in their budget and accounts documents. The paper goes on to chart a process for institutionalizing risk analysis and management as part of fiscal and macroeconomic management: first, by establishing a risk management policy, then, by requiring individual entities to become accountable for risks that fall within their mandates; instituting a central risk oversight body; and establishing central controls over risks. While this process is logical and reflects the key characteristics of countries like New Zealand, Australia, Britain and the United States, it does not represent the actual process that those countries have gone through to reach their stage of sophistication. Neither does it reflect the significant institutional differences among the advanced countries selected—for instance, Australia and the US are federations, whereas the United Kingdom and New Zealand are unitary states, with significantly different levels of complexity among them.

Beyond these points, developing and emerging market countries face a variety of significant barriers to adopting an accrual basis/BSA/risk management trajectory to fiscal policy, given the way their present fiscal management system has evolved. Developing countries have generally adopted systems based on those of former colonial powers, but with new centres of authority derived from post-WW2 decolonization and establishment of central planning commissions in many. Some emerging market economies share several these features, but others have modernized sufficiently to move towards an OECD-style model of fiscal management. Of those developing and emerging market economies that have arisen from state-controlled regimes based on the former USSR and China, fiscal management and risk assessment for many is heavily influenced by the ruling party and the considerable influence of state-owned enterprises. Many, however, are moving towards introduction of accrual basis accounts, and some towards broader coverage of the fiscal impact of the public sector; in general, the IMF, the World Bank, the OECD and other multilateral development agencies provide assistance for these efforts.

These proposals for PFM reform and the establishment of fiscal risk management are definitely worthwhile, but they understate the importance of a program of reform of accounting and reporting standards along the lines illustrated in Fig. 4.1 and described above. Making comprehensive data available through PFM reform covering the whole public sector is also an essential element to establishing fiscal policy credibility—in the sense that annual and medium-term budget statements should give a fair forecast of actual outcomes. Central direction of this system should naturally accrue to the ministry responsible for finance and treasury. Problems will remain in those countries that are under direct state control or have politically powerful planning commissions, but the technical nature of authority should enable such differences to be resolved; in all cases, advice to adopt better practices needs to give more emphasis to the importance of accounting standards and data.

Integrated Reporting: From Entity Management to GDP Reform

The IIRC's work on integrated reporting introduces a new and vital element that revises our idea of what constitutes capital and value creation. It has far-reaching implications—immediately for management of public and private entities, and much more widely and long-term for measurement of social value and well-being and hence for reform of GDP. We will look first at its application at entity level. Many of the concepts need to be further refined and codified at this level to help promote and guide widespread adoption of <IR> practices, as discussed further below.

Figure 4.2, drawn from IIRC/CIPFA (2016), illustrates the critical role that <IR> can and should play in ensuring that all forms of enterprise are

A Framework for Improving Well-Being Measurement and Fiscal... 119

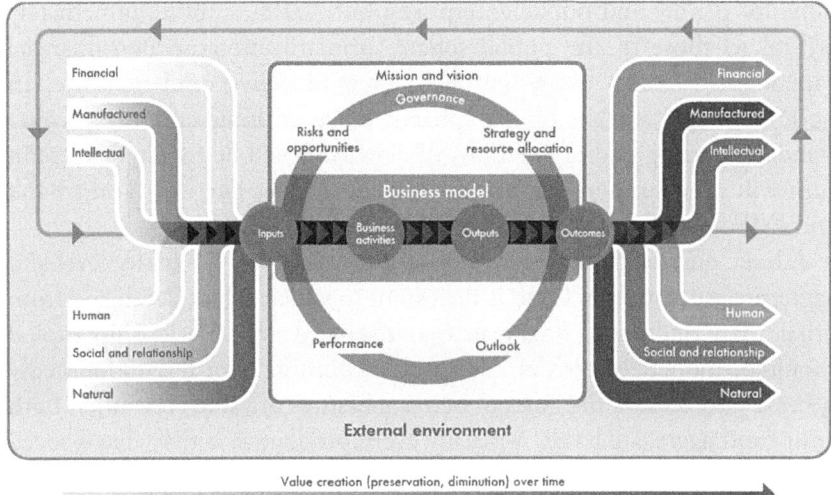

Fig. 4.2 Value creation and reporting under IIR (Source: CIPFA and World Bank Group (2016)

managed to achieve social goals. <IR> recognizes forms of capital and pathways of social value creation or diminution through output/outcome analysis beyond those of standard commercial accounting practice, most notably the impact of government and commercial enterprise on environmental and human capital. From a social welfare measurement point of view, these impacts should increasingly be recorded formally in both public and private enterprise accounts. Accounting and statistical implementation of these reforms should become an integral part of the ongoing accounting and PFM reform described in Fig. 4.1 and above.

IIRC/CIPFA emphasize establishing <IR> in the public sector as a priority. In CIPFA/WB (2016) they observe that for any organization, its main purpose is "to explain how an organization manages its resources and relationships (or 'capitals') to create value over time. All the capitals that an organization uses or affects should be considered—financial, manufactured, intellectual, human, social and relationship, and natural capitals—but only those that are material to the business need to be included in the integrated report" (p. 7). The basic processes are the same for private and public enterprises, but <IR> is more immediately critical to those in the public sphere, primarily because non-financial capital use is much more central to their objectives and mandate. In both the public and the private spheres, however, intervention via strong standards-setting bodies like IPSASB and IASB will be required; these in turn will need support from international agencies like the World Bank and IMF as well as multilateral and bilateral agencies.

A basic question that needs to be addressed at both the entity level and aggregate estimation of GDP is the extent to which values developed from other than traditional financial, manufactured and relationship capital should be monetized. Private enterprise accounting reform is undoubtedly necessary to achieve the goals of better measures of value creation at both entity and aggregate levels. Virtually every productive activity has a social cost beyond the price that is paid for the product, even oranges and apples have a peel and a core, and usually packaging, all of which must be disposed of or otherwise managed and which give rise to immediate costs and a variety of longer-term environmental costs.[7] But, because of 'free-rider' issues, governments—sometimes using private contractors—are obliged to take responsibility for disposing of waste and managing environmental impact. Some new forms of corporation[8] do acknowledge responsibility for environmental and private negotiations, and these may well take a leadership role in implementing <IR>. But these examples alone will not necessarily inspire others perhaps less inclined to take responsibility for their impact on social or environmental capital to apply the same standards.

A key issue, however, is that while corporate entities can make some estimates of the monetary value of use of, say, environmental capital, under current accounting rules these cannot be recognized formally in their financial statements. Private entities thus need guidance from accounting-standards-setting bodies as well as from government policy on pricing and valuation of use of non-traditional items—the application of carbon pricing providing the most obvious example. The case for a broader regime for estimation and regulation of non-traditional capital in the enterprise sector must thus be guided strongly by governments (aided by independent professional associations). The cooperation of enterprises that are actively recognizing their social and environmental responsibilities will also play a vital role.⁹

This combination of the recognition of non-traditional forms of capital and of using taxes and subsidies to ensure associated expenses and benefits are recorded thus has considerable implications for both social and tax policies—albeit again very long term. On tax policy, economists describe taxes as being 'distortionary' when they discourage effort or savings. Consequently, modern policies have greatly reduced high marginal rates of income and corporate tax and favoured regressive taxes on consumption.¹⁰ Development of an alternative, Pigouvian-principled, tax framework aimed at pricing the collective costs and benefits of private production as a major source of revenue for collective goods should be explored as an adjunct to the <IR> program. Such a system could both help overcome the 'free-rider' problem of financing collective goods and provide a clearer scope for tackling social and economic inequality (the latter issues are discussed in more detail in Chap. 5). Pricing mechanisms on broadly Pigouvian principles, while strongly resisted by traditional private enterprise, are advocated by economists as the most efficient way of implementing climate change mitigation policies in particular. Successful implementation of formal pricing of carbon emissions would represent a major step towards recognizing the general need for monetization of the external impacts through <IR>. The formidable political problems being encountered both nationally and globally against pricing of externalities is examined in Chap. 6 with reference to carbon pricing.

The question of monetizing value created, where applicable and practicable, is of fundamental importance to the broader objective of improving GDP as a measure of well-being. Although this objective seemed to be central to Gleeson-White's argument that the 'six capitals' and <IR> represent the 'holy grail' of accounting theory and would help create a GDP-like measurement that more closely represented well-being rather than merely commercial health. She, however, drew back significantly from that conclusion in the later sections of her book, observing that the use of multiple capitals is relatively new and that their measurement is relatively undeveloped (pp. 190–191). In her epilogue she goes on to argue that "there is a logical inconsistency at the heart of the six capitals model which will prevent it alone from saving the planet: it seeks to account for non-financial value, but can see it only in terms of financial value" (p. 282).

The <IR> introductory manual, for different reasons, takes a cautious approach to the question of monetization of non-traditional forms of capital, noting that "the concept of value is highly subjective, the <IR> Framework does not suggest or require 'monetizing' value. It highlights that value created for the organization is linked to value created for others, including key stakeholders and society at large" (p. 13). It does not reject monetization but indicates that it is not an integral objective of <IR> at this stage. Given the still-developing framework and the need for explicit government action to estimate external costs and benefits, this approach seems necessary. However, the case for making continuing and growing efforts to measure value creation from all forms of capital in monetary terms should be stated as firmly as possible as implementation proceeds and is taken up more generally by governments. Use of available measures of carbon price provides an avenue for monetizing value when GHGs are involved. Where it is not possible to do so, an alternative non-financial measure may be reported, together with an explanation of the difficulties of applying monetary measures of value at entity level.

The points regarding monetization, particularly by Gleeson-White, appear to have been heavily influenced by the views of moral philosopher Michael J. Sandel (2012), who points to the corrupting and coercive effect on social behaviour arising from the dominance of the commercial market and its extension into all aspects of life. Putting a price on everything, he argues, corrodes society's moral standards; commercialization of a whole range of activities—from signing autographs, to queue-jumping, to hiring mercenaries to fight wars, to reducing carbon-dioxide emissions—has corrupted and diminished their social value. The very act of putting a price on many activities he suggests either condones certain socially undesirable behaviors or demeans others.

I agree with many of Sandel's concerns, but his arguments apply primarily to the present neoliberal form of commercialization rather than the proposed <IR> valuation process. <IR> provides an avenue for applying deliberated evidence-based ethical considerations to purely commercial valuation. A measured estimation of monetary costs and benefits and use of the tax/subsidy system to influence market-driven commercial decisions for clearly explained policy purposes, as argued above, constitutes a legitimate and ethically defensible position. Monetary estimates of the costs of running down our environmental capital or of producing armaments versus agricultural products are likely to be more persuasive than verbal moral suasion advanced in the political arena. Monetarized estimates are, moreover, likely to be more convincing if these outcomes are translated into real prices through taxation/subsidy or some form of rights-trading scheme as advocated for climate change policy, as we discuss in more detail in Chap. 6. The real questions are political rather than ethical.

Monetization of tangible benefits and costs at the entity level thus should be actively, though judiciously, encouraged in <IR>.[11] While monetization poses some analytical challenges and its use must be clearly explained, there are huge advantages in establishing a common 'numeraire' to facilitate trade-offs between different types of value creation within an organization. Quantification of monetized value should obviously be supported by evidence, and, if rejected on principle, that principle should be clearly explained. Some indicator of value must be applied in every case; it is better that the arguments for trade-off be made as explicitly and congruently as possible. Where a monetary calculation can be made, it will allow a consistent overview of the contributions of different forms of capital. This argument becomes much more compelling when we consider the impact of many organizations nationally and globally; as noted above in relation to PBB, purely verbal or KPI-based arguments for non-financial benefits or costs tend to be ignored. It is precisely this microlevel weakness of non-comparability of financial and nonfinancial values that must be addressed in re-engineering the measurement and use of GDP.

The IIRC/CIPFA proposal thus needs to be part of a broader global governance program aimed at strengthening the measurement of social value of production by all producing entities. Strategically, emphasis should be placed first on the public sector and then move progressively to apply the principles, rules and practices of accounting against the six capitals to all forms of enterprise. The development of measurement and standards methodology is fundamentally a task that needs to be undertaken by government and professional economists, accountants and statisticians and ultimately approved through a political process. Once there is agreement on the basis for standards, the concepts fully tested, and a manual produced, the agreed standards should be mandatory for all entities, government and private, operating in these value spheres. Establishing <IR> as the basis for managing the performance of individual entities and for assessing their contribution to aggregate well-being should lead to the development of a measure of social well-being based on value creation from all forms of capital (i.e., gross domestic value).

At this stage of implementation of <IR>, while several studies are underway at entity level most are exploring initially the ways in which <IR> can best be integrated with present reporting and decision-making processes; it is recognized as a way of 'breaking down silos' and getting a comprehensive overview of the whole business. The question of monetization has been discussed, but not yet adopted, as a means of improving overall measurement of the value of the organization; some look rather at 'value' as best represented through a combination of quantitative and qualitative information. Even where environmental issues are a significant element of the entity's responsibilities (such as the UK's The Crown Estate) and these responsibilities are clearly recognized, the parties have not yet fully established monetized value in their annual integrated report.[12] The importance of monetization is well established, however, in tackling environmental issues, as discussed in Chap. 6.

Implementation of <IR>, as emphasized above, depends on a solid platform of comprehensive accrual basis accounting in both public and private sectors. As mentioned earlier, much more work is needed to consolidate reforms even in the more advanced countries. A survey of accruals practices and reform among OECD members (OECD 2016) showed that although an increasing number of countries are adopting accrual accounting, and round 40 percent of national entities such as ministries of finance or an independent standards setting board, use IPSAS (or, the survey suggests, IFRS) as the main references for developing the national standards; only 15 percent of these countries provide an overview of the public sector as a whole in their financial statements; and another 23 percent of countries do so at the federal level. Few have explicit plans to expand the coverage of their financial statements. The survey suggests practical and technical challenges as one explanation, but also points to the lack of public and governmental appreciation of the need for a full view of public finances. Many factors are at play, including austerity-influenced political reluctance to invest in continuing PFM reform, as well as the limited expertise in accrual accounting in most finance ministries. Reactivation of PFM reform in OECD countries requires a major boost.

If these points are not well appreciated among OECD countries, even more difficulties seem certain among emerging markets. Overall, the slow pace of adoption of modern accounting standards will severely limit our ability to improve identification, estimation and remediation of national and global risks to commercial health and social well-being. Forecasting complex system outcomes will always have a high degree of uncertainty, but technology is making it easier to handle numerical complexities; timely and reliable accounting and reporting are most amenable to automation. IPSAS/IFRS standards are generally fully accommodated in high-level commercial accounting packages; the following chapter will examine key issues with respect to assistance to developing countries. A great deal more work will be needed to develop and codify <IR> standards for ICT application, and this aspect could be productively incorporated in the IIRC/CIPFA program—and linked to ongoing work by the World Bank and other international organizations, as discussed in the final part of this chapter. Technology difficulties are not, however, the main problem. More crucially, the dimensions of value creation and their measurement have not yet been sufficiently recognized either administratively or politically even in the most advanced countries.

Designing such a program and reaching agreement among the multitude of stakeholders presents major and long-term challenges. <IR> is a necessary step towards a more inclusive measure of social well-being than GDP, but coordinating the variety of professional disciplines and the international and bilateral technical and financing support bodies first to build a comprehensive accrual basis platform and then to establish <IR> is an unavoidably long-term process. As developed further below, a series of country- and entity-level studies may be the best way to meet these challenges and follow up the IIFC/CIPFA conceptual work on entity and national reform of value creation and reporting; IIFC/CIPFA, as noted, are already embarking on a number of entity-level studies, but these principles also need to be taken up at the national and international level.

Better measurement of social progress at entity level is unarguably important, but deeper reforms of government institutions, particularly its statistical compilations via the SNA and the political use of these data, will be necessary for these measurements to become embedded in the social policy process as deeply as GDP has been. Evolution of SNA concepts and compilation processes necessarily proceed slowly—there are many stakeholders and many national and professional interests. <IR> should increasingly contribute to that evolution, based first on entity-level reforms and then linked to parallel development of compilation and reporting on environmental-economic accounts governed by the UN.

Weaknesses in commercial and GDP accounting have been recognized for many years, even when the System of National Accounts was being developed.[13] The driving force at that time, however, was a simpler (albeit then revolutionary) one of measuring aggregate supply and demand, then a pressing and necessary objective. Aggregate commercial demand and supply remain important measures of economic health, but they do not measure social well-being. If a much broader concept of social well-being is our real objective, a GDP measure of production, should not continue to dominate social policy discussion.

Many studies have been undertaken with the aim of providing a broader measure of social value, and indeed some (such as the UN Human Development Index (HDI), developed under the direction of Amartya Sen and Mahbub ul Haq) are used. Like many other proposals that have been put forward, however, HDI uses a multidimensional measure to augment rather than replace GDP. While many embrace the idea of a broader basis for evaluation of social policy, these proposals lack political force. HDI's impact on policy-making has been limited[14]; GDP remains overwhelmingly the dominant measure for national and global policy-making. So-called 'dashboard' alternatives like HDI have proved incapable of capturing either political or public attention sufficiently to challenge the established focus on growth of commerce as the primary statistic to guide public policy. <IR> provides a strong conceptual basis to move beyond dashboard sets of indicators towards a more integrated measure of well-being.

The most recent official study of GDP in terms of its use as a measure of economic and social development is the comprehensive review sponsored by then-President Nicolas Sarkozy of France, led by Joseph Stiglitz, Amartya Sen and Jean-Paul Fitoussi, reported in 2009. The report targeted four groups: political leaders, technical/bureaucratic policy-makers, the academic and professional statistics community, and civil society organizations. It addressed both the deficiencies in the present GDP-based measurement and many of the issues that have to be tackled in moving toward a broader measure of social progress. Once again, however, it recommended a dashboard-type solution to augment GDP rather than its fundamental replacement.

Like earlier efforts, the report's recommendations have not yet had a major impact on either measurement or policy. Continuing work by the OECD is underway to develop the findings of the Commission and to promote better measures of social progress; the OECD's better life index[15] covering eleven topics aims to allow policy-makers and the public to compare well-being across countries. Several countries or entities within countries have established similar types of dashboard indicators[16] Modification of elements of GDP to reflect non-commercial value as quantitatively as possible, while institutionally difficult, seems likely to lead to a better option for PFM practice than developing an alternative set of indices to guide fiscal policy. The base already established by GDP, however, will make it easier to apply a modified measure of fiscal well-being to policy-making.

Apart from the advantages of having a clearer aggregate target, <IR> would help change the behaviour of individual and group social actors. Moreover, <IR> should complement the work of the United Nations Statistics Division, which has been working since 1993 to develop the System of Environmental-Economic Accounts as a satellite system of the SNA.[17] Figure 4.3 gives an overview of the way in which long-term accounting reforms including eventual adoption of <IR> will link together to lead to better accountability within public and private entities and much more valid measure of social value creation: gross domestic value (GDV).

4 Measuring Social Well-Being: GDP Is Neither Accurate Nor Fair

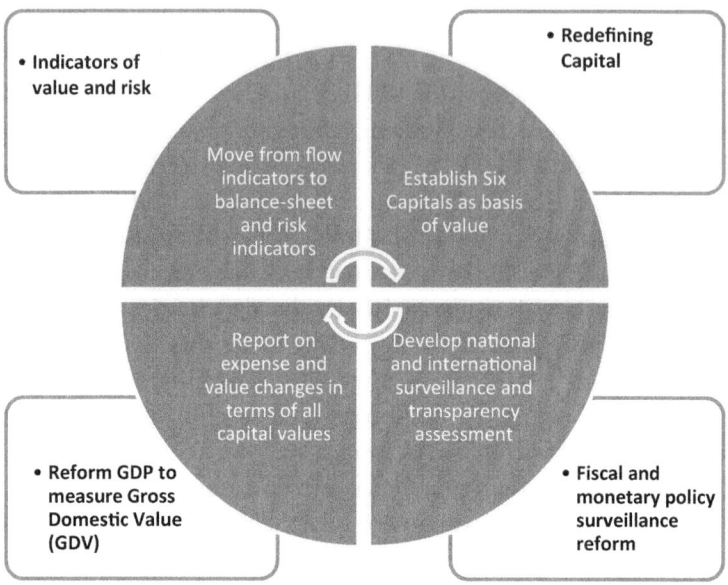

Fig. 4.3 Towards gross domestic value creation and surveillance (Source: Author)

A solid BSA and risk management platform will permit a more rapid development of <IR> and clear standards and practices to incorporate the principles of reporting in all relevant forms of capital use in both IPSAS and IFRS, as well as reconciling IPSAS and the IMF's Government Finance Statistics more fully with respect to the public reporting entity. IIRC has made a strong case that corporations and government organizations need to change basic accounting practices and value environmental and social capital explicitly as part of overall capital alongside the standard financial capital measures. Such changes would place a clear value on social and environmental concerns by all operating entities and the public. Rather than being tracked imperfectly (indeed, imperceptibly, as far as most of the public is concerned) by a battery of economic and social performance indicators, a much wider and more relevant range of social and environmental costs would be recognized at transaction level and thus taken explicitly into account in transaction flows and balance sheets; social benefits/costs and choices should thereby be reflected much more clearly under such an augmented 'invisible hand'.

Figure 4.3 thus provides a broader picture of relationships between different elements of the PFM reform program depicted in Fig. 4.1. It emphasizes the linkage between entity and aggregate accounting as a basis for more reliable surveillance of fiscal and social policy at national and global levels. The timeframe for completion of these linkages will be very long term, particularly in relation to reform of GDP measurement. Future progress will require considerable effort to improve coordination among the different disciplines and entities involved in relation to PFM and fiscal policy. The final part of this chapter considers key measures to tackle these coordination problems.

A Fresh Initiative: Improving Coordination of Standards and Practices Reform

Some of the practical difficulties of reform programs are very often related to differences in legal and administrative frameworks in different countries, and—partly consequent, partly tribal—political and public reluctance to move towards global standards. The IIRC/CIPFA and IPSASB work highlights the need for much more attention and resources to be applied to addressing these issues. It is not the case, however, that few resources are available, though the level of technical skills and political appreciation of the need to augment these skills may be lacking. Ministries of finance and treasuries across the world are aware of the standards proposed and are becoming more conversant with their merits and technical challenges.

We are now at a stage where there is a need to strengthen signals at all levels of the importance of accrual information generally and the necessity to adopt the BSA for comprehensive long-term fiscal policy and risk assessment. A lack of political will at all levels and poor synchronization among the agencies given responsibility for promoting national efforts to adopt international standards are certainly among the major causes of slow progress. In this context, we now revisit some points made in Chap. 2 regarding the roles of the Bretton Woods Institutions (BWIs) and the way that the IMF and the World Bank Group and other international organizations have evolved relative to national governments, the UN and other international organizations in the modern global framework.

Much has changed since the mid-century inception of the BWIs, in terms both of evolving roles for the IMF and IBRD/IDA and the development of regional development banks and a greatly increased role for bilateral aid agencies and commercial banks in financing development investment. The multiplicity of organizations involved has tended, however, to complicate rather than expedite the task of establishing agreed standards and accelerating government reform and value creation. Differences in and changing organizational mandates, as well as different time horizons for their tasks, account for much of these difficulties.

On establishing accounting practices in line with global standards, the IMF and World Bank Group play key roles both in interpreting and supporting the work of standards setting organizations and incorporating these standards in their own work. The IMF remains the paramount international organization for monitoring global economic activity through its surveillance activities and agreements with its near-global country membership as well as its provision of advice to multilateral international forums such as the G20. Though, at one point in the early 2000's the IMF's role seemed threatened; around 2003 the rules and practices governing global stability appeared to be nearly in place, and the Fund had relatively few major users of its resources—and consequently diminishing sources of income and influence. But the illusion of effective global policy management under the 'Washington consensus' was blown away in 2008. Since the GFC the IMF's importance has been firmly reinstated.

At the same time the IMF has had to pay much more attention to weaknesses in its surveillance and program facilities to meet fiscal and monetary crises in member countries and globally. The largely financial causes of the GFC and the magnitude of risk from the financial sector has led to a great deal of emphasis being placed on use of BSA techniques for macro-financial and fiscal and external debt sustainability analyses. The time horizon is also being widened—though the early-warning nature and need for rapid response by the IMF results in some disconnect between IMF data improvement requirements and the longer-term issues faced by member countries. The central importance of trends in stocks of assets and liabilities and the risks and uncertainties associated with these is now well recognized, but establishing a more comprehensive and longer-term BSA will require both an improvement in the interaction between national governments and international surveillance agencies and a sustained effort to build capacity and encourage national governments to adopt the agreed international standards.[18]

The urgency of producing timely early warning analyses with adjusted country data thus competes with support for longer-term and deeper reforms of country accounting systems and reporting practices. It may also, as discussed further below, reduce willingness of countries to review their PFM weaknesses. The former issue must be addressed to ensure long-term viability of global surveillance; the latter is more a question of establishing political transparency and accountability at all levels of government. For both, links between IMF surveillance and international support to improve standards and practices of data collection at country level need closer investigation and better cooperation; relationships and possible measures are discussed below.

The OECD,[19] as noted, plays a significant role in promoting better PFM standards and practices among the advanced economies. It differs in adopting a peer review approach and multilateral discussion as a means of assessing economic performance, improving PFM practices, and policy coordination among members. It also reviews non-member country practices on request, and in such cases its approach is like that of the IMF. Regional development banks and bilateral agencies are also involved in promoting better PFM standards, mainly for developing countries. Policy on developing country assistance will be considered in more detail in Chap. 5, but is worth mentioning here because the issues of standards are relevant to all countries.

As described in Chap. 3, the Standards and Codes (S&C) initiative established by the IMF and the World Bank following the financial crises of the 1990s, particularly the 1997 Asian crisis was conceived as an appropriate set of steps to encourage all countries to adopt sound fiscal and monetary practices and help prevent recurrence of such crises. Efforts to implement the broad range of practices are continuing. But coordination across practices—in the IMF, for instance, linking these efforts to both Fund surveillance and technical assistance and to development lending by other organizations—proved extremely difficult at that time.

A key assumption of the Fiscal Transparency component of the initiative (FTI) was that the market would respond to perceived improvements in a country's fiscal transparency and accountability by increasing investment and lowering borrowing costs. Empirical evidence supports the assumption that improvement in transparency is correlated with fiscal performance,[20] but this FTI hypothesis seemed attractive only to a limited number of countries (mainly those seeking EU or Eurozone membership); neither was this appeal highlighted by the financial press or taken up by the rating agencies. As mentioned above, there was considerable resistance at Board level, particularly from Asian countries, the Middle East, and many of the less developed sub-Saharan African countries.[21] David Heald (2013), in reviewing the FTI, argued that the term 'transparency' has many dimensions and, on this basis, attempted to clarify the underlying logic of the initiative and linked the FTI strongly to IMF surveillance. He suggests that difficulties of the FTI vis à vis the surveillance process were intrinsic to the FTI concept.

The original intention of the FTI, however, was simpler: it aimed primarily to encourage improvement in PFM practices,[22] not to provide stronger surveillance, and IMF management made it clear that S&Cs, including the Fiscal Transparency Code (FTC), stood outside the surveillance mandate under its articles of agreement. It was also quite explicitly concerned with transparency of flows of comprehensive fiscal data from government administrations to countries' public and press and to the international markets, not with broader meanings of the term 'transparency.' It was anticipated that disclosure of practices and a commitment to improve these, over time, would benefit countries that participated in ROSCs and undertook to reform areas where practices were seen to be deficient in some respects. However, there is little doubt that many member countries associated the initiative with surveillance and oversight of developing countries by the controlling advanced elite; many continue to believe that even technical assistance from the IMF embodies an element of surveillance.

A second major and continuing issue that complicates the FTI implementation was the reaction of other international agencies to the IMF's role in promoting PFM improvement. The Code was initially well received, and indeed, provided a template for initiatives by several other organizations; these initiatives, however, were adapted to suit their differing goals and mandates. Key organizations in this respect, were the World Bank, OECD, and the International Budget Partnership (IBP), a civil society organization based in Washington DC. The World Bank was the principal initiator of the Public Expenditure and Financial Accountability Assessment (PEFA) process[23] aimed particularly at tracking the effectiveness of PFM technical assistance and lending on improving country PFM practices and outcomes.[24]

The OECD approach, as noted, differed significantly from that of the IMF; it adopted a survey technique to build a database covering the budgetary practice of its member countries in a five-year cycle. Although aware of the IMF initiative, and many of the practices covered are very close to those included in the IMF code, its purpose was, however, simply to track progress on the basis mainly of member survey responses. The OECD reviews of individual countries, including non-members that wish to be assessed against OECD standards are quite similar to fiscal ROSC or PEFA assessments.

The IBP is concerned with ensuring that budget documentation provides a basic but broad range of information on budget policy and performance to the broad public, as well as to increase public participation in the budget process. It saw the FTC as a good basis for identifying the flows of information on accountable processes and documentation and information flows to citizens. Its survey questionnaire has been developed from the original FTC with a focus on budget documents regarding timeliness, quality, and accessibility to the public. It conducts its Open Budget Survey every two years and rates budget transparency at a national level as of 2014 in 100 countries.[25] It operates, however, on a limited budget using local reviewers who assess compliance primarily on a review of available budget and accounts documents. There is likely scope to improve the conduct of the survey to take account of the extent to which accruals and <IR> are considered. Given the OBS's broad coverage and succinct presentation, further support for this initiative is warranted.

The variety and variation among competing fiscal/budget transparency initiatives have given rise to several concerns: first, among the countries that participate in transparency-oriented reviews; and, second, to the media and broader public perception of their worth. Multiple demands on country resources to undertake assessments, differing technical requirements, and, in the case of the FTI (perhaps to a lesser extent PEFA), an underlying suspicion of external surveillance, will likely continue to create significant country reluctance to participate. In practice, country managers tend to fight for inflated performance assessment results, which negates somewhat the purpose of external objective surveys. These concerns need to be addressed. Heald's analysis, while idiosyncratic in some respects, reflects valid concerns, particularly the difficult association between the vital bilateral and global surveillance role of the IMF and its promotion of fiscal transparency.

Some of these concerns have been taken up by the Global Initiative on Fiscal Transparency (GIFT),[26] which aims to reconcile and order the variety of global norms and organizational goals that are embedded in the international fiscal transparency initiative. GIFT represents a continuing attempt to coordinate the efforts of the major agencies involved in improving PFM and governance issues. One of the issues that GIFT has focused on is the desirability of coordinating the changes to the instruments used to assess transparency and accountability of PFM administrations in countries. Petrie (2013b) has produced a useful summary of the main instruments for assessing transparency and accountability at that time, looking at the main transparency-linked instruments (but excluding PEFA because it includes PFM diagnostics that go well beyond transparency), looking at the scope, coverage, and nature of assessment. GIFT itself does not carry out assessments, but works with the main agencies to promote development of common norms, with some emphasis on public participation and strengthened legislative oversight.

Both PEFA and the FTC have been significantly updated (see PEFA 2016, and IMF 2014). In many ways, they have been technically improved, but both are technically demanding, overlap in a number of dimensions, and are directed at assessing outputs and practices that continue to invite defensive reactions from country officials and ministers. A key recommendation for both is that the introduction of modern accounting standards should play an increasingly central role in an integrated and, ideally, streamlined approach. Suggested new relationships are

A Framework for Improving Well-Being Measurement and Fiscal... 135

broadly illustrated in Fig. 4.4 below, which is consistent with the process suggested above and in the preceding figures. These suggestions should not involve radical realignment of present organizations: public sector accounting and auditing standards are already addressed in the initiatives of the main international agencies (IMF, World Bank Group, OECD); progress in these areas is accepted by all bilateral donor agencies with respect to assistance to developing countries; and IFAC and IPSASB have close connections with all national and international agencies. GIFT could play a key role in helping to coordinate this strategic focus—indeed its mandate could be extended somewhat to incorporate standards setting coordination, becoming GIFTS (Global Initiative on Financial Transparency and Standards). The emphasis presently given to improving PFM practices in developing and emerging market countries should thus be linked clearly to well-defined strategies and plans to establish accrual accounting, a balance-sheet approach to PFM, and risk management.[27] The need to address risk management is particularly emphasized in the third pillar of the IMF's revised FTC, and implementation of this critical aspect of PFM would be well augmented by a focused improvement in public sector accounting standards, as discussed above.

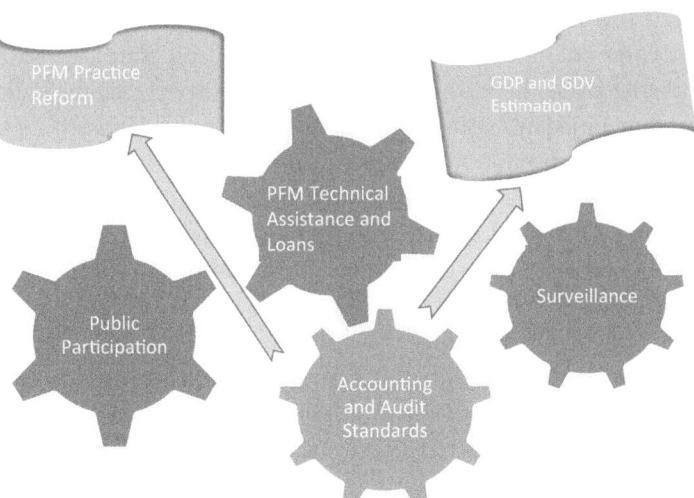

Fig. 4.4 Refocusing standards and practices reform (Source: Author)

Some rationalization of the allocation of resources to different elements of the proposed integrated strategy will be needed. IMF surveillance activities will benefit considerably from an emphasis on improved data standards, but its association with technical assistance and development lending needs to be coordinated carefully with the activities of technical assistance teams. The latter often involve several organizations. A coordinated technical emphasis on establishing robust systems for measuring and validating accounting transactions (and eventually all forms of value creation) seems likely to lead to stronger cooperation than the often dissociated assessments of PFM practice in the past. Ultimately, the benefits should be realized in terms of better fiscal and economic data—and eventually a better measure of social well-being through a UN-led reform of the GDP measure.

A continuing survey of the extent to which international standards for measuring value creation and attendant risks are being adopted and used in social policy would give a leading and objectively measurable indicator of the status of government reform. The World Bank-led Accounting and Auditing component of the S&C Initiative at present focuses on assessment of country practices with respect to application to corporations of IASB accounting standards and IFAC International Standards on Auditing. Given that the basic thrust of the <IR> initiative is to broaden the base for both corporate and government accounting and thus to narrow the differences between them, there appears to be a strong case for building a core program aimed at a continuing survey across public and private sectors of country adoption of accruals, BSA, whole-of-government and <IR> as the central driver of system reform, illustrated in Fig. 4.3.

How then to move forward? Any action must engage with practical experience and the realities of present-country administration. A practical possibility could be to undertake a pilot series of country studies to refine principles of reform for countries at different levels of PFM capacity; each participating country should have clearly articulated goals to improve that capacity. Such studies should involve the main multilateral and bilateral agencies now promoting better PFM practice standards. They should aim to identify ways in which PFM assessment methodologies could be better coordinated and streamlined to minimize overlap and improve integration with country-led PFM reform strategies. No doubt many enhancements can be suggested, but we need to move forward in this direction to capitalize on the reform efforts that are already underway.

Summary of Themes and Conclusions

It is widely agreed that our present measures of national and global well-being, based as they are largely on estimates of commercial production plus costs of government services, are inadequate. This chapter argues that these inadequacies distort government policies away from production of collective goods, other than defence and national security (which themselves provide no guarantee of global security). The need for changes in measurement is also widely acknowledged, but alternatives to the standard GDP as a measure of well-being, such as the HDI, have gained little traction either at national or international levels.

Modern developments in accounting, particularly the application of accrual basis accounting to government as well as private entities, however, are beginning to transform public (and some private) sector entities. A more recent recognition by international standards setting agencies of the role of non-traditional forms, such as natural, human and social capital, in creating or diminishing entity value promises a much broader revolution over the long term. Recognition of value creation from these forms of capital would transform entity decision-making and should ultimately lead to a much more reliable indicator of aggregate well-being at national and global levels.

But significant institutional barriers prevent rapid change in this direction, and these must be tackled to guide national, global economic and social policies towards general as well as commercial improvement in well-being. Key institutional issues identified in the chapter are, first, the need for coordination of activities among different professional cadres and national and international entities, and, second, the need for government to become directly involved in establishing values of the different forms of capital and their outputs. The latter task cannot be performed only at an entity level, and this point will be illustrated more graphically in Chap. 6 with respect to the price of carbon.

A well-designed, internationally coordinated program of accounting and integrated reporting reform implemented initially at entity and national level needs to be initiated and supported over the long term. National governments will play a key role in establishing uniform price and value regimes for all their entities, and these should become internationally consistent and incorporated in further development of the UN SNA framework for national accounts. The continuing programs to improve fiscal transparency and accountability should embody these accrual basis and <IR> standards as a basic element of their programs. Since many participating organizations are involved, there is a strong case for strengthening coordination authority.

Notes

1. Generally derived from sample surveys on a quarterly basis.
2. Evidence for this statement is derived mainly from newspaper reports in Australia (and elsewhere), and the well-established, legally condoned practice of so-called 'pork-barrelling' by Congress in the United States.
3. IPSAS standards are set by the International Public Sector Accounting Standards Board (IPSASB) covering both cash basis and accrual basis accounts for public sector entities; IFRS standards for private enterprise accrual basis accounts are set by the International Accounting Standards Board (IASB). IPSAS accrual basis standards are derived from relevant IFRS standards taking into account requirements specific to or not relevant to public entities.
4. See GFS Manual 2014 Para 2.58: *The general government sector consists of resident institutional units that fulfill the functions of government as their primary activity.*
5. However, <IR> should have considerable application in developing PBB reporting and making more effective use of output and outcome information currently seen as 'non-financial' with accounting reports of spending. An important objective for both advanced and developing countries is to integrate financial and non-financial information to assess the social value of public activities. Some work along these lines could be initiated at any stage of the PFM reform process.

6. One can argue that, as discussed in Chap. 3, the GFC came about because of hubristic belief in the financial market's ability for self-correction, and ignorance on the part of the Federal Reserve and the commercial banking sector of the potential catastrophic risk from the shadow-banking sector.
7. Although packaging in some instances improves the keeping qualities of fruit and meat and so reduces wastage. Establishing the chain of costs and benefits in any detail would be difficult; perhaps analysis of aggregate waste composition could give a reasonable guide as to the cost and source of waste.
8. Gleeson-White cites several examples of 'new kinds of corporations' that assess their impact on society and the environment as setting exemplary standards. They include: The Centre for Tomorrow's Company initiated in 1996, which proposed a 'dynamic relationship between the economy, society, and environment'; Richard Branson and Jochen Zeitz's B Team, "founded in 2012 under the banner 'people, planet, and profit,' to 'catalyse' a better way of doing business for the good of people and the planet"; Corporation 20/20; and several other initiatives that recognize the need to reconcile commercial profit and social impact (see p. 237). In contrast to the IIFC, she gives high priority to promoting corporate uptake of <IR> principles.
9. In this context, the *IIRC Newsletter* of March 2017 records that around 1500 global companies have adopted <IR>, and the IIRC has launched a worldwide call for feedback on its implementation (http://us4.campaign-archive2.com/?u=b36f6aeef75cea67e62812844&id=38c045e559&e=4ac0e9ad50#Review)
10. See for instance OECD (2010)
11. Masood (2016) strongly supports this view, based mainly on the failure of 'dashboard' solutions proposed by many highly distinguished economists (pp. 169–172). He does not, however, refer to the IIRC initiative.
12. See discussion of several <IR> entity studies in CIPFA/World Bank Group (2016, pp. 30–40). The Crown Estate has explored monetization; its *Total Contribution Report 2017* http://www.thecrownestate.co.uk/ applies an economic value to the performance metrics of all forms of capital, but these are not consolidated in its financial statements. Part of the reason for not doing so is the huge amount of data that needs to be collected and run through the Total Contribution model within a short timeframe. A high-level government and professional recognition of the

importance of calculating value creation or diminution from non-traditional sources of capital would be necessary to ensure that these important sources of well-being are appropriately recognized.
13. The history and weaknesses are well described both by Gleeson-White (2014) and Masood (2016). The latter describes in considerable detail the course of development of GDP, the roles of major players Kuznets, Keynes, Mahbub ul Haq, Amartya Sen and many others. His Epilogue, *Unfinished Revolution* (pp. 161–178) points to the formidable task of changing GDP and the ongoing work of introducing environmental indicators to GDP (now in the satellite accounts).
14. Masood (2016) attributes a significant part of its lack of impact to the lowering of US ranking from top spot to 19, as well as the elevation of Cuba (see pp. 95–100).
15. See http://www.oecdbetterlifeindex.org/
16. For instance, in Australia the Australian Bureau of Statistics produces annual Measures of Australia's Progress (MAP) surveying17 "headline dimensions of progress which cover major facets of Australian life". The Herald/Age Lateral Economics (HALE) Index of Australia's Wellbeing adjusts GDP to take into account the changes in value of the nation's stock of physical, environmental and human capital and adjusts for changes in health, inequality and job satisfaction. Its aim is to provide a better measure of national well-being than traditional economic measures; it is reported regularly in the 'progressive' Fairfax press. Neither of these measures, however, have had a discernible impact on government policy discussion or decisions.
17. See http://unstats.un.org/unsd/envaccounting/seearev/Chapters/SEEA_Central Framework_Ch1-6.pdf and Masood (2016, pp. 86–87). Notes on Australian work towards Environmental-Economic accounts are given in http://www.abs.gov.au/ausstats/abs@.nsf/PrimaryMainFeatures/4655.0.55.002?OpenDocument, which includes a quote from the Stiglitz Commission: "[W]e often draw inferences about what are good policies by looking at what policies have promoted economic growth; but if our metrics of performance are flawed, so too may be the inferences that we draw." (p2 of 12)
18. The IMF's efforts in this area have been extensively reviewed by the IEO, the Independent Evaluation Office of the IMF (see IEO 2014 and 2016). The technical range and complexity of these reforms are described in some detail by David Robinson (2014). Emily Poole (2015) gives an overview in line with that of IEO including an emphasis on the need that

IMF advice be seen as even-handed, since the worth of its surveillance lies in its power to change domestic policies in countries being surveyed. IEO (2016) emphasizes the importance of establishing reliable country data and notes the practice of IMF surveillance teams to use staff estimates where member country data is found to be inadequate or inconsistent, as well as the need for better integration of country data within the Fund as it is between area departments and the Statistics Department.

19. The Organisation for Economic Co-operation and Development (OECD) (developed from the Organisation for European Economic Cooperation (OEEC), established in 1948 to run the US-financed Marshall Plan for reconstruction of Europe) was established in September 1961 to help foster a new era of European cooperation. It now has 35 members, drawn mainly from advanced Western economies, but also includes Japan and Korea and some emerging market economies, Chile, Turkey and Mexico, and it provides technical advice on budget and accounting management to a range of developing countries. See http://www.oecd.org/about/history/
20. See Hameed (2005) and Glennerster and Shin (2008).
21. In some cases, where the ROSC was made publicly available, the local press tended to highlight the deficiencies indicated in the report rather than the areas of good performance.
22. The 1998 Fiscal Transparency Code aimed to identify the range of good PFM practices that would establish a flow of information on any government's fiscal position and prospects to inform policy-makers, the international markets, and the general public on the status of the country's financial management. The 2001 Manual on Fiscal Transparency provided more detailed advice on the importance and scope of each element of the code as well as country examples of these practices.
23. Now under the auspices of a PEFA Secretariat, located at the World Bank in Washington, DC. The Secretariat is supervised by a Steering Committee, comprising representatives of the partner agencies (World Bank, IMF, EU and several bilateral donor agencies (see https://pefa.org/content/history).
24. A useful detailed comparison of approaches up to 2007 is given in http://blog-pfm.imf.org/files/note.pdf
25. For the surveys see http://survey.internationalbudget.org/
26. See http://www.fiscaltransparency.net/about/

27. The CIPFA (2016) two-volume publication *Public Financial Management—A Whole System Approach* gives a valuable technical oversight of the relationship the elements and components of PFM processes. This chapter focuses on the need for better coordination among international agencies aiming to improve PFM practices, primarily by emphasizing the critical role that progressive improvement of accounting standards should play for all countries.

References

CIPFA (Chartered Institute of Public Finance and Accounting). 2016. *Public Financial Management – A Whole System Approach*, Volumes 1 and 2 (http://www.cipfa.org/policy-and-guidance/reports/whole-system-approach-volume-1).

CIPFA and World Bank Group. 2016. *Integrated Thinking and Reporting <IR> Focusing on Value Creation in the Public Sector: An Introduction for Leaders.* Washington, DC: World Bank Group.

Gleeson-White, Jane. 2014. *Six Capitals: The Revolution Capitalism Has to Have – Or Can Accountants Save the Planet.* Sydney/Melbourne/Auckland/London: Allen & Unwin.

Glennerster, R., and Y. Shin. 2008. Does Transparency Pay? *IMF Staff Papers* 55 (1): 183–209.

Hameed, Farhan. 2005. Fiscal Transparency and Economic Outcomes, IMF Working Paper, WP/05/225, December 2005.

Heald, David. 2013. Strengthening Fiscal Transparency, Chapter 33. In *The International Handbook of Public Financial Management*, ed. Richard Allen, Richard Hemming, and Barry H. Potter, 711–741. New York: Palgrave Macmillan.

IEO. 2014. *IMF Response to the Financial and Economic Crisis: An IEO Assessment*, Independent Evaluation Office of the IMF, November, 2014. Washington, DC: IEO.

———. 2016. *Behind the Scenes with Data at the IMF: An IEO Evaluation*, Independent Evaluation Office of the IMF, February, 2016. Washington, DC: IEO.

IMF. 2014. New Fiscal Transparency Code (http://www.imf.org/external/np/fad/trans/).

———. 2016. *Analyzing and Managing Fiscal Risks: Best Practices.* Washington, DC: IMF (PDF http://www.imf.org/external/np/pp/eng/2016/050416.pdf).

Masood, Ehsan. 2016. *The Great Invention: The Story of GDP and the Kaing and Unmaking of the Modern World*. New York/London: Pegasus Books.

OECD. 2010. Growth-Oriented Tax Policy Reform Recommendations, Chapter 1. In *Tax Policy Reform and Economic Growth*, (OECD PDF). Paris: OECD.

———. 2016. *Accruals Practices and Reform Experiences: Results of the OECD 2016 Accruals Survey*, Handout for 16th Annual OECD Public Sector Accruals Symposium, 21–22 March.

PEFA. 2016. The PEFA Framework (https://pefa.org/content/pefa-framework).

Petrie, Murray. 2013a. Managing Fiscal Risk, Chapter 28. In *The International Handbook of Public Financial Management*, ed. Richard Allen, Richard Hemming, and Barry H. Potter, 590–618. New York: Palgrave Macmillan.

———. 2013b. *The Current State of Fiscal Transparency: Norms, Assessment, and Country Practices*, PREM Notes, September 2013, No. 4. Washington, DC: World Bank.

Poole, Emily. 2015. The IMF's 'Surveillance': How Has It Changed Since the Global Financial Crisis, Reserve Bank of Australia. *Bulletin*, March Quarter.

Robinson, David J. 2014. *The IMF Response to the Global Crisis: Assessing Risks and Vulnerabilities in IMF Surveillance*. BP/14/09 Independent Evaluation Office of the International Monetary Fund.

Sandel, Michael J. 2012. *What Money Can't Buy: The Moral Limits of Markets*. New York: Farrar Strauss, and Giroux.

5

Tackling Inequality and Social Justice: A Global Imperative

Economic and social inequality has long been an accepted part of life. In the early twentieth century, however, with respect to economic inequality Keynes[1] suggested that "[a]varice and usury and precaution must be our gods for a little longer", but, he suggested, if we can sustain economic growth our grandchildren will enjoy sustained prosperity.[2] He did caution that we must control population, avoid wars and civil dissent, entrust to science those matters that are properly the concern of science, and control the rate of accumulation.

Aggregate economic performance has certainly been interrupted by many of the factors that Keynes warned against, but the promises for the future remain unfulfilled mainly because commitment to the goal of social justice has not been taken up, but rather sidelined, particularly in recent years, by an overriding concern with market-driven economic growth. Achieving the broad sharing of growth that Keynes envisaged, however, has not been part of modern economic theory—and less of political practice. This goal has not been envisaged as flowing naturally from the operations of the market. Its achievement has not been incorporated in economic equilibrium theory; to do so would require that we separately establish clear goals, understand the mechanisms of distribution of income and wealth, and establish ethical and practical ways for social groups, nations and global society to set equity goals and design effective redistributional mechanisms. Some concerns and tentative trends towards a bolder vision are emerging, which we explore these in this chapter.

Economic theory and policy in recent years have generally tended to the view that the focus of government should be to encourage rapid aggregate growth rather than aim to redistribute income or opportunities. 'Trickle-down' proposals (not really theory) considered it unnecessary to redesign redistribution mechanisms, assuming that all would eventually benefit from a larger national income pie rather than competing for shares that would slow the rate of growth of the pie. The Pareto principle, requiring only that no one should be made worse off by investment or program proposals, has justified economists' focus on efficiency and growth objectives and has played a significant role in limiting political commitment to affirmative redistributional and social justice policies. Modern economic and social theory is, however, beginning to tackle these issues in a way that is becoming more consistent both with Keynesian cautionary advice and his broad social vision.

Recent evidence shows that while income inequality decreased substantially in advanced countries up to the 1980s, it has increased sharply over the latter part of the twentieth century through to the present. A variety of reasons, including the Great Depression and the build-up of the welfare state post-WW2, have been advanced to account for the mid-century improvement. Much more attention is now being paid to the current trend towards greater inequality and its possible consequences. Globalization and technological change are seen as key factors that help explain this trend in the advanced economies. Different and more complicated explanations apply to differences between advanced and developing economies. While global inequalities have been reduced through market-based development mainly in China and India, measurement of the gap between GDP per capita in the US and regions of the developing world show that the gulf between the world's poorest and the very rich has increased, in part because within-country disparities in developing economies have increased[3]; prospects for sub-Saharan Africa appear particularly grim.

Currently available data thus suggest strongly that the problems of inequality should become more central to the policies of national and global government—and, as a corollary, that its measurement should be improved. The concept of inequality, however, has many dimensions. Danielle Allen (2016), drawing on some aspects of Michael Walzer's work, has distinguished moral, political, social and economic spheres, and emphasizes the importance of treating them together; this chapter aims to do so, looking particularly at linkages between economic and political disciplines and institutions. We look first at the efforts of distinguished social thinkers to define principles for governments to apply towards achieving practical social justice. Second, based on recent studies of economic inequality, the chapter reviews recent trends in industrialized countries and globally, and proposals for the way forward. The third and major emphasis of the chapter is on the question of divergence between rich and poor countries and the necessity to develop governance and genuine self-government in the latter group as both the critical step to achieve sustainable social justice and a necessary step towards global governance and justice.

The Dimensions and Aims of Social Justice

Eminent social philosophers Amartya Sen, John Rawls and Jürgen Habermas have all tackled the question of how society should think about treating its disadvantaged and move toward a just society in terms of establishing principles of redistribution. Michel Foucault also approached these issues, but in a very different way. As we discuss below, the first three have been concerned primarily with principles of decision-making founded on free individual choice that are consistent with accepted principles of liberal democracy. Foucault, as described in Chap. 1, focused mainly on historical/genealogical analysis of forces that have led to the creation of institutions like prisons, asylums and schools, and with the implications of these for social interaction.

Social ambitions to reduce inequality, as observed earlier, have been secondary to those of sustaining aggregate material production in most liberal democracies. Are market-dominated liberal democracies better placed to tackle these issues than more centralized states? Certainly the balance of liberal opinion favours transparent processes and public participation over autocratic rule, but both over-dominance of commercial markets and resort to populist policies present dangers in democracies that must be taken into account. We will return to these broad institutional questions in Chaps. 7 and 8. All forms of political organization need to start by examining the current ways in which questions of social justice are being addressed and why. The contributions of social philosophers should not continue to be set aside; political and professional decision-makers must commit to question and improve these ideas and translate them into practical programs.

Sen (2009) dedicated his book *The Idea of Justice* to the memory of John Rawls, though he makes it clear at the outset that he doesn't accept Rawls' 'transcendental institutional' approach, which sets basic principles of justice that are to be agreed to unanimously and then implemented through progressive constitutional and legislative stages. Rawls' primary goal of establishing universally agreed principles and institutions faces immense practical obstacles; its implementation seems to be feasible only by achieving some form of global sovereignty. Sen takes a more pragmatic, empirical and incremental approach, one based on modern social choice theory, to which he has been a major contributor. He advocates the development of a comparative, realization-focused understanding of justice[4] as a framework that will guide society both to improve its perceptions of what constitutes justice and to lead to more just outcomes for individuals and groups within society.

Sen's approach embraces Rawlsian principles only as possible candidates for determining just principles, institutions, procedures and outcomes, but all aspects should be continually open to critical debate. All elements of the idea of justice should be able to "survive challenges from *informed* scrutiny coming from diverse quarters" (p. 45, emphasis added), a position which he argues is consistent with those of both Rawls and Habermas. He clearly sees the process of establishing justice in any global (or indeed national) sense as very long term and inescapably tied to the development of sound public deliberative processes.

His approach thus appears somewhat more pragmatic, incremental and attuned to attainable political change than that of Rawls. His major area of disagreement is with the concept of the share of Rawls' primary goods (income and wealth, powers of offices, and citizenship and political rights) as the key measure and instrument for achieving justice. Sen argues at length on the importance of not just recognizing disparity in distribution of primary goods but also in the distribution of *capabilities* to use opportunities afforded by possession of primary goods. Capability ultimately determines the extent to which the less well-off can take advantage of improved opportunities. Sen's view contests the existing order of things more than does Rawls' and seems to offer a way to tackle the issues progressively. But this solution too faces practical obstacles that seem insuperable without a sea change in political institutions. The information requirements for informed public debate of reform centred on even marginal change in capability distribution are enormous. The lack of political willingness or incentive to promote such a debate, however, is by far the more important hurdle. Current political institutions have shown few signs of establishing processes and programs to give prominence to either Rawls' or Sen's views of justice—though some changes are emerging, as we discuss in the following parts of the chapter.

Habermas (1979) tackles these issues from a Kantian, transcendental perspective. His aim is to establish fundamental principles for social communication, discursive validity, legitimation of political orders and, ultimately, social evolution toward a deliberative democracy. He defines much of the territory to be covered in moving toward a deliberative state, but his starting point of ideal individual deliberation of sincerely held and expressed values of ethical and factual truth is not easily connected to the realities of modern states. The ideas of Habermas, like those of Rawls and Sen, must be validated by their application in actual states. All, to varying degrees, have promoted practical application of their ideas, but no major agency of government appears yet to have engaged seriously in their further development and implementation.

This last point is the obverse of Habermas' views on establishing principles of legitimizing modern political orders. The nature of a modern state, he argues, implies acceptance of the obligations of correcting the deficiencies of justice in the capitalist economy, but systematic normative principles for doing so have not been applied. While Habermas proposed criteria for validating socio-political decisions according to factual and ethical principles of discourse, no government has yet adopted a mechanism for applying such formal principles and rendering itself accountable in a way that compares to commercial accountability. As discussed in Chap. 4, radical changes proposed in accounting and use of Integrated Reporting may ultimately provide some foundation for improved forms of accountability and public discourse. But the principles of reducing inequality differ significantly from those of using all forms of capital effectively and accountably.

Adam Smith's invisible hand worked in part because all parties gained tangibly from private commercial transactions. Records were maintained as a matter of course and these became the basis for private and public accounting systems. Commercial valuation is thus already part of the institutional framework; establishing the institutional capacity to address social, moral and ethical decisions is much more difficult. Along with embracing the need for a broader definition of capital suggested earlier, governments need to acknowledge socially committed and evidence-based approaches to reducing inequality. Only governments—not commercial markets—can drive these principles.

Foucault's analysis is in fundamental contrast to the abstract approaches of Habermas, Sen and Rawls and may help governments move in this direction. His concern has been to understand how society is driven by its biopolitical relationships, not to develop principles that 'ought' to be applied to develop a more just society. His method, as described in the opening chapter, through its historical detail and conjectures on the emergence of social relationships conveys an empirical and challengeable appreciation of the evolution of institutions of confinement to treat disability, criminality and mental illness. That thinking applies equally to the assessment of public and political reaction to problems of inequality.

The economic framework in which Rawls, Sen and, to an extent, Habermas, worked also rests on the assumption that the issue can be resolved within our current form of capitalism. The case being made in this chapter is that attainment of social justice will be possible only by modifying market capitalism to incorporate agreed principles of just transactions in social institutions governing private and public corporate entities.

How can such incentives be developed in a mixed capitalist economy? Optimum provision of social justice is a form of collective good different from that of managing the environment or human capital discussed in other chapters. Both are a basis for value creation or diminution if properly recognized as forms of capital for which government and private enterprise share responsibilities (as argued in Chap. 4). Inequality, however, arises not just from an exchange and value creation process but through the distribution of power, as well as use of juridical and military force, resulting from these exchanges. Inadequate knowledge of the distribution of income and capabilities or how to modify market and political processes in favour of reducing inequality is a further major factor impeding development of social justice policies. Growth of knowledge in these areas is unlikely to be supported by commercial enterprise; it must be driven primarily by government and civil society. Support for such policies thus will depend on government-driven research and public communication. While this area of knowledge creation will add to human capital and will benefit all units within society, it constitutes a separate dimension of governance from direct value creation because it changes the nature of the system.

Because of their game-changing and long-term nature, redistributive policies would best be considered in a separate frame from the established routines of economic management and direct value creation.[5] Regular reviews of inequality would likely centre on, say, a five-year review process for each country, including annual measures of national inequality and extensive research on past trends and implications of distributional change on the economy. A global review would be carried out in much the same pattern, building on and guiding national efforts. While the process would occur in a separate cycle it would mesh with and complement the annual, medium-term and long-term economic and social capital review process outlined in Chap. 4.

These proposals are fairly consistent with Danielle Allen's view that 'politics trumps economics' in the sphere of justice for the United States. She proposes developing institutions and laws that "[bolster] political equality throughout the lower and middle layers of the US federalized political system" to improve policy contestation at local and regional levels (p. 28). Such an approach would be formidably difficult and would meet certain political opposition from present incumbents. The challenge of inequality will not be met in other than a very long-term timeframe. If it is to be met at all, however, institutional change of this magnitude and kind will be required and ways to address such long-term obstacles to needed institutional reform must be found. We will return to these issues in Chap. 7.

Some elements of this kind of understanding are emerging. Much research has been undertaken in recent years on the nature of inequality and the long-term significance of a failure to address it. The next two sections of this chapter examine these issues, first with respect to trends in advanced countries, and second with the global existential issue of how the problems of the bottom two income quintiles of the world population are being addressed and how that process must be redirected to achieve global well-being and security.

Inequality and Growth: Advanced Country Experience and Issues

Income and wealth inequality is of course recognized as a matter of concern in the economics discipline, and economists and statisticians have developed a range of ways to measure its extent. Currently, however, there is a range of opinions on the nature of the problem and on the appropriate technical and political responses; measurement of inequality is certainly among the major issues to be tackled, though not yet the most critical aspect.[6] By far the most pressing issue is establishing the importance of inequality vis-à-vis the survival and development of global society. We start by looking at the recent experience of the most advanced economies, emphasizing first the political economy dimensions.

Pierre Rosanvallon (2016) has charted the evolution of the 'age of equality' that arose in the late nineteenth and early and mid-twentieth centuries. Much of the incentive for political promotion of egalitarian policies in those times, he argues, arose from the force of public and political opinion to compensate the working poor for the conditions imposed by industry and the massive personal costs to the military and civilians of the two World Wars. In modern times, he suggests, these forces have diminished. The current attitude of the public, and likely of many politicians, is "the product of a strong moral revulsion at excessive inequality combined with a weak consensus on the theoretical grounds for acting to reduce it" (p. 16). Only the tragedy of war or depression can convince the public and their political representatives to take action on social justice.

The contemporary environment, after the collapse of communism and prolonged experience of peace in the nations involved in WW2, Rosanvallon goes on to argue, has removed much of the moral pressure towards reducing inequality within these nations. On the contrary, concerns have grown about external threats and the costs of maintaining the welfare state. One can add that the emergence of market fundamentalism in the late twentieth and early twenty-first centuries, as described in Chap. 3, would have gained political support because of this changing balance of public sentiments. Somewhat similarly to the social philosophers discussed in the preceding part of this chapter, he sees support for positive social justice policies as emerging from a political acceptance of the need to balance individual *singularity* and rights against *reciprocity* among individuals and groups and *commonality*—the "development of some sense of community for society as a whole" (pp. 21–22).

These views capture the nature of an ideal political debate about social progress; however a Foucauldian view of the way that biopolitical forces interact to determine actual social progress helps a great deal. Much depends on the strength of the economic and social case relative to the political and juridical environment. Fortunately, a stronger economic case on the need for inequality to be established as an integral part of socioeconomic policy is being put in place. These emerging trends need to be acknowledged at a political level and appropriate policies put in place, results that will likely be difficult to achieve in the political environment of 2017.

The facts of income inequality across OECD countries have increasingly been recognized. Martin and Förster (2013) reviewed OECD country trends, noting that the overall gap between rich and poor had reached its highest level in 30 years, but also that there were very substantial variations across countries: in general, the Scandinavian countries and Northern Europe showed much lower income inequality (measured by the Gini coefficient) and relative poverty compared with relatively large gaps in the US, Israel, Mexico, Turkey and Chile. They noted also a substantial difference between inequality as measured pre-tax and after tax. European countries generally, however, were assessed as providing more tax and social service relief to lower income groups than most of the countries identified as having greater income inequality. They argue that growing inequalities are not inevitable: the challenges of globalization and technological change can be tackled by policies that promote appropriate employment, intensive human capital development and effective tax/-transfer mechanisms.

Thomas Piketty (2014) has forcefully put economic equality back at the centre of economic and political debate. His analysis of trends in income distribution in the United States and other Western countries based on tax records tracked developments in these countries from the eighteenth century demonstrated clearly that although income inequality diminished in mid-century, it has grown very rapidly since the 1970s. He attributes this new trend to technology and increasing returns to capital, which reduce opportunities for employment and labour income. So long as the rate of return on capital exceeds the overall rate of growth, inequality must increase.

A number of economists and social scientists disagree with elements of his overall thesis. Tyler Cowen (2014), for instance, in his review of Piketty's book, suggests that he is not completely clear on what he means by the rate of return on capital and suggests Piketty has not taken sufficient account of risk-taking in the stock market. He argues that growing capital wealth in the case of the US allows for a "dynamic circulation of financial elites", suggesting also that the present elites' fortunes will be surpassed by future "innovators and tycoons". These points, however, seem peripheral to Piketty's central case, that accumulation of wealth in a few hands does occur and, as Cowen concedes, reduces opportunities and upward mobility for lower-income groups.

David Harvey,[7] anthropologist and geographer, suggested that because capital is a component in the process of exchange and value creation,[8] the value placed on capital assets reflects its anticipated earnings from a stream of future income—and thus ultimately depends heavily on the rate of growth. Piketty himself makes similar points (pp. 172–176), but stresses that his objective is not to predict or prevent stock or asset bubbles (which may intervene), but to establish an empirical relationship over time between growth, savings, and inequality.

Joseph Stiglitz (2016) has also been critical of Piketty on several grounds. One point he raises, based on his longstanding opposition to privileged rent-seeking, is not dissimilar to Harvey's. He argues that Piketty's definition of capital includes rental assets which, to the extent that value rises only in response to rising prices, do not contribute directly to a more productive economy. As noted in relation to Harvey's points, Piketty separates the bubble effects of speculative house price increase witnessed in the 2008 GFC from secular trends in investment and capital value. Rent for Piketty represents a normal and broadly justifiable return to construction of dwellings. His charts showing changes in the capital/income ratio for Britain, France, Germany and the US indicate that housing assets constitute a large and growing component of wealth/capital over the period that he considers in his coverage of advanced countries.

This defence is not to say, however, that government policies to encourage housing investment and home ownership are not problematic. Indeed, as noted in Chap. 3, the continuing rise in house prices in many advanced economies due to incentives and concessions to homeowners (and as a haven for foreign investors) is increasingly causing intergenerational inequity by rewarding richer property owners and developers and putting home ownership out of reach for younger purchasers, particularly those in the lower income brackets. This point brings us to Stiglitz' more general concern with Piketty's thesis: the difference between the rate of return to capital and economic growth cannot, he argues, be the full explanation of a continually growing gap between wealth and income. It is necessary to identify in more detail the forces that govern the rate of return to capital as well as their potential impact on growth. Stiglitz and his team offer a wide-ranging institutionalist approach to the issue of inequality, based on his own work and that of many other economists.

Institutional economics in many respects raises questions regarding the value of equilibrium theory, including Piketty's work. Piketty's policy suggestion of an international agreement to adopt a global tax on wealth to reduce returns to capital, which arises from his powerful but over-simple model, has been widely criticized as being impractical (and indeed recognized by him as being utopian). More is needed; as Stiglitz states, "rules matter and power matters" (p. 10). A deeper study of policies, politics and institutions is necessary to define and analyze the policy framework in sufficient detail to determine a range of appropriate policies to address the threat of inequality. As we discuss further below and in Chap. 7, institutional theory, while adding important dimensions, has its own limitations.

Before going on to look at Stiglitz' approach to inequality in the American economy, however, mention must be made of Branko Milanovic (2016), who, like Piketty, has undertaken a great deal of research using national household survey data for a wide range of countries. He agrees that inequality has risen dramatically in advanced countries, but his explanation of global inequality is different. Milanovic's proposal is based on a development of Simon Kuznets' 1955 paper (referenced in Stiglitz) on economic growth and inequality, which suggested a natural cycle of development where inequality is low at low levels of development, rises as development progresses, and then falls as economies mature. Milanovic argues that countries experience cycles of rising and falling inequality because of Kuznetsian 'benign' or 'malign' forces (economic growth or war/disease/depression) and modern technological change and globalization (pp. 53–58). Thus he argues that neither Kuznets' equality nor Piketty inequality are inevitable for maturing economies; these will undergo a new cycle as a consequence of the prevailing forces. But this theory provides an insufficient basis to predict inequality or to guide global policies against inequality: it appears to suggest that the capitalist system will simply work its way through to the next stage of renewal. He also presents a favourable picture of reduced global inequality among countries, though these effects are very much a result of the rapid development of the Chinese and, to a lesser extent, Indian economies over the last three decades. The situation for developing

Inequality and Growth: Advanced Country Experience and Issues   157

countries in Africa is vastly different; we take this latter issue up again in the final part of this chapter.

In his book *Rewriting the Rules of the American Economy*, Joseph Stiglitz presents a strong case that the current trend towards inequality in the US and globally has been caused primarily by the choices that recent US administrations have made to allow private corporations to extract maximum rent from the rapidly evolving global economy. He uses an iceberg analogy. The tip of the iceberg is the widely acknowledged fact of growing inequality and the pain suffered by those at lower levels of income and employment opportunities. The global causes, the base of his iceberg, are summarized as globalization and technology, which in 'trickle-down' terms should increasingly create the means for global growth and adequate shares for all. The intermediate component, the rules that structure the economy, however, determines how the base forces affect the outcomes at the tip and for the remainder of the economy.

Recent rules in the US have not been aimed at promoting greater equality, but instead have been governed largely by the belief that corporations should be unhindered by constraints on their operations and profitability. The US has led the way in reducing monitoring of anti-competitive practices and monopoly behaviour and progressively deregulating to 'free' the market. Intellectual property rights, intended to ensure that innovators are properly encouraged, are now used mainly to allow companies to extend profitability through various forms of patent extension. Combined with globalization and tax competition among countries these values have helped tilt the balance of economic power very much against workers in the advanced economies—and by the same token has helped workers and the middle class in emerging markets. Stiglitz argues that the US "could and should have used [its] position as the largest economy in the world to set rules that helped all parties" (p. 37). Perhaps so, but given the political climate and general reluctance in most US administrations to advocate global principles, this failure is scarcely surprising—and appears to be completely ruled out by the 'America first' doctrine of the Trump administration.

Nonetheless, it is vital to recognize that the rules that evolved from the 1970s onwards have not served to meet the challenges of the globalized economy and have undoubtedly contributed to the emergence of inequalities in the US and other advanced economies. The growth of the financial sector in the US and elsewhere is one of the most alarming features of the inequality story and its deregulation and failure of oversight a central cause of the GFC. As Stiglitz argues, the massive salaries and bonuses collected in the finance sector are quite unwarranted and have radically changed the incentives in both the financial and non-financial economy. As an aside, gifted mathematicians are now more likely to be drawn to financial modelling than science (and, as *The Big Short* illustrates, this is to the detriment of both fields of productive thinking).

Regarding the impact on the rest of the economy, and more broadly, austerity rules are being and need to be contested. IMF staff (Ostry and others 2014 and 2016) have highlighted the costs of austerity policies in terms both of increased inequality and the negative impact that increased inequality has on level and sustainability of growth. They carefully suggest that neoliberalism has been oversold, and that some policies have increased inequality and possibly endangered durable expansion.

The case that the present rules are quite inadequate and need to be rewritten to meet the coming challenges of the rest of this century seems strong. Stiglitz advocates a broad and bold two-part strategy: 'taming the top', and 'growing the middle'. Both involve an extensive list of government regulatory and macroeconomic policies. The first part will require government to reduce monopolistic market power and restore competition; the second requires fiscal action to expand investment and improve access to employment opportunities. Both seem necessary, but who is going to rewrite the rules? And what is the timeframe? Changing institutions (or rewriting the rules), as Douglass North (1992) points out is constrained by the present framework (or path-dependent). Neoliberalism is still very strongly represented in US politics—and indeed elsewhere; politicians of that persuasion will be in no hurry to endorse a program to favour those who have been unable to get a decent wage or are unemployed and to increase taxes on the privileged financial sector.

The Stiglitz agenda for the US is one that certainly should be considered in a deliberative and professional process. Some degree of partisanship is unavoidable; as Thomas Kuhn has shown, even in scientific peer review processes it takes time for strongly held paradigms to be replaced.[9] The United States Constitution is designed to promote competition and independence among the branches of the federal government and between levels of government, and these principles and the current political climate make it difficult to envisage such a proposal progressing politically without a high degree of professional agreement and public education.

To go back to our political economy overview of this topic, the first step should be to reach agreement at a high level that now-available data and analysis provide a convincing case that inequality should be a central topic of government socio-economic policy—a topic that should be debated on a regular basis. Given that status, its extent should be measured and reported regularly to each branch and level of government. Public and private investment should be encouraged in a range of activities linked to understanding and combating causes of inequality. 'Investment' to achieve these objectives should include health, education and social welfare spending, currently treated simply as recurrent spending and evaluated at cost. As argued in Chap. 4, <IR> techniques should be applied to assess monetary values of these uses of capital. Government spending on social research, development and application of measurement techniques, and assessment and reporting on effectiveness of government, corporate and civil society programs to address inequality, all represent important social value creation processes.

Ideally in the US, a joint commission or other high-level administrative body could help establish the central importance of tackling inequality within the country and globally, as advocated by Stiglitz. But there seems little chance of the Trump administration promoting such an agenda. The global dimensions of this issue are extremely important, and progress, or lack thereof, in the US will affect progress everywhere. Continuing lack of US will to address this fundamental social issue will have profound long-term effects. Domestically, it will likely fail to meet the aspirations of the dissatisfied groups who supported Trump; even more likely it will slow global commercial growth—and obviously the growth of well-being, the most relevant measure of progress being advocated in this book.

The consequences of continuing increases in inequality will prove to be serious for advanced and emerging market countries. The issues being faced by low income developing countries need even more urgent attention. Apparent reduction in global inequality because of growing opportunities for wage earners in China and India does not foreshadow likely progress for the very disadvantaged countries. Much of sub-Saharan Africa faces the triple disadvantage of low income, high population growth and poor governance. As we discuss in the last part of this chapter, improving the last factor is crucial to tackling the first two; a high-level international commitment to reduce poverty, it is argued is insufficient and can only result in sustained improvement by giving much more emphasis to improving governance in these countries. Failure to do so will see increasing civil unrest, which ultimately seems likely to rebound in increasing costs to handle refugees and civil and global violence.

Developing Countries: Poverty, Demographics and the Central Role of Governance

The factors applying to programs promoting economic development and social justice for less developed countries differ in kind from those relating to inequalities within advanced countries. International development assistance and investment, trade and private sector growth are generally regarded as the key drivers of development for low income countries. As described in Chap. 2, the historical genesis of these developed/developing country inequalities has established a profoundly different legacy. Trickle-down theory, suggesting that laggards will eventually catch up, fails to address the continuing governance barriers faced by those nations left behind in the past two centuries of industrial revolution, imperial expansion, colonization and decolonization.

The prevailing assumptions that most problems are economic and can be handled by economic capacity-building, investment and access to markets need to be and are being challenged; the need for strengthening internal governance of developing countries is recognized, but not yet sufficiently. At the beginning of the new millennium, however, a much greater emphasis was given to planning for the benefits of economic growth to be more widely shared and towards addressing the worst consequences of past failures of development. In 2000, the UN set eight Millennium Development Goals (MDGs), each with targets to be achieved by 2015. Some, including a significant reduction in global poverty, were achieved—though much, as noted earlier, was due to China's rapid economic growth. In October 2015, agreement was reached to continue these UN-anchored efforts by setting seventeen Sustainable Development Goals (SDGs) to be achieved by 2030.[10]

Governance and the SDGs

These efforts appear to denote the beginning of a global commitment to share economic growth more equitably among the world's population groups. But two serious issues regarding the nature of the 'partnerships for development' mechanism have not been sufficiently addressed:

First, the way in which the MDGs and SDGs have been determined by global consultation and are then expected to be entered as a commitment into national plans and budgets gives far too little emphasis to the state of preparedness, the political and administrative cultures of different regions and countries, and the nature of the pressures they face. All of the goals represent normal responsibilities of any national government, but the most vulnerable countries lack many of the basic capacities to fulfil these responsibilities. Any global program to address social failures must consider the basic standards of governance and administrative responsibility that apply at country level and the extent of improvement required to face regional and national challenges; implementation of global goals needs to be interpreted in light of these pressures.

Second, the UN and allied agencies (particularly the Bretton Woods Institutions (BWIs) and multilateral development banks (MDBs), prior to the millennial commitment, had already established efforts over many years to support a variety of sectoral programs in health, education, fiscal and financial management. These recognize specific national and regional pressures, but they do so under severe funding constraints—and compete with one another for financial support from the pool of technical assistance and loan funds available through the international aid financing system (public, private and philanthropic).[11] The MDG/SDG initiative adds another layer of complexity to these arrangements, explicitly to improve coordination and produce tangible, measurable results. The implicit assumption is that a focus on measurable development outcomes will overcome poor governance.

Developing country governments, like all governments, are responsible for achieving SDG objectives such as reducing inequality, better maternal and child healthcare, better education and so forth, as well as overall fiscal management to ensure stable sustainable growth for the benefit of all citizens. When governments fail to perform these tasks effectively, it is not at all clear that setting global targets and assigning responsibilities for their achievement by those apparently non-performing governments is the appropriate answer. Some form of assessment of country PFM and fiscal management and assistance to strengthen it would appear to be vital elements of engagement to ensure that SDG implementation plans are sound. Unless full government control over fiscal policy, priority-setting and implementation is established in low income countries, their prospects for achieving SDGs, or even ensuring basic fiscal progress, are not high. It may seem persuasive that an external agency should interfere, or even directly provide the needed services in the interests of vulnerable citizens, but these remedial steps will be unproductive in the long run unless the quality of government is also improved. Sustainable development outcomes must be achieved *through* government, not *despite* bad government. Improving governance is, of course, recognized among the MDGs/SDGs, but if anything its visibility has decreased in the transition to sustainability.

This chapter puts the case that strengthening government in developing countries is a strategically necessary underpinning for all efforts to reduce inequality and, eventually, eliminate poverty. This view is not far out of line with critical comments made by Jeffrey Sachs (2005), the intellectual leader of the MDG program. His deep concern with the international community's response to its implementation challenges, which he describes as 'incoherent in practice',[12] reflected his view of the importance of deep engagement with individual countries. Implementation of the MDGs was under the broad guidance of the Bretton Woods Institutions (i.e., the World Bank and the IMF), but, he argues, guiding multiple sources of development finance as well as satisfying the existing mandates of the BWIs proved difficult. Sachs describes the relative ineffectuality of coordinating recipient country needs and donor country contributions through 'country-led' Poverty Reduction Strategy Papers (PRSPs).[13] It is as Sachs (2005) argued difficult to see a direct linkage between the PRSPs and achievement of the MDGs. The former were not designed as complete blueprints for implementing the latter. From the IMF's point of view, they were one among many instruments used to guide developing countries toward establishing macro-economic frameworks linked to national strategies and budgets.

Sachs' interpretation that the BWIs, particularly the IMF, place most emphasis on fulfilling their own mandates was and is unsurprising. The IMF has been tasked with surveillance of global macroeconomic stability, and its involvement with MDG implementation necessarily had to take that role into account. At the time, moreover, establishing stable growth was seen as a prerequisite for attaining more equitable distribution. Since then, however, as discussed in Chap. 4, the IMF is deeply rethinking its role in relation to long-term risk and stability assessments, and also reconsidering aspects of the links between inequality and growth (as discussed in Chap. 4 and further below).

Sachs' earlier work advocated that the UN Development Programme (UNDP) would be better placed to take full charge of international efforts to implement the MDGs. The reality then and now is that our present international institutions have bureaucratic mandates rather than political direction and all have considerable pressure to continue with their current mandates. Bilaterals, on the other hand, are torn between their own political constituency and that of the recipient country, not always to the benefit of the latter. Nonetheless, evolutionary change is clearly needed. Stronger coordinating mechanisms, ideally under UN/BWI tutorship, would be desirable. Much closer working arrangements between the IMF and the development-oriented agencies (as Sachs indeed suggested) is an important aim. And, as we argue here, even more important, we need a much clearer articulation of how to strengthen the capacity and role of developing country governments.

For sub-Saharan Africa, Sembene (2015) provided econometric evidence that PRSPs did not significantly impact the incidence of poverty or improve the income share of the bottom quintile; on the contrary, the top quintile was able to increase its income share. These findings suggest that growth-led strategies in the absence of a strong and committed administration will be unlikely to achieve SDGs. Country strategy papers to replace PSRPs must go beyond statements of intent; they should demonstrate explicitly that underlying PFM and country administrative capacity is adequate or is being strengthened to put needed PFM measures in place and sustain them to achieve the relevant SDGs. Work to develop a stronger framework is underway both in the IMF and World Bank, but in both cases appears to be aligned with their existing mandates, and modifications are in early formulation stage.[14] The preceding chapter and this one make the case that strengthening public financial management, particularly through strengthening accounting and risk management practice and transparency, is essential to achieving fiscal and monetary stability and SDGs. This objective should be progressively and strongly embedded in the SDG framework.

The issue of country responsibility within partnership arrangements has thus not yet been well handled—and the transition from 8 to 17 goals (see further discussion below) appears, if anything, to have compounded the difficulty of creating bottom-up action to match top-down aspirations. Questions of some aspects of governance and accountability have certainly not been neglected (see UNDESA (2015); the MDGs and SDGs involve a massive investment in statistical tracking of every element of each goal and of each partner. By far the most important, but neglected, level of accountability, however, lies with the developing countries themselves. Chapter 4 has described development of modern accounting practices and its potential to transform government accountability at all levels of development. Less developed countries are, however, also least prepared to apply these techniques to their own governance. They will need sustained support in this area. Plans to achieve SDGs must affirm country, regional and national standards for accountability and transparency much more than was achieved for the MDGs.

The need to establish accountability for use of development loans and grants in the recipient country by DPs using country systems for disbursement, planning, budgeting, payments accounting, reporting and auditing was emphasized and agreed as part of the aid effectiveness agenda following the 2005 Paris Declaration on Aid Effectiveness. These principles are equally applicable to implementation of the MDGs and SDGs.[15] The practical reality, however, is that principles of dual accountability have not been widely implemented either as an aid management practice or as a principle of partnership in attaining the MDGs and SDGs. Improving the standards and practices of country PFM systems and management practices, including a deeper integration of the relevant SDGs with country planning and budgeting systems, is essential in order to provide a satisfactory platform for PFM and development reform in developing countries; it is the basis for a genuine partnership for development. Its absence makes failure more likely. PRSPs were developed as an instrument to achieve this ideal for the MDGs, but the integration process is still at a superficial level and needs revisiting.

The transition from 8 MDGs to 17 SDGs, however, reveals a continuing top-down mechanism; the results confirm that the fundamental problem of anchoring policy on improving the capacity of participating governments has not been sufficiently appreciated. The new structure adds a layer of complexity to partnerships for implementing the goals. For instance, MDG 8—to 'develop a global partnership for development'—has been transmuted into no less than 6 'partnership' elements of the 17 SDGs. These encompass: 'work and economic growth' (8); 'industry, innovation and infrastructure' (9); 'sustainable cities and communities' (11); 'responsible consumption and production' (12); 'peace, justice, and strong institutions'; and finally, goal 17, which corresponds broadly to the intention of the original MDG 8, and emphasizes the importance of establishing partnerships to strengthen national and global data collection, maintenance, and the way it is used to bring government and corporate data systems and management to address the world's development and sustainability problems. The new range of goals sets out the areas of economic growth and institutional strengthening that must be tackled to enable governments to tackle inequality and poverty. But how is this to be done without a major effort to build stronger PFM systems in developing countries? Sembene's study noted above suggests that inequality-reducing goals must be firmly embedded in growth strategies; too often in Africa (and more generally for resource-rich countries) the result is the enrichment of the powerful and already wealthy.

The SDG process appears to have become more layered and complex at most[16] levels. In addition to goal 17, the goal of eradicating extreme poverty and hunger, MDG 1 has become SDGs' (1) no poverty, (2) zero hunger and (10) reduced inequalities. This seems likely again to set targets that partnerships will be unable to meet—and those that contribute will likely again come from governments that define and tackle their own problems and, as needed, seek help to tackle them. Reducing inequality, however, is a general goal that this book and other analysts very much support. Priority should be given to deepening understanding of the extent of inequality and strengthening the mechanisms to address these issues—of which poverty and hunger are prominent symptoms. We will return to the question of how MDG 7, environmental sustainability, has been treated in Chap. 6.

Much of the problems arise from the way that international intervention has evolved. Development assistance has emerged in the past century or so as a vast set of international, governmental, religious, civil society, philanthropic and commercial enterprises. Aid goals and programs are diverse, often competitive; each agency responds to its interpretation of needs within the terms of its own political or agency constituency. Objectives are correspondingly varied: those of voters and political parties in recipient countries differ from those in donor (development partner)[17] countries; bilateral donors' objectives diverge from those of international agencies, which differ from those of diverse civil society and philanthropic groups. While many high-level conferences have been held and declarations made to eliminate extreme poverty and increase the effectiveness of aid delivery, progress towards this emotionally powerful goal has been much less than should be expected from such a prominent global program.

The accepted model of focusing on technically defined development outcomes and achieving global goals through international expertise and cooperation appears deeply flawed. The present array of divergent multilateral and bilateral organizations is insufficiently coordinated to set strategic targets for individual countries. Neither does the multitude of development agencies have the capacity to give financial support and technical advice in the places and areas most needed to help the recipients to set their own priorities. In practice, austerity has become an increasingly important principle constraining international cooperation. Neoliberalism combined with political and public disenchantment with aid has moved international development guidelines even more firmly towards 'more with less' and 'aid for trade' doctrines. Wasteful aid spending undoubtedly does occur, but correcting these symptoms will require sustained support and effective coordination of efforts to focus on PFM reform as the key instrument for sustainable development performance.

Country Experience: Ghana's Long Road to PFM Reform

Individual country experience provides vital empirical and contextual information to allow assessment of the importance of country management capacity. In 2005, Sachs highlighted the importance of Ghana's experience to illustrate his points. It remains a good representative case of issues encountered in aiding developing countries and the links between improving government performance and achieving the MDG/SDGs. Although Ghana has not developed as rapidly as many had hoped, it continues to be a prime example of the potential of sub-Saharan African countries.[18] It has established, consistent with Sachs' earlier description, a vigorous and fairly contested democracy and has taken a generally progressive approach to PFM reform. But it also illustrates many of the continuing problems of even the progressive sub-Saharan economies.

Since Sachs' overview Ghana undertook a considerable amount of work to build up its PFM capacity using modern information technology (ICT).[19] From 2009, work has been underway to establish a fully operational Government Integrated Financial Management Information System (GIFMIS),[20] which was supported by the World Bank, the UK Department for International Development (DFID), the European Union (EU) and Danish International Development Agency (DANIDA).[21] Creation of GIFMIS was and continues to be seen as crucial to establishing effective control over fiscal policy and control of spending within limits authorized in the annual budget. The GIFMIS project was concluded in 2015 and had completed most of its agreed objectives. However, in terms of achieving its full impact on PFM, much remains to be done; its full integration as a fiscal management tool still requires longer-term strengthening of critical aspects of the bureaucratic and political framework, as well as extension of coverage and strengthening linkages with other fiscal management systems, such as revenue collection, bank reconciliation, and cash and debt management. Such scenarios are very typical of the experience of implementing GIFMISs and, more generally, of successfully establishing credible fiscal control in developing countries.

A central issue for Ghana and other developing countries is that many weaknesses lie outside the formal PFM system processes. Fiscal institutions are weak. Many legal and technical barriers are difficult to address within a project framework because their resolution requires action by other arms of

(continued)

the bureaucracy or political assent. For instance, at the time of initiation of GIFMIS neither the budget nor the accounts in Ghana covered all elements of general government spending: notably many charges and fees are retained by government departments (they are shown in the budget but only partially brought to account in the financial statements); significant extra-budgetary funds are not reported in the budget and accounts; and most donor funds are reported in the budget but not reported in financial accounts statements. These issues were clearly identified and are being addressed as part of the GIFMIS project and its successor Public Financial Management Reform Project (PFMRP). Their practical resolution has, however, proved difficult and time-consuming.

Very importantly, however, some investment priorities continue to be set outside the formal budget process, and fiscal risks arising from state-owned enterprises (SOEs) also continue to be a significant contributor to accumulation of payments arrears and consequent budget overshoot and need for adjustment. Cabinet-established policies on pay and civil service employment also have a continuing impact on budget outcomes—though in recent years, these pressures are being overcome. Because of these real and sustained pressures—many of which arise outside the formal budget approval system—Ghana has been unable for some time to exercise effective control over budget outcomes and had to seek IMF adjustment support from 2014. These adjustments, however, need to be supported by deeper changes in the fiscal decision-making environment. IMF policy suggestions thus are being considered in the context of Ghana's technical and institutional progress, including development of its own PFM reform strategy.

PFM reform cannot be achieved through a single GIFMIS project, a critical point recognized by both the Bank and the Ghanaian authorities during GIFMIS implementation. Establishing a PFM reform strategy, one that aimed at encompassing and coordinating all PFM-related projects in the medium term expenditure framework (MTEF), was therefore established as a condition for mounting the follow-up PFMRP; resources to implement the strategy, however, were and remain tightly constrained. The Ghana GIFMIS was assessed by Hashim and Piatti (2016) with a relatively high rating on technical grounds, but downgraded overall because of poor coverage of bank accounts in its nascent Treasury Single Account (TSA), a continuing significant portion of transactions conducted outside the GIFMIS, and a still inadequate policy environment. Fiscal risk assessment capacity, encompassing risks from the SOEs, is a recognized weakness. The enactment of a stronger Financial Management Act in 2016 should, in combination with an effective strategy, help address the policy environment weaknesses. In 2016, Ghana once again demonstrated its democratic credentials by a peaceful transition to a new government. The incoming government has a major task of building on the significant accomplishments in PFM reform so far.

(continued)

> The events in Ghana over around two decades exemplify both the fragmented way in which discussions on interlocking development issues are held between country officials and DPs in most developing countries and the need for long-term international commitment. They reflect the inherent complexity and time dimensions of discussing, agreeing to, and designing changes to the institutional framework in any country. Professional organizations like the IMF, World Bank or advanced country aid agencies too often overestimate their understanding of drivers of institutional change in specific country settings and underestimate the time and resource requirements to encourage change. Too often also they divide issues into compartments according to technical specialty and donor interests, and severely underestimate the importance of working together to build institutional structure and linkages among DPs and national administrations.

Demographics, Population Policy and Governance

An even stronger argument for strengthening governance and PFM capacity in low income countries is that many of them face enormous challenges in managing their growing populations and handling conflict and displacement within-country. The consequences of failure to respond to these pressures pose existential threats to the countries facing them and to the global community. Population and demographic statistics are widely available but are open to varying interpretations. UN projections of current trends in population growth in developing economies, and particularly in sub-Saharan Africa, indicate pressures that only a strong, well-informed and judicious government can manage. If the responsible governments are not able to modify the current drivers of development, world population and demand pressures will be as represented by the projections in Chart 5.1.[22] Africa's demographic future looks bleak.

From a global point of view, as well as for the nations that currently have a young and rapidly growing population, their situation can offer opportunities that good government can exploit for long-term advantage. A combination of rapid economic growth and declines in child mortality and fertility will produce a 'bulge generation', which means a high proportion of workers and fewer dependents; the demographic dividend.

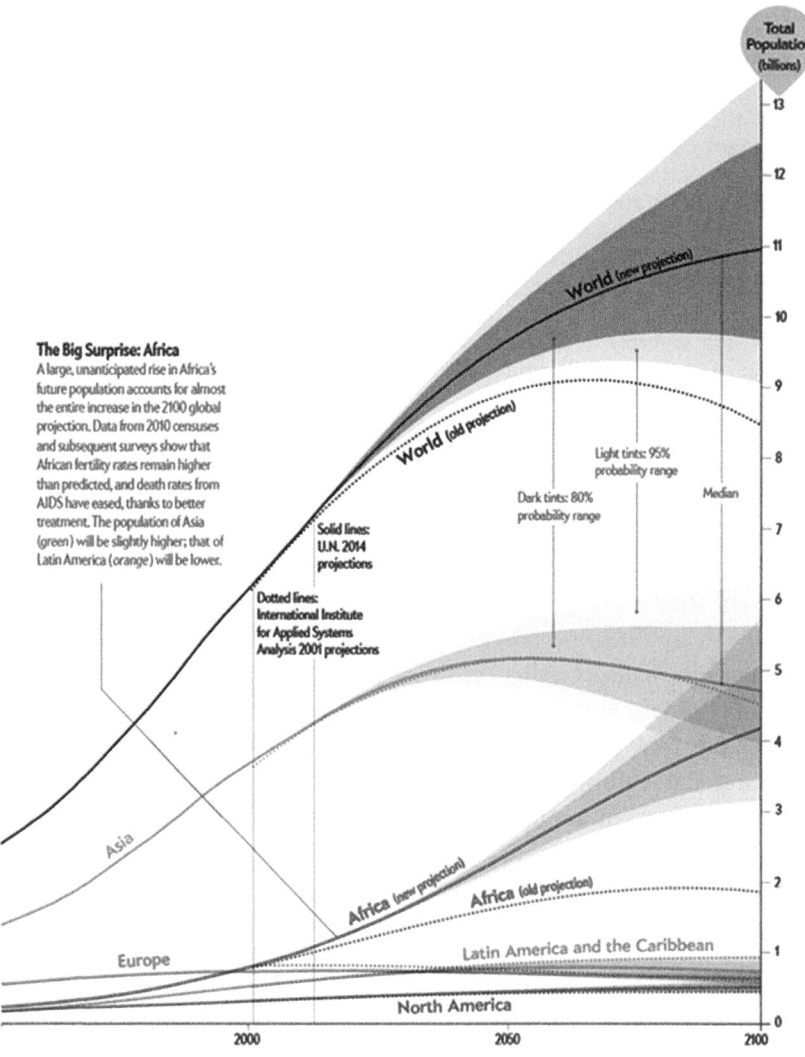

Chart 5.1 Population pressures among the most vulnerable (Reproduced with permission. Copyright 2014, Scientific American, a division of Nature America, Inc. All rights reserved. https://www.scientificamerican.com/article/world-population-will-soar-higher-than-predicted)

The 2015 report for the World Bank by David Canning and others, *Africa's Demographic Transition: Dividend or Disaster*, presents a picture of Africa's current situation and a positive agenda of interventions aimed at achieving such a transition—giving the subcontinent countries "a menu of options available to speed up the transition, improve investment in the resulting youth cohort, expand labor markets, and encourage savings". They point out, however, that achieving such a transition is neither easy nor automatic (p. xvii). The economic risks in present times are high. East Asia's successful demographic transition came at a time when global growth was strong, and the emerging regional economies, particularly China, were able to offer efficient services and a high demand for resources, which, in turn helped stabilize global growth in the pre and post-GFC years. Conditions for Africa are much different because of the stage of development of the region, more uncertain complementarities (more of a source of resources, rather than a target of labour-intensive investment) and the continuing fragility of the global economy.

Africa's potential to reap a demographic dividend thus depends crucially on putting the right policies in place nationally and regionally. Even more importantly, the measures taken by the rest of the world should aim to ensure global growth and stability and to take into appropriate account the current needs of Africa as well as potential global threats from failure. Current population trends are full of uncertainties, and depend among other things on health and education policies in developing countries. The Canning report suggests some cause for optimism in Africa because of declining child mortality rates and fertility rates in several countries. However, as illustrated in Chart 5.1, UN projections of population growth show likely greatly increasing pressure on available resources and potentially massive international spillover consequences.

These population growth patterns, combined with low economic growth, can only add to internal conflict and displacement with continuing repercussions for neighbouring countries and the rest of the world. According to UNHCR (2016), sub-Saharan Africa and the Middle East and North Africa accounted for around 24.1 million or around two-thirds of the world's internally displaced people because of conflict or violence. For the Middle East and North Africa much is due to recent displacements in Iraq, Syria and Yemen. The number in sub-Saharan Africa has remained around the same level (11.9 million) because of the chronic and continuing nature of the problems. Nigeria, the Democratic Republic of the Congo, Sudan and South Sudan account for around 8.5 million of the total for the subcontinent. Country-strategy and governance-based approaches in Ghana, Sierra Leone, Liberia and Senegal are giving some promise of tackling fiscal management and social improvement as central to their economic future, but these approaches need much more publicity and coordinated effort from international organizations. Governance-oriented policies in more progressive countries may help establish a process that can be emulated elsewhere; in every case, however, sustainable improvement in attaining SDGs will be dependent on strengthening governance.

Neither the SDGs nor specific policies aimed at transforming health and education will by themselves change this projected future sufficiently; technocratically defined objectives can only be taken up successfully by an effective government. To be sure, much can be learned from successful policies from other African countries and other regions, many of which are detailed in the Canning report. But the world and its fragile regions face a series of existential threats that need to be evaluated as phenomena—complex interlocking processes—not as a set of discrete technological problems. Effective implementation of the SDGs in vulnerable nations will thus depend critically on helping them tackle the nationally relevant issues as a central element of their planning and fiscal administration processes.

Achieving such a result in turn requires in-depth reconsideration of the way in which international and bilateral agencies involved in promoting SDGs, population research and policies, and country fiscal management and policy interact with one another and individual country partners. The UN and its related agencies have performed a very important service by identifying a linked set of goals that if achieved would transform the opportunities for a very significant part of the global population: as Jeffrey Sachs (2008) observed just before the GFC, a new approach to development practice in line with both a recognition of the most pressing needs of vulnerable populations and the immense potential of modern science, technology and the social disciplines. This book places the need to develop self-governance and national governance promotion as a paramount goal, very much in line with UN and Sachs' ideals of a common wealth for all.

Institutional strengthening to achieve technocratic goals will not happen automatically; it involves an intensely technical investigation of appropriate standards and a socio-political investigation of how these standards could best be promoted and adopted. Some important elements of this set of tasks are discussed in the previous chapter and are continued in this and the next. Inspiration towards improving government and aid effectiveness in achieving improvements in development indicators should continue, globally and by universal human values, but distinct national and regionally appropriate strategies need to be added to the mix.

Regions and nations face distinctively different governance/developmental issues, and strategies or assistance for addressing these must reflect these realities. Sub-Saharan Africa represents many of the least privileged communities of the world; security and sectarian concerns predominate in much of North Africa, the Middle East and South Asia; potential hegemonic conflict and strategy will be central in East Asia/Pacific and Eastern Europe; and Central and South America, North America and Europe all face their own distinctive governance problems. The potential for regional governance issues to spill beyond their boundaries, however, is a huge and growing global concern that places enormous pressure on the weak, undersupported and underfunded UN resolution processes. The US, as the dominant hegemon, should take these issues on board and use the UN more constructively to achieve broader agreement—though, as Chaps. 3 and 7 discuss, such a change in direction will be difficult to achieve in the current political environment. The emergence of 'America first' policies combined with a refusal to recognize the need for objectively challengeable debate represents a retreat into past failed policies of mercantilism and imperial arrogance. A broader thrust towards multilateralism is essential for our global future. More global public resources need to be deployed to develop institutions that will lead to socially rational and objectively defensible solutions. These arguments, however, need to gain political and public credibility, and should do so as we move beyond neoliberalism and the current trend to micro-nationalism and populism.

Their fundamental importance should be taken on board now. To move on this path, I propose three priority areas for governance reform that would provide critical inputs to coordinate SDG implementation and continuing sectoral programs fostered by multilateral, bilateral and civil society agencies.

First, give high priority to governance and aid effectiveness in sub-Saharan Africa—while obviously not neglecting other highly vulnerable areas. Sub-Saharan Africa has progressed least in achieving the MDGs and has achieved modest economic growth, but its major demographic challenges and continuing governance problems threaten progress in achieving a more just distribution of the continent's rich resources, as well as being a global threat. Strengthening governance surely deserves special attention. As discussed, Ghana is one of the better governed countries in the region and has made significant progress in building a solid PFM infrastructure, but it still needs to establish a transparent policy dialogue to ensure that government works effectively for the population as a whole. Government in many other African countries is much worse; a strong region-wide program is needed to strengthen government so that it can address these problems more effectively. A series of intensive case studies focusing on development of PFM strategy and reform is warranted for sub-Saharan Africa to establish a pathway that countries in the region can emulate. In most sub-Saharan countries, work on PFM systems is already underway, and it should be feasible to mount a cross-country review to identify new inputs required to ensure adequate linkage between PFM capacity and implementation of SDGs.

Second, strengthen coordination and continuity between the short- and medium-term macroeconomic guidance provided by the IMF area departments and longer-term institutional reform provided by the IMF, the World Bank and other DPs. Two key measures suggested are: (i) direct involvement of IMF area department staff in institutional strengthening programs; and (ii) longer-term commitment of technical staff from all DPs to ensure continuing and effective dialogue on the country PFM strategy.[23]

Third, harness ICT as an integral part of governance reform for entity, national and global management and control of our social destiny. At a basic level, Government Financial Management Information Systems (GIFMISs), given long-term support, and when executed within a broad PFM reform strategy, will play a central role in controlling rent-seeking by empowered officials, discipline of political decisions within sustainable fiscal space, and, ultimately, management of all forms of commercial, social and environmental capital. Rigorously applied, GIFMISs can serve both government and society in strengthening public financial management administration, particularly where low-level rent-seeking is endemic, but much more importantly in providing real-time information to all decision-makers regarding the extent to which fiscal and financial policy standards are being met.

On this last point, Dorotinsky and Watkins (2013) rightly emphasize the long-term nature of GIFMIS 'projects', the many technical and institutional problems that must be overcome, and the considerable investment that the World Bank alone has made in automating PFM processes (US$ 2.2 billion at the time of their writing). They suggest the starting point is to anchor the IFMIS project in a broader PFM reform strategy—and the need for a strategic framework is illustrated in the Ghanaian experience. A fundamental point, however, and not just for developing countries, is that GIFMIS is no more an option but an essential tool for governance; it must be implemented in both developed and developing worlds simply because accounting and reporting are essential tools of fiscal management for all countries and ICT is necessary both for efficient data processing and control of all stages of the commitment to payment process. ICT is now an integral part of any PFM strategy.

Unavoidably, automation requires long-term commitment. Implementation of a GIFMIS is a learning process, and will take longer the more basic is a country's starting legacy system. But the notion that institutions must first be changed before implementing an automated system is simply wrong. The experience of implementing a GIFMIS over its inevitably long gestation and growth enables fiscal administrators and governments to understand the tangible benefits that can be gained from pursuing these difficult programs to their logical and necessary conclusion. Too often these programs are abandoned because of the difficulties of sustaining support over several decades. GIFMIS commercial technology is steadily improving and offers all countries the option of eventually controlling their own fiscal destiny, even though that path is a long one. For several reasons, adoption of commercial, off-the-shelf (COTS) software is preferable to custom-developed, primarily because large commercial companies can continually update the technology, whereas home-country development is less likely to keep up with technological progress and can build a dependence on local (often connected) suppliers. The downside of COTS is that the market becomes monopolized by a few major suppliers and is difficult to manage internationally, particularly for small low income countries.

No one can claim that GIFMIS is a panacea; its effectiveness depends ultimately on institutional change. But it is an essential tool of governance reform that should be wholeheartedly embraced by the development community. GIFMISs have a central role in helping to achieve accountability and public awareness of governance issues, but of course themselves need to be under transparent government control. At the most practical level, developing country GIFMISs provide the means for establishing both national and development partner accountability for use of all resources. Modern systems have the capacity to record all government transactions, however financed, from receipt of funds and commitment through to payment and bank disbursement and audit. These systems can provide full accountability for receipt and spending of all public moneys to national governments and citizens, to contributing DPs and to the international community. Though their technical and institutional effectiveness must continue to be rigorously monitored, continued investment in their development and implementation, particularly in developing countries, is essential for society to understand and value its own progress and deficiencies.

On a much broader front, the very rapid and competitive emergence of new technologies poses massive new challenges and governance problems that governments are presently ill-equipped to handle. We will return to these issues in Chaps. 7 and 8, which discuss society's profound needs to review long-established institutions and establish effective forums for deliberative discourse.

Summary of Themes and Conclusions

Economic inequality has long been recognized as a problem that should be addressed more effectively by governments, and visions that rapid economic growth would provide enough resources for all to enjoy a leisured and fulfilled life have not come to pass; the benefits of rapid economic growth have not trickled down far enough, and increasing inequality threatens grave risks to many people. Proposals by eminent economic theorists and philosophers on principles that would lead to more equal distribution of resources, opportunities or capabilities have not had a major impact on government policies in recent years.

Inequalities were reduced in many of the advanced countries following the Great Depression and WW2, largely because of growing employment and targeted social welfare programs, but recent research has shown disparities in distribution of income and wealth both in OECD countries and between developing economies and the rest of the world. Some OECD countries, mainly in Europe, have handled the issue of inequality through effective social welfare policies, others have continued to emphasize the need to reduce the role of government and encourage economic growth via monetary policy, deregulation and low company taxes. Globalization and technological change, however, are generally recognized as contributing to continuing growth in inequality. Many analysts see the diminishing opportunities for low-skilled workers as providing a platform for discontent and a factor in the rise of nationalism, fear of immigration and rejection of the established political parties in many countries. The need to tackle inequality is now well appreciated at a professional level, but it requires substantial policy reform and institutional change, much of which seems unlikely to be supported by the new US administration. The chapter argues that government spending on human and environmental capital investment should be part of the mix. Globally, however, much depends on the way the many strengths of the US administration are deployed to tackle these increasingly well-understood problems.

Despite a major effort to revitalize international aid efforts through the UN's MDG and subsequent SDG program, the issue of inequality between the less developed economies and emerging market and advanced economies remains; inequality between rich and poor nations has decreased mainly because of globalization and growth in China and India; lower income but educated groups could increase their manufacturing and technology sectors at the expense of advanced countries. Most of Africa does not have this opportunity, and few of the countries have established strong PFM capacity. The MDG/SDG programs are designed, to a very limited extent, to support stronger governance, but for the most part are designed to provide external inputs to achieve SDG outcomes more directly—essentially bypassing national governance. The chapter argues that this relative neglect of governance support endangers sustainability.

The chapter includes a description of two decades of reform experience in Ghana, one of the more promising of African democracies, illustrating the nature of governance problems that must be faced in even relatively stable and advanced countries in Africa. Global failure to support national governance programs will likely see increasing civil unrest, and this seems likely to give rise to increasing costs to handle refugees and civil and global violence. Demographic pressures in sub-Saharan Africa are, likewise, a responsibility that must be faced by African governments with international support; the so-called demographic dividend should be reaped by the African people rather than through transfer of the most talented to other countries.

Notes

1. Keynes (1930) *Economic Possibilities for Our Grandchildren*.
2. Robert Skidelsky and Edward Skidelsky (2012) have suggested, first that "[t]he awkward question Keynes did not face was how far the rich should go in postponing the arrival of their own "Bliss" to help the poor" (p. 23), which they label 'Keynes' mistake'. They provide a definition of what Keynes might have defined as the common good and suggest a set of policies that could move toward an explicit government commitment to achieve the common good rather than just continuing material growth. However, too many factors in the current democratic institutional framework are likely to work against initiating such a reform program in the near future and the task of gaining political and public support would also need to be explicitly considered, as this book discusses.
3. Data on developing countries is not of high quality, which limits definitive assessment. However, Cristoph Lakner (2016) a colleague of Branko Milanovic, used available data to argue that inequality in developing countries "remains at a higher level than during the 1980s...and is substantially greater in the developing than in the developed world".

See also Jason Hickel citing World Bank data https://www.theguardian.com/global-development-professionals-network/2016/apr/08/global-inequality-may-be-much-worse-than-we-think. Measurement of inequality, particularly in less developed economies, raises a host of problems regarding reliable measurement.
4. Sen links the proposed framework to the concept of *Nyaya* in classical Sanskrit jurisprudence literature, where realization of justice is seen as a matter of judging society in its entirety not just its institutions and rules.
5. These characteristics are similar to those of fundamental science and research—and free-rider effects have likely limited the level of investment in all such potentially game-changing, but highly uncertain, forms of public policy including reducing inequality.
6. Alan Auerbach and Lawrence Kotlikoff (*https://newrepublic.com/article/131517/weve-measuring-inequality-wrong*) argue that for the US inequality should be measured by after-tax spending and taking into account lifetime spending, not at a point in time. Their analysis shows that spending inequality is much smaller than income inequality because of the progressivity of the tax system—and argue against more progressive taxation. There is no doubt that many issues regarding measurement need to be considered, but both globally and in the US data showing growing inequality present a strong case for a major effort to investigate the problems in greater depth, including more analysis of the most appropriate set of measures to address the problems and propose solutions.
7. See http://davidharvey.org/2014/05/afterthoughts-pikettys-capital/
8. See also discussion of various forms of capital in Chap. 4.
9. See discussion of memes and paradigms in Chap. 1.
10. See https://unstats.un.org/sdgs/report/2016/The%20Sustainable%20Development%20Goals%20Report%202016.pdf (PDF)
11. As a practitioner in this area for many years, I consider that PFM reform has experienced a low priority in this competition for funds in large part because it cannot be characterized by so-called SMART indicators of performance in comparison with programs that have easily measurable outcomes such as power generation, roadworks or child mortality-related programs.
12. See pp. 270–274, where he lays much of the blame on the Bretton Woods Institutions—the IMF and World Bank—who were given joint leadership roles in guiding implementation. But he says they "reveal split

personalities, championing the MDGs in public speeches, approving programs that will not achieve them, and privately acknowledging, with business as usual, that they cannot be met!" (p. 271)

13. Initiated by the IMF and the World Bank in 1999 and required governments in low income countries to prepare formal papers describing the macroeconomic, structural and social policies to be undertaken over the medium-term to promote growth and reduce poverty. By January 2014, 126 full and 59 interim PRSPs had been prepared. Mechanisms for ensuring coordination have not been clearly elaborated and PRSPs have since been replaced with country strategies and planning documents.

14. An outline of policy can be gained from the websites of each organization. At a summary policy level neither organization articulates the need for high priority to be placed on improving PFM as a means to ensuring sustainability. In practice, both have encouraged PFM reform for many years and the Bank has lent a significant amount to computerization of accounting systems, which have been supported by PFM technical assistance from both organizations as well as from bilateral sources and the multilateral development banks.

15. As indicated in UNDESA (2015), the evolution of the Aid Effectiveness agenda up to the 4th High Level Forum and key aid management issues are covered in Allan (2013).

16. Other SDGs have changed the notion of development partnership in different ways: MDGs 4, 5 and 6 are put in more general terms, as are MDGs 2 and 3, and likely this move is more in accord with improving coordination with work that is already underway and flexibility of goal setting at the national level.

17. This term is now standard in development assistance documents to emphasise shared responsibility for results between recipient and donor countries. The language is aspirational, but it denotes a significant objective.

18. My comments in this chapter, while based partly on experience with the World Bank in PFM reform associated with its GIFMIS project from 2010 through to the present, is drawn from several sources, including published Bank and IMF reports.

19. Progress in using country systems, the importance of ICT in helping to establish greater use of country systems, the necessity of doing so as part of improving PFM, and practical difficulties of implementing the Paris Declaration on Aid Effectiveness are described in Allan (2013).

20. As emphasized by William Dorotinsky and Joanna Watkins (2013) the term GIFMIS is overused to describe Government Financial Management Information Systems (GFMISs), which very often simply represent automation of budgeting, accounting transactions without covering the full range of PFM functional requirements or integrating planning, budgeting, accounting, reporting and auditing on a single database. The Ghana project has not yet fulfilled all of these aims (as indicated in the text) but is being designed as an integrated system, which will serve as the platform for implementing its PFM reform strategy.
21. This project was built on earlier efforts to develop an integrated PFM Reform Program (PUFMARP) incorporating a computerized Budgeting and Public Expenditure Management System (BPEMS), which was initiated in 1996 and supported by the World Bank, DFID, the EU and CIDA (see review of PUFMARP by Mary Betley and others (2012).
22. See also Robert Engelman (2016).
23. The present way of providing support is largely due to limited resources available either for technical assistance or for IMF surveillance and oversight of fund support programs. Both the IMF and World Bank tend to provide technical support on a regional basis by providing a single advisor to cover several countries and periodic high-level support to advisors through short 'missions from HQ or a regional office. These policies are also sometimes fuelled by concerns that long-term advisors may be 'captured' by the administration and become less effective over time. The present system is far from being effective.

References

Allan, William. 2013. Managing Foreign Aid Through Country Systems, Chapter 25. In *The International Handbook of Public Financial Management*, ed. Richard Allen, Richard Hemming, and Barry H. Potter, 540–554. Basingstoke: Palgrave Macmillan.

Allen, Danielle. 2016. Equality and American Democracy: Why Politics Trumps Economics. *Foreign Affairs* 95 (1): 23–28.

Betley, Mary, Andrew Bird, and Adom Ghartey. 2012. *Evaluation of Public Financial Management Reform in Ghana 2001–2010*, Final Country Case Study Report, Joint Evaluation 2012.

Cowen, Tyler. 2014. Capital Punishment: Why a Global Tax on Wealth Won't End Inequality. *Foreign Affairs* 93 (3): 158–164.

Dorotinsky, William, and Joanna Watkins. 2013. Government Financial Management Systems, Chapter 36. In *The International Handbook of Public Financial Management*, ed. Richard Allen, Richard Hemming, and Barry H. Potter, 797–816. Basingstoke/New York: Palgrave Macmillan.

Engelman, Robert. 2016. Six Billion in Africa. *Scientific American* 314 (2). https://www.scientificamerican.com/article/africa-s-population-will-soar-dangerouslyunless-women-are-more-empowered/

Habermas, Jürgen. 1979. *Communication and the Evolution of Society*. London: Heinemann, (German text 1976).

Hashim, Ali, and Moritz Piatti. 2016. A Diagnostic Framework to Assess the Capacity of a Government's Financial Management Information System as a Budget Management Tool, IEG Working Paper 2016/No.1.

Lakner, Christoph. 2016. *Global Inequality: The Implications of Thomas Piketty's Capital in the 21st Century*, Policy Research Working Paper 7776. Washington, DC: World Bank Group (PDF http://documents.worldbank.org/curated/en/323831470153290439/pdf/WPS7776.pdf).

Martin, John P., and Michael Förster. 2013. Inequality in OECD Countries: The Facts and Policies to Curb It (PDF http://insights.unimelb.edu.au/vol15/pdf/Martin.pdf).

Milanovic, Branko. 2016. *Global Inequality: A New Approach for the Age of Globalization*. Cambridge, MA: Harvard University Press.

North, Douglass C. 1992. *Transaction Costs, Institutions, and Economic Performance*. San Francisco: International Center for Economic Growth Publication/ICS Press.

Ostry, Jonathan D., Andrew Berg, and Charalambos G. Tsangarides. 2014. *Redistribution, Inequality and Growth*, IMF, SDN/14/02X. Washington, DC: International Monetary Fund.

Ostry, D., Prakash Loungani, and David Furceri. 2016. Neoliberalism: Oversold. *Finance and Development* 53 (2): 38–41.

Piketty, Thomas. 2014. *Capital in the Twenty First Century*. Cambridge, MA/London: The Belknap Press of HUP.

Rosanvallon, Pierre. 2016. How to Create a Society of Equals: Overcoming Today's Crisis of Inequality. *Foreign Affairs* 95 (1): 16–22.

Sachs, Jeffrey D. 2005. *The End of Poverty: How We Can Make It Happen in Our Lifetime*. London/New York: Penguin.

———. 2008. *Common Wealth: Economics for a Crowded Planet.* New York: The Penguin Press.

Sembene, Daouda. 2015. *Poverty, Growth, and Inequality in Sub-Saharan Africa: Did the Walk Match the Talk Under the PRSP Approach*, IMF Working Paper WP/15/122. Washington, DC: IMF.

Sen, Amartya. 2009. *The Idea of Justice.* Cambridge, MA: The Belknap Press of HUP.

Skidelsky, Robert, and Edward Skidelsky. 2012. *How Much Is Enough? Money and the Good Life.* Kindle ed. New York: Other Press.

Stiglitz, Joseph E. 2016. *Rewriting the Rules of the American Economy: An Agenda for Growth and Shared Prosperity.* New York/London: W.W. Norton.

UNDESA (Department of Economic and Social Affairs). 2015. *Transitioning from the MDGs to the SDGs: Accountability for the Post-2015 Era*, CDP Background Paper No. 25 (ST/ESA/2015/CDP/25). New York: United Nations.

UNHCR. 2016. Global Report on Internal Displacement, UNHCR, Internal Displacement Monitoring Centre.

6

Managing Environmental Capital: The Case of Climate Change

Climate science has established that emission of GHGs and the greenhouse effect provide the best available explanation for potentially catastrophic rising global temperatures being experienced, but distrust of 'inconvenient' science has become entrenched in market fundamentalist ideology. Facile rejection of climate science and evidence-based reasoning has also been a feature of Trumpist populism memeologies[1]; together, these are playing an unpredictable role in determining the pace and direction of policy-making on climate action, as well as other vital global policies. Indeed, the willingness to reject evidence-based and peer-reviewed science and ignore conventional, or any recognizable, standard of truth in public discourse by too many politicians looms as a much more troubling development than the neoliberals' somewhat more contestable faith in unconstrained markets as the best determinant of social progress.

    The problems now being faced emanate from a stark contest among neoliberal beliefs in market forces, populist political manipulation of public opinion, and deliberative processes of science and government. These developments, while not entirely unexpected given recent turmoil, are very disturbing in terms of a belief in humanity's capacity to understand and control its own development. Doubt and refutation of scientific theory are essential elements of the scientific method; populist dismissal of well-documented science without proposing a coherent alternative theory or examining the body of evidence undermines the very basis on which scientific knowledge and human progress has been based. Neoliberalism has some basis in ideas that are being vigorously contested and are likely to be replaced by better social theory; populism gives no such assurance. The institutions allowing this apparent slide towards erratic, poorly based decision-making must be understood more clearly. Our capacity for measured discourse must be restored. Climate change and environmental decay are vitally significant issues around which the principles of reasonable, evidence-based political decisions must be renewed.

The issue of human induced climate change has, as Nordhaus (2013) describes, been recognized by most scientists in a wide range of disciplines. Tackling this issue enjoys wide public support (though that dimension should be interpreted carefully in a political context, as we discuss both in this chapter and Chap. 7). Tackling it successfully, however, should lead to a much wider public and political recognition of the virtues and necessity of international and coordinated national action to meet the challenge of climate change, as well as a model for tackling other issues that require collective rather than commercial responses.

Guided by the United Nations Framework Convention on Climate Change (UNFCCC), established in 1992, a massive effort has been made to develop a policy framework aiming to avoid the potentially catastrophic consequences of continuing present levels of greenhouse gas emissions. These efforts over more than two decades have led to the setting of global targets for GHGs, and they illustrate both the complexities and possibilities of political action to address global collective issues; they also demonstrate the worth, indeed the necessity, of the United Nations. Only through the UN would it have been possible to coordinate the work of so many scientific and environmental national and civil society groups in a globally organized effort to meet this existential worldwide threat. No doubt efficiency and effectiveness of the UN can be improved, but tackling these extremely challenging administrative and governance tasks is more likely to occur and to succeed once the UN's importance is more widely acknowledged and supported by the community of nations.

We first review the broad nature of the problems posed by climate change and the impressive steps that have been taken so far to move towards a global solution. Second, we examine political and administrative experiences in establishing climate change policies and practices at a national level to illustrate the kinds of commitments needed and issues that may be faced in ensuring that global agreements can be honoured. Australian experience over the past decade or so is taken as an example. The political and administrative difficulties faced here, if nothing else, demonstrate, perhaps extremely, the problems that can arise even in generally well-governed countries when ideology dominates balanced and evidence-based debate. Mitigating and adapting to climate change are issues of fundamental importance for global and national governance. Success on climate management on a global scale could establish a pattern for a successful approach to investigation, measurement and discourse on a broad range of threats to humanity's stability and security; but failure, even in a few countries of influence, could have long-term negative effects well beyond national borders.

The UN and Global Governance of Climate Change

Global efforts on mitigation of climate change have been guided since the early 1990s by a long process of international conferences under the UNFCCC aimed at setting a binding cap on global emissions and establishing a commitment for individual nations to establish effective control regimes to meet that global target.[2] At the Conference of the Parties (COP) to the UN Framework Convention on Climate Change in Paris on December 2015 (COP 21), 195 of the 196 parties agreed to limit global warming to 2 degrees Celsius on the basis of the intended nationally determined contributions (INDCs) to emissions reduction submitted by more than 185 of the parties.[3] This agreement is now regarded as having significantly increased momentum towards limiting emissions. But it is already acknowledged that even if all INDCs are fulfilled, the global target of limiting global warming to 2 °C will not be achieved. Experience and some ominous signs from key participants suggest that many of the INDCs will not be fulfilled, but on the other hand over-performance by others, particularly China, may help the achievement of the global goal. Serious repercussions from global warming now seem unavoidable, but each nation must continue to recognize their responsibilities for supporting continuing surveillance and, as part of this global contract, to seek the most efficient ways to control emissions and help those most vulnerable to climate impact to adapt.

On this last point: the periodic reviews of country progress towards fulfilling the INDCs will play a critical role. Parties will next take stock of their collective efforts in relation to progress towards the goal set in the Paris Agreement in 2018, and a global stocktake will be undertaken every five years to assess the collective progress towards achieving the purpose of the Agreement and to inform further individual actions by Parties.[4]

Given the experience of international cooperation and conflict over past centuries it should not be too surprising that self-interest of nations, corporations and individuals prevails over common public interest. Well-established economic theory argues that self-interest simply doesn't work in resolving problems of collective choice. Mancur Olson's *The Logic of Collective Action,* published in 1965, provided the basis for the now generally accepted economic explanation of failure to invest in collective goods through individual contributions towards their acquisition. Ronald Coase (1960) famously argued otherwise, suggesting that producers and affected citizens would negotiate an optimal solution if transaction costs were sufficiently low. In Olson (2000), his last book, Chap. 3 provides a convincing case that private action cannot in most circumstances replace properly conducted political contracts. Put simply, individuals have little incentive to contribute unless their personal benefit exceeds their contribution. They then become 'free-riders' willing to enjoy the benefits if a group decision to support a collective good is made, but they are not prepared to volunteer a contribution. Private negotiations in major areas of disagreement, such as climate change, has demonstrably failed to work.

Todd Sandler (2004) has very succinctly consolidated and extended Olson's work and linked it to a more comprehensive game theory framework that covers both contributions to collective good investment and withdrawals from a common resource pool (the 'tragedy of the commons'), and more generally any generation of external costs or benefits from private activity. Briefly, any transaction involving external costs or benefits that cannot be captured in formal commercial exchange requires some form of negotiation among groups to agree on fair shares of payment. This requirement applies particularly to pure public goods that consumers cannot be excluded from sharing once it is produced (non-excludable), and those that can be consumed by anyone without reducing consumption by others (non-rival). National defence is commonly given as an example of a good that exhibits both properties (though, as I pointed out in Chap. 2, that example is less convincing in a global context). Two problems emerge from this economic approach to collective action. The first that Olson's solution to such problems was to propose financial incentives/disincentives to overcome free-rider reluctance. But, comparably to Olson's rebuttal of Coase, this approach also understates the difficult institutional and political questions of how a Pigouvian approach to collective choice can, in practice, be established. In very many cases the political opposition is simply too strong to allow a price-based solution.

Climate change policy is a clear example of these difficulties. It is a particularly complex area of collective choice involving many powerful defenders of the profitable status quo and many others simply concerned with their cost of living and unprepared to support any political action that endangers their financial future. Sandler's game theoretical analysis, while broadly supportive of the Olsonian logic, suggests that there are simply too many players in the game of climate change response to be confident of the outcome. He contrasts the climate change problem with that of restoring stratospheric ozone layer protection, which was being depleted by chlorofluorocarbons (CFCs) and similar product emissions.[5] The effects of the latter and its dangers to human health were suggested in 1992, and the linkage between CFCs and ozone layer depletion were solidly demonstrated in the mid to late 1980s. Following substantive scientific verification, decisive global action was achieved through a series of UN organized treaties and protocols. Following the Montreal Protocol in 1987–89, there was international agreement on progressive reductions in production in halocarbons, and these were implemented successfully.

Success in this case was due to practical, political and scientific factors that do not apply to climate change: (i) the number of polluters was relatively concentrated: "[a]t the time of ratification of the Montreal Protocol, just 12 countries caused over 78% of the emissions" (p. 217); (ii) all countries would suffer from ozone layer depletion; and (iii) the relative ease in developing substitutes meant that producers could quickly succeed in establishing alternative profitable products. We will consider again, however, a more general question of mathematical game theory and equilibrium theory versus real-world biopolitical games in Chap. 7.

While GHG emission reduction meets the Olsonian criteria of non-rivalry and non-excludability for pure public goods, the political task of reaching global agreement on action to reduce emissions, as Sandler argued in 2004, has proved vastly more difficult. The process has been so challenging because fossil fuel and energy production are much more widely distributed, change of technology is much more difficult, and profits from fossil fuel extraction have been very high—and remain substantial for low-cost producers. The economic case for increasing the price of carbon-based fuels is very strong, given that the costs of not controlling emissions are potentially catastrophic, though much of these costs will be passed on to future generations. Continuation of a current market price basis for fossil fuel production is thus not only inefficient in terms of our use of natural resources and environmental capital, it is inequitable both as between generations and between industrialized rich countries and developing and emerging-market economies. For most of the twentieth century economic growth in the industrialized world was driven by cheap coal and oil, but producers and nations that have enjoyed these benefits are not easily going to support a dramatic change in their market environment.

These factors notwithstanding, perseverance has worked. From the first World Climate Conference in 1979, establishing the scientists' Intergovernmental Panel on Climate Change (IPCC) in 1988, setting up the UNFCCC Secretariat in 1996, adoption of the Kyoto Protocol in 1997, the non-binding pledges agreed to at the Copenhagen Accord (COP 15) in 2009, through to the adoption of the Paris Agreement in December 2015 to cap GHG emissions in line with country INDCs—all have together established a sound, well-researched and publicly supported global commitment to take action on climate change. This game is by no means over, but a record of soundly based and scientifically supported goals plus political commitments from virtually all parties to the UNFCCC is in place and is well supported by the public of most countries. The risks of not fulfilling the promise of the Paris Agreement arise mainly from fossil-fuel or linked-industry opposition and political compliance with that opposition.[6]

What humans cause, one can reasonably argue, they can also mitigate or protect against through technological advances that will change the outcome. Possible limitations on human population and production have been recognized at least since the time of Malthus, and up until now technological improvement has come to the rescue and growth has continued with little hindrance. When present technology is the major part of the problem, however, it needs either to be replaced with clean alternatives, such as non-GHG producing renewable sources (wind, hydropower or sunshine), geothermal or safe nuclear power. Alternatively, technology could be applied to reducing the level of GHGs in the atmosphere—the so-called geo-engineering solution. In principle, therefore, once the problem is clearly identified and acknowledged, the likely most cost-effective solution should be calculated and enough invested in science and technology to get the best answer. These steps are by no means simple, but they are necessary. Assuming that the market and private profit motives will seek the right answer and invest in the right technology without strong government help and international coordination is not realistic, given the well-established estimates of climate change threats.

Capping global and national emissions requires clear mechanisms to ensure control by all national signatories. Most professionals agree that setting a clear price on carbon emissions is the most efficient way to achieve that objective. Accordingly, many countries are beginning to put systems in place for setting prices on carbon emissions. The International Carbon Action Partnership (ICAP) estimated in 2016 that more than half of INDCs include some form of carbon pricing. The EU has made the largest contribution towards establishing a carbon price by establishing an emission trading system (ETS) in 2005, though its early experience has been less than satisfactory because of its issuance of an excessive volume of emissions allowances. Nonetheless, the EU has provided a guide for future developments and many lessons on how a more extended trading system must operate. ICAP (2016) indicates that international coverage of ETS increased very little from 2005 (2150 $MtCO_2$) to 2011 (2300 $MtCO_2$), but has since accelerated to 4590 Mt CO2 by 2015. They forecast a substantial expansion by 2017. The ECOFYS (World Bank) 2016 Carbon Pricing Watch shows that a few countries (mainly, Northern Europe and Scandinavia) use quite high rates of carbon tax to control emissions, while most of the others use forms of ETS or cap and trade mechanisms, but at rates of US$25 per tonne of carbon or less (noting that prices are not necessarily comparable among countries).

The principles of controlling GHG emissions are well established, but putting these principles into practice at the national level has proved politically difficult in many countries. In the US, the Obama administration was a strong proponent of action on climate change, but congressional dominance in his second term, particularly, forced him to rely heavily on his presidential executive powers. As Tim Flannery (2015) records, the deal brokered between Presidents Obama and Xi at the APEC meeting of November 2015 did much to ensure the eventual success of the Paris Agreement. The agreement that was reached is not legally binding, but from the point of view of consolidating international agreement on climate change it has given rise to the 'atmosphere of hope' supported by Flannery and many others. Its current reliance on US presidential executive action, which President Trump continues to threaten to reverse,[7] may pose future problems; early actions with respect to the US Environmental Protection Agency have been extremely negative, and conservative proposals for a form of revenue-neutral carbon pricing seems unlikely to garner much Republican support. Globally, we need to face these possibilities by continuing to strengthen international cooperation.

Advances in renewables-related technology in recent years have, however, somewhat changed the nature of the problem by greatly reducing the costs and efficiency of photovoltaic cells and battery storage, thus making solar generation more directly competitive with fossil fuels and helping to overcome the problem of grid stability for all renewables. This development does not change the need to apply a price signal to fossil fuel generation to reflect its (now largely accepted) long-term impact on the environment. But, as pointed out in *The Economist* (February 25, 2017) and in several other forums, it presents major problems for existing fossil fuel power companies, particularly coal-fired plants, and requires substantial rethinking of grid design, power pricing and likely some assistance to phase out the dirtiest forms of power generation. These issues would best be addressed in the first instance by professionals in the relevant fields, but government support for a coordinated energy and emissions-reduction plan seems weak in some key countries—Australia and the US are two examples. Public opinion while generally in favour of climate change action has not been a driver of political responses.

Does Public Opinion Matter?

Politics in some powerful and influential countries thus threatens to slow down climate change action to potentially ineffectual levels. Public opinion, on the other hand, has in most countries appeared consistently to support government action to mitigate climate change by reducing GHG emissions. Chart 6.1, from PEW Research Center, shows that over 75 percent of the population in the sampled countries favour government action to control emissions—importantly, as part of an international agreement. Opinion was less strong on how important the issue of climate was as a global issue, but around half indicated that it was regarded seriously. Public opinion polls, however, are very difficult to interpret in the context of politically contentious policy in a deeply divided political environment, and indeed in controlled or autocratic polities. A key issue in democracies, where elected representatives are expected to take due account of the opinion of their publics, is that elections are based on multiple policies and many dimensions of political performance. The complexity of choice and process issues, while of critical importance, played a limited role in the 2016 US Presidential and Congressional elections.[8] In a similar vein, the unusual experience of Australian politics over the past decade has avoided clear presentation of policy issues in favour of dog whistle political manoeuvres; obviously, a US reversal will have a much more significant effect on international policy. In neither

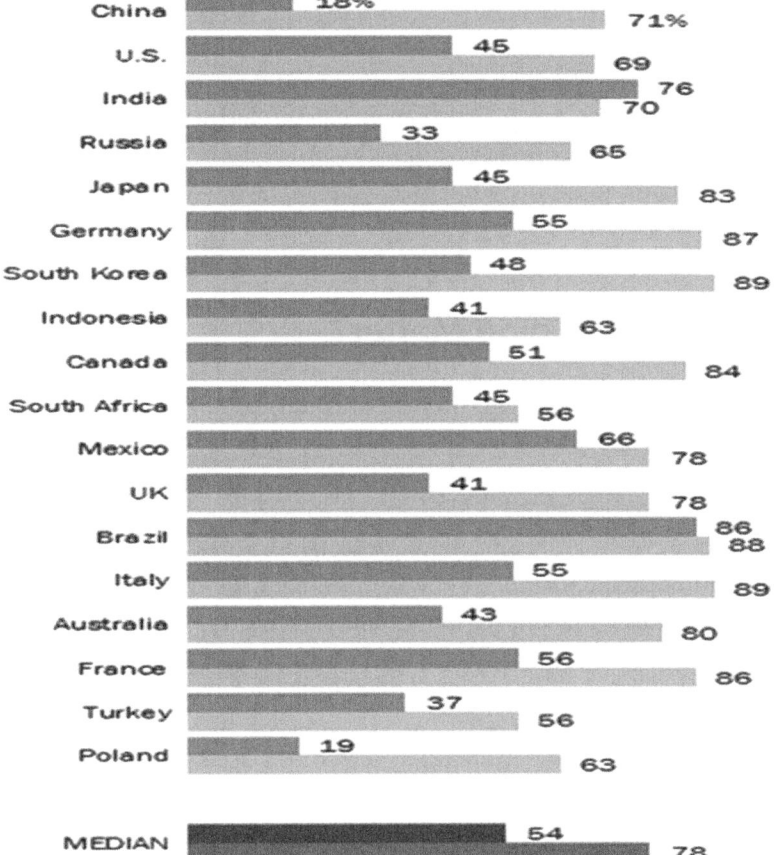

Chart 6.1 Public support for climate action

case, however, was climate change a determining factor in the election results, but in both, the electoral victors claimed a mandate to reverse national climate change policies. The eventual outcome for implementation of global and national climate policies, will nonetheless have a significant long-term effect on the well-being of their own publics and globally, particularly the most vulnerable. We will return again to the question of public opinion in Chap. 7 in relation to behavioural theory, public opinion dynamics and the institutions that govern political and social outcomes.

We also need to look back to Chap. 4 and the question of measuring value creation from non-traditional forms of capital as well as the strong case for making both government and enterprise accountable for the outcomes arising from their operations. A broader global program of reform to accounting practices to require external costs and benefits of enterprise and government entity productive activity, as being promoted by the IIRC, would transform the relationship between government and the market sector regarding environmental management. Climate change effects of burning fossil fuels represents an extreme example of this phenomenon, but because of its extreme consequences it provides an opportunity for a thinking society to seek effective ways for adjusting its mechanisms of accountability and socio-political behaviour wherever private action diminishes natural capital.

For decades, powerful enterprises profited from fossil fuel extraction and use; persuading both industrial and individual consumers of the need to break the dependence on fossil fuels is an extreme challenge, one that political institutions at the national level have not yet managed to meet successfully. Modestly successful piecemeal negotiation is not sufficient to reaching the ultimate goal. The critical long-term challenges for a modern thinking society are to ensure, first, that social outcomes are comprehensively measured, second, that entities responsible for these outcomes are accountable for performance for all uses of capital, and, third, to establish institutions that maintain standards of measurement and accountability for performance. Global level agreements cannot create the needed national institutions (though, as noted above and earlier, they can help set standards); these must be put in place by individual nations consistently with the goals of national climate action commitment. The

Australian climate action experience outlined below, while extreme in some respects, illustrates many of the critical issues that must be faced by all national governments. It is important that international efforts recognize these nation-level difficulties; in the end governments' efforts play a determining role in achieving lasting international cooperation.

> **Economics, Politics and Climate Change Action in Australia**
>
> A powerful political case and economic plan was developed in Australia for introduction of emissions trading to redirect the economy towards clean energy sources. The plan was initiated by the Labor government following the election of Labor under Kevin Rudd as Prime Minister in 2007. Australia had emerged from the GFC in the early years of the Rudd/Gillard administration relatively unscathed due both to its relatively limited banking exposure and a successful moderately expansionary fiscal policy.[9] The political case was initially presented forcefully by Rudd, who appeared to be deeply committed to supporting the UNFCCC program of global climate change action in the years leading up to COP 15 and the proposed Copenhagen Accord set for December 2009. Robert Manne, in the November 2008 *Monthly*, gave a broadly favourable overview of Rudd and his agenda. However, he expressed deep disappointment at Rudd's proposals on climate change action. Calling the previous Howard government's performance on global warming "a complete disgrace", he was, I think for the time, overcritical of the Rudd proposals for action leading up to COP 15. Much worse was to come, but subsequent developments were much more the consequence of disastrous political missteps than an overly cautious proposal on the part of Rudd and his advisors.
>
> Rudd, as portrayed by Manne and others, saw himself as an internationalist and significant player on the world stage who would lead Australia beyond its attachment to the US alliance to a significant role in the Asia-Pacific region. He staked a great deal on the success of the Copenhagen negotiations and prior to the Copenhagen meeting had made speeches that included the phrase, "Climate change is the greatest moral, economic and social challenge of our times." In his speech to the UN just prior to COP 15 he expressed similar strong commitments to the global process.[10] The Copenhagen Accord has generally been interpreted as a failure because it did not succeed in getting a binding commitment from the developing world. Certainly, many were disappointed and there was a loss of momentum, but the UNFCCC process continued and much credibility was eventually restored in Paris five years later. The Copenhagen outcome, however, was perceived by Rudd as a major setback, and from that point his commitment and that of the
>
> (continued)

government to climate action failed very badly to live up to his earlier rhetoric. Strong work to build a climate action program continued under the government at public service and advisory level, as we discuss further below, but these efforts were eventually badly undermined by the political developments that followed.[11]

Just prior to Copenhagen, Rudd had reached a deal in November with then-opposition leader Malcolm Turnbull on amendments to Labor's Carbon Pollution Reduction Scheme (CPRS); see further discussion below. However, largely on this issue, Tony Abbott replaced Turnbull as leader on 1 December and began orchestrating a massive attack on Labor's climate action policy, aimed particularly at the CPRS and any action that would increase energy prices or endanger jobs and investment in the energy sector. These moves combined with the Copenhagen outcome melted the resolve of the Rudd government and greatly weakened its internal cohesion and its commitment to a strong climate action program. While Rudd had the option to call an election because of his climate change policy being rejected by the Senate—and strong climate action still retained public support—he chose to delay the emissions trading scheme until 2013. A loss of confidence in Rudd's leadership led to his replacement as Prime Minister by his deputy, Julia Gillard, in June 2010. The failure to contest the election earlier because of a clear difference of policies on the importance of an economically sound approach to climate change action was perhaps the clearest indication that retaining power was more important than taking the 'moral challenge' to the people. In the event, both were lost.

In 2011, major efforts were made to consolidate the machinery of government action on climate change. Garnaut (2011) proposed arrangements similar to those applied in the UK to achieve multiparty agreement. The government agreed to establish three independent bodies to implement and administer Australia's carbon price arrangements: an independent scheme regulator, an independent committee to advise on targets, and an independent agency to advise on trade-exposed industries. These were legislated and worked well for the following two years, but cross-party harmony on this vital topic was not to be achieved.

The internal conflicts of the Labor Party, and Gillard's proposal to introduce a carbon tax as an interim measure towards an ETS after earlier promising that there would be 'no carbon tax', led to the return of Rudd to lead the government just prior to the election—and subsequently to the election of the Abbott-led Coalition government in September 2013. The new government claimed a mandate for its 'direct action' policies on climate change and vigorously pursued plans to eliminate all policies linked to carbon-pricing as a means of changing behaviour away from fossil fuel towards use of renewable energy. However, the real political shift was much more due to public reaction against the power struggle within the Labor Party and

(continued)

dissatisfaction with its overall management capacity. Public views on climate action, while shaken, were not altered significantly and should not have provided a basis for avoiding considered and objective bipartisan discussion of efficient and effective policy alternatives.

Politics thus effectively negated much of the technical and administrative foundations for climate action in Australia. At a technical level, Ross Garnaut's 2008 *Climate Change Review* for the Australian federal government had recommended adoption of an ETS in carefully designed transitional stages: the CPRS. It described the problem of persuading the public and politicians to take the necessary steps to mitigate the effects of GHGs as "a diabolical problem" but "with a saving grace".[12] On the first point, considerable stock was taken of the complexity of climate change as a collective action problem and the costs of transition to fossil fuel producers, workers and consumers affected by changes in prices that would affect profits, cost of living and potentially jobs. Accordingly, the recommendations emphasized a relatively modest initial pace, allowance for time to adjust and income compensation for additional costs to lower income earners. The saving grace that the report relied upon was the fact that the Australian public appeared very supportive of the need to bear extra costs in the cause of the common good. On this matter, however, public support for climate action counted for little, in part because the public were never really drawn into the debate on the most efficient and effective ways to achieve climate action goals. Public opinion in any case cannot and should not operate at this level of choice; in earlier years, these matters would have been examined in detail by a strong civil service with sufficient authority and independence to talk truth to power.

Garnaut's 2011 review aimed towards this end. From December 2013, however, politics became increasingly divisive and dominated by the neoliberal and conservative forces in the Liberal/National Party Coalition. The political environment eliminated any possibility of objective review of benefits and costs and bipartisan discussion, even though Malcolm Turnbull, who lost the leadership by a single vote, had previously agreed in principle with a market-based emissions trading scheme.

In the international arena, as described above, most economists had agreed that the costs of environmentally destructive behaviour through GHG emissions would be most efficiently countered by introducing some form of carbon pricing. Globally, nations had agreed to a cap on emissions, and INDCs defined the nationally approved contribution of each party to the COP 21 agreement. The current Australian government's policy, however, is to the effect that it agrees to the cap and argues that it will achieve that target, but does not accept that a clear mechanism for costing climate impacts represents the most cost-effective solution. In a deliberative democracy, government policies would be examined by independent experts, the

(continued)

conclusions of the experts would be debated within government and be open to public examination, and policies revised and implemented accordingly. The Australian government since 2013 has, so far, not met these standards and has greatly reduced opportunities for its public service to provide independent analytical advice. These aggressive techniques are becoming more common in neoliberal-leaning democracies. They raise very serious institutional problems, including a virtual ruling out of multi-partisan agreement; their trajectory and consequences are relevant well beyond Australia.

Australian experience thus underscores the critical role that politics plays in determining the extent to which independent professional opinion is sought or used. It is also instructive on the inherent difficulty of coordinating different levels of government and establishing clear criteria for assessing government climate change-related spending proposals. While mining and energy-producing enterprises should be obliged to acknowledge their responsibility for managing our natural and environmental resources,[13] so too must the agencies of government take clear responsibilities for environmental management and set clear criteria for selecting and managing government's climate change programs.

These latter concerns were taken seriously in the early stages of developing the climate action framework. The Rudd government initiated a comprehensive review of federal and state activity in 2008 to ensure that all levels of government operated within the principles established internationally and applied by the Garnaut report were consistently adopted by all relevant agencies and programs at federal and state level. Its review (the Wilkins Review[14]) of existing climate change policies and measures, led by the then Department of Finance and Deregulation (DoFD), examined current government practice and budget processes to help ensure that federal and state government programs were consistent with the proposed climate change action policy as directed by the federal government and defined by the Garnaut Review.

Wilkins was quite critical of the capacity at federal and state level to coordinate a climate change policy: "[P]rograms have proliferated across a range of departments often with poorly defined objectives, inconsistent results and no exit strategy. In many cases, it is difficult to come to a judgement as to whether the results sufficiently justify the expenditure" (p. 40). This observation is not wholly surprising; it reflects the difficulty in all countries of changing existing patterns of spending by established government agencies to meet newly defined challenges. Government agencies in general tend to change their business processes slowly. Moreover, the scientific and political debate over the significance of climate change was as intense and determining the most appropriate response was as difficult in Australia as elsewhere. Climate change-linked administration in Australia has been

(continued)

subject to major transformations from the initial creation of an executive agency, the Australian Greenhouse Office, in 1998 to the consolidation of key climate change functions within the super-portfolio under the Department of Industry, Innovation, Climate Change, Science, Research, and Tertiary Education in 2013. Bureaucratic processes become much more difficult after 2013, and the whole structure of government business was restructured round the Coalition's strategy of direct action and hardline rejection of any kind of carbon pricing mechanism.

The Wilkins Review set out a roadmap for aligning government climate programs with a cost-benefit proposition: all mitigation policies of the government should be consistent with the carbon price determined by the market through the emission trading system. The report advocated a review of policy measures largely in terms of whether the implicit carbon price embodied in a climate change program was lower than the market price for carbon. He also advocated that a single Commonwealth department be given responsibility for existing and new climate change programs. It was envisaged that Commonwealth programs would be coordinated under these principles with the more than 200 state-level programs then underway. Under the aegis of the Council of Australian Governments (COAG), states were to review their climate change programs against a set of complementarity principles consistent with the Wilkins report.[15] Each jurisdiction reviewed its existing climate change mitigation measures, and all indicated that many of their existing programs would achieve complementary status with the CPRS and a number would cease. The total of continuing programs remained substantial, however; many were continued because they were deemed justified on other grounds. The government at the time also recognized that Australia is highly vulnerable to the effects of climate change and set out key elements of a national framework for assessing national progress in adapting and managing climate change risk—emphasizing that governments at all levels, businesses and the community have important complementary and differentiated roles in adapting to the impacts of climate change.[16]

The structures initiated under the Rudd–Gillard–Rudd regime were far from perfect, but they established the beginnings of a shared set of responsibilities for climate action among all levels of government, energy industries and energy consumers. Much of that was swept away when the Abbott government came to power, and little has been restored under the Turnbull-led Coalition. A definitive first act in 2013 was the abolition of the Climate Commission, set up originally in 2011 under Tim Flannery. It had been tasked to "provide the public with facts about climate-change science, economics and international action" (Flannery, p. 70). This act changed the nature of climate action debate in Australia. As Flannery observed regarding the Climate Commission, "[S]ome five days after its demise

(continued)

[it] was crowd-funded back into existence, and [now] runs as the Climate Council, an A$1.75 million a year not-for-profit institute" (p. 70). However, as a consequence, climate change debate has become a major socio-political divider. Government is no longer acting as a unifying force seeking to lead industry and the public to meet the moral, scientific and economic challenge of climate action; it is a partisan defender of the status quo and denies on ideological grounds the need either to examine lower cost options to its 'direct action' plan or the need for a continuing emphasis on fundamental climate science. On the latter point, as well as abolishing the Climate Council, it cut staff numbers in the CSIRO divisions primarily involved in climate science, largely because of its market-oriented view that the CSIRO should work more closely on industrial technology.[17] A widely supported contrary view is that the CSIRO, the Bureau of Meteorology, and the Climate Council should work cooperatively, obviously with due regard to scientific independence and peer review, to ensure that the government and the public get the best possible data and climate theory developments to guide policy.

The Olsonian argument, as presented earlier, on handling external costs (and benefits) of private activity is that government should intervene as necessary to provide fiscal incentives to ensure adequate provision of the collective good—in this case investment in fundamental science and in reducing the risks of environmental damage. Instead, the current Australian government provides subsidies to encourage industry to provide alternatives to its current environmentally damaging production, and, at the same time, cuts investment in fundamental research to establish understanding of the progress and likely impact of climate change. Effectively, the government is acting as a free-rider in science investment, although Australia's contribution to climate science has been significant, and the potential impacts of climate change and climate events in this country remain very serious. Internationally, the threat of climate events is gaining wider recognition (Otto and others 2015).

An underlying problem for all governments is that of assessing, monitoring and evaluating their own programs, most of which do not have commercial outputs. Climate action programs increasingly should be assessed in terms of their economic impact in terms of mitigating climate change using the best available estimate of the carbon price—as advocated by Wilkins in Australia. Like most OECD countries, Australia has developed its budgeting system over the past three decades to focus on accrual basis accounting, medium-to-long-term budget outcomes, and clear agency and ministerial responsibilities. Its accrual-outcome budgeting system is regarded as being close to best practice in terms of international standards of public financial management. Despite these advances, however, the system is not yet well designed to handle multi-agency programs like climate change. Even more importantly, like other OECD countries, its processes of accounting

(continued)

monitoring, and evaluation of its programs, have not yet addressed the issues of integrating social impact information with either cash or accrual accounting. The emphasis for government programs continues to be primarily on costs. As we discussed in Chap. 4, the development of <IR> accounting methodology, which is particularly relevant to assessing value impact of an environmental program, could help transform the assessment and management of climate action programs at all levels of government.

Australian PFM administration continues to emphasize formal outcome assessment, but these assessments are not easily accessible to the public and rarely attract the attention of the media, old or new. Expected program outcomes are required to be clearly articulated in the Australian PFM/Budget system, and the information on outcomes is reviewed by the legislature—with some emphasis on the role of Senate committee review at the Commonwealth level in Australia. Senate reviews are publicly available when budget proposals are tabled in Parliament. The main instrument (under direction of the Department of Treasury) to achieve an outcome focus is the Portfolio Budget Statement (PBS) submitted by each department of government to "provide information, explanation and justification to enable Parliament to understand the purpose of each outcome proposed in the Bills".[18] Currently, PBSs cover only general government (each state jurisdiction reports separately, however, and these are not consolidated). The statements require (i) a *portfolio overview* listing top ministerial and administrative responsibilities and all departments and general government agencies within the portfolio, and a summary of resources available for the year; (ii) for each agency within the portfolio, a *strategic direction statement* that lists all of the agency's programs and conveys a sense of goals and priorities; a definition of outcomes for each program, the resources to be allocated to each outcome, and its expected *deliverables* and *performance indicators*. Among other things, this information is intended to give information to parliament and the public that will enable them to establish the value obtained from public spending. It also provides a stronger basis for the Australian National Audit Office (ANAO) to carry out performance audits.

These features tick many of the boxes usually applied in assessment of PFM standards. However, in practice the system has not in the past and does not yet deliver all critical decision-making or public transparency benefits necessary to manage highly complex cross-functional programs like climate change. Key weaknesses in PBS implementation apparent in recent years are as follows:

- PBSs define outcomes within agencies and programs within the departmental portfolio; they are not required to consider dependencies on, or critical linkages with, agencies outside their direct portfolio responsibilities.

(continued)

- Deliverables and performance indicators are too often defined in very broad qualitative terms (such as 'quality policy advice to the minister')—comments along these lines were made in the Wilkins report and in an ANAO audit of the climate action programs in 2009/10.[19]
- PBSs give little indication of how much was achieved over the several years prior.
- ANAO audits are agency-centred and tend to look at a sample of programs rather than overall policy implementation. Earlier ANAO reports on climate action are no longer available on the internet, and current reports appear to focus on efficiency issues.[20]
- PBSs are highly technical, bureaucratically structured documents and are not easy to read. Their impact in Parliament seems slight and the impact on the public almost nonexistent. This is a complex issue that raises questions of government communication apparatus and commitment to transparency (including the apparent reduction of material on climate change issues in Australia) and the role of the media in using available material to explore policy issues in depth.

The above issues are by no means unique to Australia. The tasks of appraising, budgeting, monitoring and evaluating complex government programs have yet to be fully defined and comprehensively designed in all countries, at all levels of development, involved in tackling this global problem. In terms of PFM, linking technical performance analysis and reporting to budget decision-making and policy formulation and review is recognized as a problem in most of the OECD countries.[21] The developments in Australia are concerning for many of its citizens in the light of global concerns with climate change and its government's apparent unwillingness to encourage fundamental science or nonpartisan debate on the challenges that Australia and the world unavoidably faces. These issues are not unsurmountable, but under any genuine liberal tradition they should demand close objective investigation, open discussion and public involvement. Such measures are not being applied in Australia in 2017, but Australia is not alone in this predicament.

National Governance and Policies Will Determine the Effectiveness of Global Climate Action

Climate action policy in Australia, while unusual, is not unique. All nations must face the internal pressure from companies and other interests that gain from fossil fuel production of energy. In all cases, the failure to do so arises from lack of recognition by many of the concerned entities of their responsibility for environmental as well as commercial or administrative management. Kevin Rudd was right in his identification of climate change as one of the greatest moral challenges of our times. He failed to follow through with action to address that challenge, but in that failure he was not alone. Managing our environmental capital is a responsibility of both private and public sector entities and of members of the public. Public opinion has not yet played a central role in ensuring that these responsibilities are taken up by our representative governments—and government in many countries has been able to exploit the fragility of public opinion to claim a mandate for minimal action on addressing the need for action suggested by the best available evidence. It is time for governments everywhere to heed science and their citizens. Effective climate action is ultimately dependent on the actions of all the nation-states that are party to the Paris Agreement. Each is vulnerable to internal pressures from interest groups and to their own weaknesses in assessing and implementing climate change programs.

Climate change, it has been agreed at the global level, poses an existential threat, particularly to many of the world's most vulnerable communities. Effective action following the Paris Agreement, however, depends critically on ensuring that sufficient signatories to that agreement establish governance practices that will ensure their INDCs are not only fulfilled but exceeded. Climate change effects are increasingly being measured and monitored and their economic impacts becoming measurable and more predictable. It is thus becoming feasible to consider the environmental effects of human activity as a measurable component of GDP and to set these activities within the scope of national and global fiscal management control.

Global action on climate change is thus not only vital to ensure a stable and secure future for much of the world's population; it is an opportunity to redefine how nations and the global community measure and control their future, and an important step towards a redefinition of GDP as a measure of human progress. It depends critically, however, on a majority of influential nations accepting these responsibilities.

Summary of Themes and Conclusions

We have reviewed progress made in establishing an effective global program to tackle global climate change by examining the roles and interactions among four main groups at national and international levels: producers and users of fossil fuel energy, scientists and economists, the public, and politicians. Establishing a coordinated program to tackle climate change by reducing GHG emissions presents what has been described as 'diabolical' policy and practical problems at both national and international level. It is so described because the collective need to avoid potentially catastrophic future climate-related events requires assent from many powerful, politically connected, special interests that gain from the fossil fuel-linked industries but have no obligation to contribute to climate change mitigation or adaptation efforts.

Despite the many difficulties, the UN-organized global response has been remarkably successful, starting from the World Climate Conference in 1979 and establishing the Intergovernmental Panel of climate change scientists in 1988 through to the Paris Agreement in December 2015; it has managed to establish a sound, well-researched and publicly supported global commitment to act on climate change. Fulfilling the national commitments made at Paris, however, will require continuing efforts by all parties to the agreement, and there are troubling signs emerging of some countries backing away from the pledges made.[22] The case of Australia illustrates the dangers of political power politics in a small, though generally well-governed country; populist politics in the US has given rise to much more extreme dangers for global policies.

An avoidable rise in global temperature is one of the most significant crises that future generations will face. UN action so far has shown that we can deploy our global expertise to analyze the problems and point to feasible solutions. Public opinion in most countries has consistently viewed climate change as a very serious problem requiring action. But neither of these factors has proved decisive. Public opinion on this issue has not translated into political commitment in all countries; votes are determined by a range of factors and climate action has not proved decisive in shifting political priorities.

Elite professional opinion on climate change has been immensely valuable because it is accountable under well-established standards of peer review. But in recent times 'elites' are categorized as privileged minorities by populists, and neoliberals have regarded market forces as sufficient determinants of public policy. The issue of climate change action challenges both propositions; their rational resolution in this vital area should be regarded as an important landmark for well-designed intervention in all areas where private activity significantly reduces public value and long-term social development.

These issues, however, require a deeper investigation of the institutions, or 'rules of the game' that determine national and global governance; these rules—and broader philosophical implications—are examined in the final two chapters.

Notes

1. President Trump during his campaign and subsequently has used the social media ruthlessly to promote a set of favoured beliefs/memes spread by modern media ('climate change is a hoax', 'drain the swamp', 'make it in the USA or pay a border tax'). This technique, aimed against professional 'elites', poses extreme social dangers because of rapidity and simplicity of transmission and difficulty of presenting more complex counterarguments. The role and importance of professional elites is developed more generally in Chaps. 7 and 8.
2. See http://unfccc.int/essential_background/items/6031.php
3. The Agreement entered into force on November 4, 2016, thirty days after ratification by the threshold of 55 parties. 125 parties had ratified prior to COP 22 held in Marrakech. See http://unfccc.int/paris_agreement/items/9444.php
4. See http://unfccc.int/paris_agreement/items/9485.php
5. See Sandler (2004), Chap. 10.
6. In fact, President Trump did confirm his intention to pull out of the Paris Agreement at the G7 Summit. The ramifications of this action are discussed in the Epilogue.
7. See Epilogue.

8. As discussed further in Chap. 7, the Trump campaign went well beyond what has been earlier described as 'dog whistle' tactics. John Zaller's analysis of the Clinton and Trump campaigns, referenced in that chapter, gives a fuller and more worrying interpretation.
9. See Garnaut (2013) for a description of Australia's fiscal trajectory prior to the GFC, immediately after, and the likely 'dog days' ahead.
10. See http://www.smh.com.au/federal-politics/political-opinion/rudd-speech-to-the-united-nations-20090924-g3nn.html
11. A very useful timeline of these events prepared by the Australian Broadcasting Commission (ABC) is given on http://www.abc.net.au/news/2014-07-10/carbon-tax-timeline/5569118 The ABC also aired a three-part television documentary series, The Killing Season, by Sarah Ferguson, covering the political events. See http://www.abc.net.au/news/programs/killing-season/
12. See Garnaut (2008), Introduction: "Observation of daily debate and media discussion in Australia and elsewhere suggests that this issue might be too hard for rational policy making. It is too complex. The special interests are too numerous, powerful and intense. The time frames within which effects become evident are too long, and the time frames within which action must be effected too short.

    "But there is a saving grace that may make all the difference. . . . A high proportion of Australians say that they are prepared to pay for mitigation in higher goods and services prices. Most of them say that they are prepared to pay even if Australia is acting independently of other countries. There is a much stronger base of support for reform and change on this issue than on any other big question of structural change in recent decades, including trade, tax and public business ownership reform. . . . Public attitudes in Australia and in other countries create the possibility of major reform on emissions reductions, despite the inherent difficulty of the policy problem."
13. Implicitly, many major oil enterprises, such as Exxon-Mobil, already do so by applying a shadow oil price to guide their investment decisions. No doubt this tactic is primarily a defensive one to avoid overinvestment in the expectation that a global scheme to limit GHG emissions will eventually be put in place. Likely, however, some within the industry acknowledge the value of climate change science.

14. Roger Wilkins (2008), *Strategic Review of Australian Government Climate Change Programs*, Department of Finance and Deregulation Financial Management Group.
15. Council of Australian Governments (COAG), (2010), Final Report: Jurisdictions' Reviews of Existing Climate Change Mitigation Measures, Complementary Measures Sub-Group.
16. The Wilkins report emphasized the likelihood that Australia would suffer significantly from climate change and that too little was being done in this area. It suggested that, while the Commonwealth should take the lead in mitigation response, states and local government should have lead responsibility for adaptation, since the effects would be specific to localities. The report added that the role of risk analysis and the pricing of risk were not well integrated into decision-making. It recommended establishing a panel to provide advice to COAG on adaptation priorities, cost-effective responses, and the role of government. Policy documents of the time include: *Adapting to Climate Change in Australia: An Australian Government Position Paper* (2010) and *Roles and Responsibilities for Climate Change Adaptation in Australia* (adopted by the cross-jurisdictional ministerial Select Council on Climate Change as a statement of common understanding on 16 November 2012).
17. See https://theconversation.com/csiro-cuts-as-redundancies-are-announced-the-real-cost-is-revealed-59895, The CSIRO and the Bureau of Meteorology do, however, continue to undertake climate-related research as part of the overall global effort—see https://theconversation.com/state-of-the-climate-2016-bureau-of-meteorology-and-csiro-67717
18. For the 2016 Environmental portfolio, see http://www.environment.gov.au/system/files/resources/cf243495-d7df-4dc8-84fd-4411be7f4df7/files/environment-pbs-2016-17.pdf
19. ANAO Report 26, 2009–10.
20. See https://www.anao.gov.au/work/performance-audit/management-machinery-government-changes
21. See Hawke, L., Performance Budgeting in Australia, *OECD Journal on Budgeting* 7(2) (2007).
22. As the Epilogue examines, the United States under Trump did indeed back away from its pledges.

References

Coase, Ronald. 1960. The Problem of Social Cost. *Journal of Law and Economics* 3: 1–44.

Flannery, Tim. 2015. *Atmosphere of Hope: Searching for Solutions to the Climate Crisis*. Melbourne: The Text Publishing Company.

Garnaut, Ross. 2008. *The Garnaut Climate Change Review: Final Report*, Commonwealth of Australia. Port Melbourne: Cambridge University Press.

———. 2011. *The Garnaut Review 2011: Australia in the Global Response to Climate Change* (PDF http://www.garnautreview.org.au/update-2011/garnaut-review-2011/garnaut-review-2011.pdf).

———. 2013. *Dog Days: Australia After the Boom*. Collingwood: Redback.

ICAP. 2016. *Emissions Trading Worldwide: Status Report 2016*. Berlin: ICAP.

Nordhaus, William. 2013. *The Climate Casino: Risk, Uncertainty, and Economics for a Warming World*. New Haven/London: Yale University Press.

Olson, Mancur. 2000. *Power and Prosperity: Outgrowing Communist and Capitalist Dictatorships*. New York: Basic Books.

Otto, Friederike E.L., and others. 2015. Attribution of Extreme Weather Events in Africa: A Preliminary Exploration of the Science and Policy Implications. *Climatic Change* 132 (4): 531–543.

Sandler, T. 2004. *Global Collective Action*. Cambridge: Cambridge University Press.

Wilkins, Roger. 2008. *Strategic Review of Australian Government Climate Change Programs*. Canberra: Department of Finance and Deregulation Financial Management Group.

Part III

Understanding Our Institutions, and Ruling Ourselves and Our World

Chapter 7, the first in this part, examines the proposition that the kinds of reform advocated in Part II are determined or critically influenced by existing institutions. Broadly, it accepts this proposition but argues that the current rules of the game themselves need to be defined and challenged. Both democratic and guided capitalist forms of governance need to be open to critical examination to allow global society to establish a common core of rules. The UN, while subject to many criticisms from powerful national governments, has made striking overall progress towards this global view of humanity. Chapter 8 draws from all the preceding explanations, from Foucault to modern social science, to model and summarize the way in which we have begun to understand and govern ourselves in modern terms. It reflects a battle between deliberative 'slow thinking' social mechanisms, and the turmoil of individual and social quick-fire thinking and social media exchanges. Much depends on society's ability to achieve a Foucauldian/Nietzschean will to knowledge and power to govern ourselves and the world justly.

7

Institutions and Behaviour: New Rules of the Game

Recent developments in institutional theory, behavioural theory and political science point strongly toward the need to re-examine the way in which our democratic institutions use economics and other disciplines to address local, national and global aspirations and needs. This chapter takes up many of the issues raised earlier of how needed reforms can be put in place; often the rules must first be changed. While we accept the fundamental importance of institutions, the key question remains: How are these barriers to be overcome? We focus first on the field of institutional economics, which has brought consideration of the rules of the game into economic theory but has yet to clarify sufficiently either the precise nature of the rules or the boundaries between institutional economics, law and political science. Second, we look at the nature of democracy itself as an evolving basis for liberal and equitable government. A closer integration of the many political and economic strands of institutional theory seems a necessary step towards a modern theoretical framework that can better link emerging theory to social practice.

Institutional Economics: An Incomplete Framework

Institutional economics, drawing on the work of Douglass North and many others, emphasizes the need to look at the rules governing economic decisions to enable individual rationality to guide market and social behaviour. It places great emphasis on establishing better institutions or 'rules of the game' as the necessary basis for economic growth and policy-making. Much of the proposed institutional basis, such as ensuring property rights and observance of the 'rule of law', is expressed in very general terms, however, and most require more thorough explanation regarding their specific nature and how they can be put more effectively in place. The concept of the rule of law is deceptively simple: formal laws should be in place and all—including lawmakers—should observe these laws. But we know that laws are open to conservative and progressive interpretation,[1] and we also know that in most legal systems, whether adversarial or inquisitorial, financial and political power plays a huge role in outcomes—usually to the great disadvantage of those on lower incomes. President Trump's opening barrage of administrative actions appears to directly challenge both conservative and progressive interpretations of the application of the rule of law in the US. A standard institutionalist position, noted in Chap. 2, is that the state should have a monopoly on violence. But this can scarcely be considered a rule that is effectively pursued in many modern states; and in the US is constitutionally hampered by its Second Amendment, quite appropriate for 1791, but much less evidently so now.

A great deal more work is needed to define the many dimensions of the rule of law more clearly and apply these to better design of legal systems and their administration. Towards this end, the World Justice Project has established a major program to compile a multi-dimensional index of factors that the 'rule of law' comprises[2] and to allow some degree of international comparison of the extent to which that set of standards has been established.

The World Bank's *World Development Report 2017* (WDR) has used this data to show that the degree of implementation of the rule of law is strongly correlated with high income. Such a result is expected, but a great deal more work is required to understand causal relationships and begin developing strategies to establish rule of law where it is not yet established. The WDR makes some suggestions regarding possible modes of transition (see pp. 96–97), but progress in this area depends on much deeper understanding of the relation between the established systems, often linked to elements of customary practice, and the different types of formal law practiced in advanced countries.

A fundamental assumption of much development economics, and more generally economic theory, which is reflected in WDR 2017 analysis, is that professional elites can influence economic and development outcomes directly.[3] The alternative thesis advanced consistently in this book is that while elites are very important in helping to guide and strengthen sovereign policies, their main significance is their role both in refining and questioning the rules of the game and in communicating these rules to both decision-makers and the broad public.

Economic theorists are increasingly drawing on other disciplines to address these issues more thoroughly. As emphasized in preceding chapters, accurate and fair measurement of social well-being is a critical requirement if society is to be sure of recognizing, debating and achieving its considered goals. This task itself requires considerable rewriting of existing rules of the game. Beyond that, however, the structures and rules that determine how social data are used in making decisions, and how the various stakeholders interact, needs much deeper analysis. Institutional theory takes us some steps in this direction, but much broader and deeper investigation of the nature of the rules, both of democracy and rival forms of government, is required. We will begin with economic theory.

One basis of institutional thinking in economics originates in the work of Ronald Coase (1960), who argued that if transaction costs in a market or internally in a firm were low, participants would reach a bargain over all exchanges, and regulation by government (or internally in a hierarchical firm) would be unnecessary. The Coase theorem has been interpreted by many economists as a sufficient argument against government intervention in the market, and by and large it has been used as a defence of the status quo (see, however, earlier discussion in Chap. 6 of Olson's refutation of Coase).

Transaction costs have since been defined by North (1992) as the "cost of measuring the valuable attributes of the goods and services or the performance of agents in exchange that is the fundamental key to the cost of transacting" (p. 7). He argues that efficient markets arise from institutions—or rules—that provide low cost measurement and enforcement of contracts. Changing institutions to improve efficiency, however, is unavoidably constrained by the existing framework—or it is path-dependent. He sees political markets as inherently imperfect, but notes that imperfection has made it possible to alter the direction of some economies. Notions of transaction costs and path dependency as guides to possible economic reform, while emphasizing the importance of existing institutions, say little about how these rules can be changed or about their quality and the impact of existing rules on broader institutional reform.[4]

Continuing renovation of the existing government model is needed for all countries and for management of a just and prosperous global economy—a task that goes well beyond that of encouraging economic growth, as argued throughout this book. But the task of prescribing the measures needed to change existing institutions for even the narrower objective of growth is not yet clearly addressed in much of the literature of institutional economics. Olson's *Power and Prosperity* and Acemoglu and Robinson's *Why Nations Fail* both highlight institutional factors as being critical to national and, by implication, international success, but neither escapes the catch-22 that the failing institutions themselves need to be changed to allow market-augmenting changes to occur. Olson suggests financial incentives to change behaviour, but weak institutions may not respond to market signals and weak governments are unlikely to allow Pigouvian intervention in the tax and price structure.

Acemoglu and Robinson are highly critical of the present framework for administering foreign aid and argue that inclusive economic and political institutions need to be created to allow a population to break out of the cycle of poverty (pp. 450–455) caused by the installation of extractive institutions that concentrate power in the hands of an elite—often based on the methods of the earlier colonial powers (p. 80). They argue that inclusive political institutions are pluralistic, establish state monopoly over violence and centralize power appropriately (pp. 79–83). But while they compile evidence spanning many centuries, they do not describe the nature of the rules in any detail, nor do they describe how such institutions can be created if they have not been established historically, nor, as Jeffrey Sachs argues, establish fully the case that the elements they identify are the most critical factors in promoting growth and efficiency.

Sachs (2012), a strong proponent of international aid, has vigorously criticized the Acemoglu/Robinson thesis that the characteristics of the institutions put in place over past centuries are what determine whether nations succeed or fail. He does agree that institutions are important and their historical research valuable, but many other factors, such as "geopolitics, technological discoveries, and natural resources" can encourage or impede economic growth. As argued earlier in this book, there is little doubt that the impact of imperialism and colonization or settlement has had a lasting impact on the governance of the colonized countries even after independence, and Sachs agrees that Acemoglu and Robinson's thesis provides important evidence in this regard. But institutional economic theory needs to go beyond merely asserting that inclusive institutions should be created. At the very least its practitioners must identify more precisely what barriers exist to prevent the development of better rules; they should also look towards the institutions that would be needed to establish new rules at country and international levels.

Sachs' invocation of other factors such as geography and natural resources, however, does not really diminish the importance of institutional reform. He cites the case of Botswana, where clearly diamonds provided a sound basis for prosperity, but as Acemoglu and Robinson point out, Botswana is one of the rare examples in developing countries where natural resource wealth was exceptionally well managed. The difference between it and other resource-rich developing countries lay in tribal traditions largely untouched by colonization as well as the emergence of good leadership leading up to independence (pp. 408–409). Neither Sachs nor Acemoglu and Robinson address the question of the nature of intervention needed to establish good governance rules in countries that now operate under extractive institutions.

We earlier discussed the case of Ghana, cited by Sachs in his 2005 volume; he linked country governance to the basic institutions of democracy that had been established, and he assumed that international support for achievement of MDG targets would provide the necessary impetus. But improvement of the processes that ensured observation of good fiscal policy practices was not sufficiently addressed—and, as we noted, further obstacles to full success must be overcome. Implementing needed institutional strengthening in Ghana and other developing country PFM practice has proved extremely difficult and requires a long-term commitment. External aid providers are often reluctant to make such a commitment to projects that generate not easily measurable outcomes and that take a long time. Long-term programs and strategies of PFM reform are needed.

This book suggests an approach based much more explicitly on establishing well-defined accountability standards and self-governance building blocks—in governments generally, but with a major emphasis on less developed economies. The need to improve measurement of well-being and to build these measurements into entity, national and global governance structures was elaborated in Chap. 4. External aid without tangible improvement in national governance cannot ensure sustainability of reforms. That chapter argued that establishing strong standards for accounting, accountability and transparency for all entities and all forms of capital is an essential pillar of institutional reform for good governance. But here we are arguing that tackling the existing rules of the game is often an essential prerequisite to support technical reforms. Development of political commitment and a clear strategy should surely form part of changing the rules of the game. Some countries that would almost certainly fall under the 'extractive' label are considering this kind of institutional change; a continuing emphasis on progress at the political and legal level could help lead these countries towards more inclusive rules.

Tackling the deep-seated issues of institutional change will play a critical role in realizing the reforms outlined in Chaps. 4, 5 and 6. Climate change action, covered in Chap. 6, likely represents the most immediately significant area of potential change—and contesting challenges to the global agreement on climate action requires a strong mechanism for supporting its scientific basis and just treatment of future generations and vulnerable countries and social groups. Democracy itself needs to be examined in this context.

The Institution of Democracy: Governance in Progress?

Democracy, as writers like John Dunn (2005) and John Keane (2009) make clear, has a long and complex history, and its institutional development is very far from finished. Dunn rightly questions the existence of a "single cosmopolitan standard" by which the legitimacy of political authority can be judged. Rather than attempting to measure the extent to which countries have achieved loosely defined democracy, we should identify those features of democratic institutions that are achieving tangible and good results for society and its individuals. As well as the aspects discussed above, we need to be much clearer about what democracy means in all of its dimensions, what its weaknesses are and what can be done to address these.

Keane puts a strong case that democracy is very far from a fully developed arrangement between governments and the governed. He has elegantly explored the genesis of modern forms of democracy from the life and death of Athenian and pre-Athenian developments of *assembly* democracy,[5] to the tumultuous emergence of *representative* democracies from the tenth to the eighteenth centuries, to the present era. For the last 60 or so years, however, he submits that government for much of the West and West-influenced countries has evolved into what he describes as *monitory democracies*. These are characterized by the development of a multitude of official and civil society organizations that critically examine and report to the public on performance of government in delivering services. He highlights the role of civil society watchdogs, suggesting they confirm "Madison's law of Free Government: no government can be considered free unless it is capable of governing a society that is itself capable of controlling the government" (p. 713).

Keane did not, however, consider the present system to be working well nor envisage a smooth transition to the next stage of democracy. His penultimate chapter, Memories from the Future, paints a bleak picture. Monitory democracy's breakdown will start, he suggests, from the people's misgivings about politicians, parties and parliaments; it will be compounded by populist control measures that ultimately are used by politicians to manipulate the public; a range of international pressures governed by powerful hegemonic contenders will lead to internal conflicts and cycles of violence within countries; and nationalism will become rampant, as will terrorism, leading ultimately to a new unipolar world order dominated by China. These proposals, though presented as a warning rather than a structured prediction, contain clear echoes of our current concerns. Such trends, however, are not inevitable. The main points I think to be drawn from Keane's overall scholarly treatment of democracy's development are: that democracy contains the elements of good government, but its many dimensions and the social reactions it creates need to be understood more deeply; and democratic institutions should be open to review, just as argued above for a finer definition of the rule of law.

Society and social science must draw much more on the study of the complex reality of democracy as an evolving institution rather than as an established system. The problems of Keane's 'monitory democracy' can be tackled by a society that seeks to understand these trends and governments and political leaders that accept responsibilities for managing non-commercial as well as commercial capital. In important respects, the establishment of better systems of accounting, accountability and transparency by both government and private enterprise, as described earlier, will help to establish a greater level of trust in our present system of monitory democracy. It would create a more inclusive set of measures of social progress and mechanisms of reward for achievement against these measures by all units of society. But technical improvements in accounting and reporting in themselves provide no real assurance that these improvements will be taken up under the prevalent rules of the game. Those in power have great incentive to maintain the status quo. The power structure and the rules themselves need to be assessed as objectively as possible.

The Varieties of Democracy (V-Dem) project,[6] co-hosted by the Department of Political Science at the University of Gothenburg, Sweden, and the Kellogg Institute at the University of Notre Dame, in the United States, has established data and a research program that should help address the problem of defining current institutions more clearly. More than 50 social science scholars are involved in the collaboration, which includes around 2500 local and cross-national experts working in 177 countries. It is one of world's largest social science databases, compiling country data from the year 1900 onwards and covering over 350 indicators on democracy and political systems.

Michael Coppedge and others (2011) provide a description of the V-Dem methodology and early results from the research program. V-Dem aims to establish fine-grained measurement and analysis that overcomes the shortcomings of the commonly used composite indices of democracy and allows examination of how specific aspects of democratic institutions are changing over time—and thus which element is likely to be most important for policy-makers to address. As Coppedge et al. (2016) describe, more detailed measures of the dimensions of democracy provide much deeper understanding of individual country institutional development; and they explain how different dimensions of democracy are applied in different countries. The paper charts quite dramatic differences in five dimensions of democratic institutions in the trajectory of democracy development in five countries (Denmark, Russia/USSR, South Korea, South Africa and Egypt). Unsurprisingly Denmark showed the highest score for all dimensions over most of the period (other than during WW2 occupation).

Below are the five key components of democracy used in the study (where 'component' is defined by indicators that make up its most distinctive attributes, and overlap among components is avoided). Each is measured by a set of detailed indicators that generally use point predictions based on Bayesian factor analysis. In summary, the components are:

- *Electoral*—assessing the core value of making rulers responsive to citizens through periodic elections, using indicators of key characteristics of representative democracy;

- *Liberal*—assessing protection of individual and minority rights from state repression, using indicators of legal protection of civil liberties and limitations on executive power;
- *Participatory*—assessing non-electoral forms of participation by citizens in all forms of political processes, using indicators of popular participation at different levels of government;
- *Deliberative*—assessing the extent to which decisions are informed by reasoned discourse, using indicators of public policy justification by political elites; and
- *Egalitarian*—assessing the distribution of power and resources, using indicators of equality in both dimensions.

Measurements along these lines should help improve both national and global discourse on the impact of country institutions on achieving well-being goals at both national and global levels. While the spectre of path dependency may, even in this case, invoke defensive reactions from ruling elites in many countries, objective research widely distributed should in the long run overcome such inbuilt conservativism. Support for extending application of V-Dem measurement and reporting on individual countries is most likely to come from our present international infrastructure of the UN and BWIs, as well as the coalition of universities already involved in V-Dem and others likely to make use of the V-Dem database.

As useful as this line of research is, it may be even more helpful in promoting governance reform both nationally and globally if linked more explicitly to the concerns of those disciplines already involved in promoting accountability and transparency, and of others, like Keane, contemplating a breakdown in established democracies. To address both sets of concerns, the following approaches may be worthwhile: (i) extending the scope of analysis to consider conceptions not only of democratic governance but of various forms of autocracy; and (ii) subdividing the elements of the 'deliberative' component to cover more specific dimensions of accountability and transparency defined in ongoing programs of PFM reform. Figure 7.1 below suggests how such a review may be set up. The Venn diagram uses the five components of democracy defined in V-Dem

The Institution of Democracy: Governance in Progress?

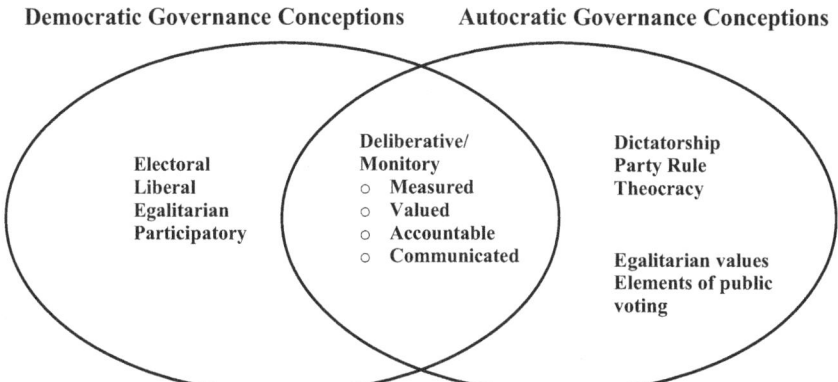

Fig. 7.1 Dimensions of governance and democracy (Source: Author)

('majoritarian' and 'consensual' components previously considered within the V-Dem array have, for the time being, been set aside).

The deliberative component, however, is modified, first, to incorporate Keane's conception of monitory democracy, and then, measured by the key elements that are tracked in accountability and transparency dimensions in PFM work; each may have several indicators. Many of these elements may be shared by some forms of autocracy, as shown—and the extent to which this is so under these regimes' forms of autocracy would be worth tracking. For the most part, other components of democracy are not part of autocratic rule, though elements may be emerging in some. A further point worth investigating is that there are many different forms of both democratic and autocratic government. The latter are summarized in the diagram, and democracies may be classified as either constitutional monarchies or republics, in each case further subdivided into unitary or federated states. It would be of interest to investigate the differing development of the components of democracy under all kinds of regimes. The V-Dem program thus promises to bring a variety of testable explanations to advance our understanding of the relationship between institutions and governance and to help establish which institutions are most likely to lead to improvement of social well-being.

A counterpart to objective investigation of institutions, however, is that of developing a better understanding of the behaviour of citizens, who are expected to obey the rules of the game, elite professional groups, who help define issues and guide policies, politicians, who are expected to cooperate and set rules that will guide citizens towards socially desirable action, and media, who are expected to provide objective interpretation of policies and their basis to citizens. Behavioural theory has begun in recent years to provide greater assurance that economic and social theory and practice are based on a sound understanding of individual and social reasoning processes and interactions.

Behavioural Theory I: Explaining Rationality and Its Flaws

The work of Daniel Kahneman (2011), his late colleague Aaron Tversky and other behavioural specialists has brought about a paradigm change in the way economists now regard human rationality as the basis for economic and (by neoliberal extension) other social choices.[7] Kahneman's book describes a distinctively different view of individual and public choice from that derived from an assumed utility-maximizing *homo economicus*.[8] The wide range of studies carried out by Kahneman and Tversky, or cited by Kahneman, however, show that actual individuals and social institutions, sometimes even highly professional ones, tend to operate by heuristics or 'rule-of-thumb' and, as a consequence, their decisions are characterized by many systematic biases; Kahneman labelled such instinctive processes 'fast-thinking'. But people are also capable of applying rigorous logical and empirically based reasoning to decisions when they recognize their complexity, and use appropriate analytical tools; such are science and math-oriented 'slow-thinking' processes.

Both individuals and groups thus employ two systems of thinking, and the reliability of decisions and maximization of value will depend on which mode of thinking predominates. System 1, or fast-thinking, will be more unreliable and prone to bias because of reliance on heuristics, perhaps the natural tendency in day-to-day life. System 2, or slow-thinking, comes to bear when we are faced with problems that demand careful calculation, such as solving mathematical problems, as encountered in school or in professional life. For individuals, attention control is shared by the two systems.[9] He suggests in Chap. 2 that system 2, while having all the attributes of a star performer, is also characterized by laziness: the natural human tendency is to over rely on day-to-day routine system 1 responses. These characteristics are often compounded by the way decisions are presented—as Kahneman describes, by "framing effects, where decisions are shaped by inconsequential features of choice problems".[10] The overall message delivered, and largely now accepted within the social sciences, particularly economics, is that complex decisions should be supported by rigorous analysis, and routine analysis even at a high professional level should itself be examined to test for systematic biases of the kind identified by Kahneman, Tversky and many other behavioural specialists.

The main implications for the governance issues with which this book is concerned are, first that market decisions (many of which have relied on sophisticated mathematical models in the financial sphere) and broader social decisions made by governments are both prone to systemic bias and require strong oversight mechanisms. Second, decisions are very much subject to the way in which choices are presented. Our present economic models are too dependent on assumptions of investor and consumer rationality and that individual decisions will lead to optimal personal and social outcomes—though evidence to the contrary is growing.

The proposal that governments should compensate for individual and social reliance on fast-thinking by using communications techniques to guide the public towards more informed decisions is now widely recognized—though often resisted by the industries affected. Kahneman cites the positive effects that have been influenced by the Richard Thaler, Cal Sunstein book *Nudge*, which he describes as the "basic manual for applying behavioral economics to policy".[11] These proposals encouraged the US government to require fuel efficiency and environmental data to be compulsorily provided on all new motor vehicles. A critical point, however, is that the government itself must recognize and be willing to act upon the potential dangers and costs to society. Both governments and advertising agencies have long recognized the power of framing.

Neoliberal governments have tended to downplay such effects and strongly support industry resistance to over-regulation and red tape. It seems unlikely that their populist and nationalist successors will act much differently.

Better governance implies strong government commitment to establishing system 2-based mechanisms to guide the public. It is not apparent that many governments yet accept these responsibilities; as argued in Chap. 3, neoliberalism has greatly weakened the position of professional advisors relative to politicians, and it seems likely that their populist successors will continue this trend. This book puts the case that we must continue to seek a deeper understanding of the way in which the frailties of system 1-thinking affect the dynamics between politicians and the voting public. Some key aspects are discussed below.

Behavioral Theory II: Understanding the Dynamics of Public Opinion

The frailty of individual and group rationality described above in turn inhibits the development of rational public discourse sought by Foucault and a primary goal of deliberative democracy. John Zaller, in his 1992 book *The Nature and Origins of Mass Opinion*, developed a basic model of the dynamics of public opinion formation, its interpretation and impact through survey responses, and shifting support of political parties. His analytical perspective drew on the classical work of Walter Lippmann, particularly his reference to 'news stereotypes' whereby complex situations (such as a WW1 battlefield) outside the experience of average readers are simplified by reference to images—'pictures in our head' of the leaders of the different forces as they may be portrayed in a painting. Since it is impossible to convey the full picture, what Zaller describes as 'elite discourse' becomes the only way in which the everyday citizen can form an opinion on national and world events. Lippmann's 'news stereotypes' have become 'frames of reference' in modern parlance, and bear more than a passing resemblance to Kahneman/Tversky 'framing'. The technique of summarizing and contextualizing news can easily become manipulative—as we argued in Chap. 3 on the role of the neoliberal press; whereas Lippmann was concerned with the social consequences of framing and manipulation, the Murdoch press in the US, Australia and the UK has seen it as both a political and business tool.

Zaller has developed an important model of the dynamics of public opinion formation and measurement based on these perspectives and from what he describes as Phillip Converse's "most important insight—that differences among citizens in their levels of political conceptualization and awareness are as consequential as differences in values and interests" (Zaller p. xi). Measured public opinion, he argues, depends on how people acquire information from the political environment and how they then transform it into responses to public opinion surveys. His basic model of public political opinion response is a process whereby people *receive* new information, *accept* it, and then *sample* from the range of views they hold at the time of questioning—abbreviated as the 'RAS model'. Overlaying this personal response model are the links between elite, professional and political discourse, informed minorities within the broad public, and mass opinion. Mass opinion depends therefore, first, on the effectiveness with which elite discourse is conveyed and received by informed minorities and the wider mass public, and second, on the predispositions of the members of public. Zaller also emphasizes that the measurement of public opinion cannot be considered as a neutral act because responses can change depending on the way the question is framed (again consistent with Kahneman/Tversky conclusions on framing). He has tested his model in several areas using the extensive American National Election Studies (ANES) database, housed in the University of Michigan, and demonstrated its analytical usefulness in examining the factors influencing attitudes to the Vietnam War and shifts in voting allegiance in US House elections. He recognizes that more work must be done. Gregory Markus (1994), who reviewed Zaller's book and pronounced it a masterpiece, did express a few reservations, particularly regarding the possible implications of future changes that enhance message flows from citizens to elites. Major changes indeed have occurred with the rapid evolution of social media; though information, not necessarily elite discourse or truth, now flows in many directions.

But the continuing development of modern media and the way it is used certainly doesn't negate the need for more work to be done on analysis of the dynamics of public opinion formation, and Zaller's work remains an important starting point. His posting on the Democratic and Republican campaigns in 2016,[12] while not particularly dependent on his theory of public opinion formation, makes powerful points regarding the development of dynastic politics in the US, the consequent failure of either party to select truly candidates that could sell their core policies to the electorate, and Trump's success in appealing to voters with no allegiance to either set of standard policies. He puts a major share of blame onto the nominating process, which relies on registered voters, and these do not represent a decisive majority of the electorate. Almost half of the electorate is unaffiliated with either party. Such a process, he suggests, does not answer to "even a minimum notion of democracy".

We will look at the necessity to re-examine even long-established institutional arrangements below. In Chap. 8, we consider the broader philosophical and social implications of Kahneman and Tversky's two-system model of rationality and the Zaller model of public opinion dynamics in Chap. 8. Both point to the growing needs to deepen our understanding and reassess the nature of democratic institutions and to establish a more holistic view of governance issues.

A Clash of Institutions: The Difficult Path to Multilateral Governance

Foucauldian state panopticism, as described in Chap. 1, likely provided one basis for development of juridical frameworks up to and beyond the eighteenth century. However, in the industrialized fiscal-military states that emerged from the Industrial Revolution, particularly after the American and French revolutions, these rules and the differences among them became widely entrenched in written national constitutions. As Zachary Elkins and others (2009) record, constitutions have varied considerably both in longevity and content since the first and longest-lasting was enacted in the USA in 1789. They have, as part of their continuing comparative constitutions project (www.comparativeconstitutionsproject.org.), identified and collected most of the constitutions produced since then, and are codifying these along a variety of dimensions.

In their introduction (p. 1), they note the exchanges between Jefferson and Madison on the lasting relevance of constitutions; Madison strongly supported constitutional longevity, whereas Jefferson argued that they should not be held in 'sanctimonious reverence', indeed they should be rewritten every generation—even suggesting an expiration date of nineteen years based on actuarial tables available at the time. Elkins et al. indicate from their current research that the actual average span of constitutions is much closer to Jefferson's estimate than Madison's, but the factors contributing to the relatively short lifespan of many constitutions are mainly military and elite rivalry and successful power grabs by entrenched power groups. By no means has a case been made in favor of a Jeffersonian solution. But there is ample justification for avoiding 'sanctimonious reverence', and its corollary, continual objective examination of constitutional provisions in line with changing times and understanding.

The United States Constitution is of global significance, not least because the US has developed into the most powerful and richest country in the world. As noted in Chap. 2, US success stems in large part from its unparalleled opportunities of settling a land rich in natural resources, occupied by peoples with limited technology to resist invasion, and, it can be added, widely separated from potential external invaders. US actions unavoidably affect global security, trade and development. The implications of its Constitution for internal governance and external relations are thus of as much significance for the rest of the world as for American citizens. The basic principle of the US Constitution to limit executive authority and to invest the citizens with power to choose their representatives is undoubtedly sound and widely accepted by other countries. But it is becoming increasingly recognized that the principles of separation of powers among the legislative, executive and judicial branches of government set in the first three Articles, and those of federalism and state rights and responsibilities, set in the following three,[13] set significant hurdles for reaching consensus and adjusting to changing circumstances.

And these factors, as we discuss below, have contributed to growing ideological confrontation in recent years.

The work by Elkins and others suggest that the US Constitution is one of the most inflexible due to the need for two-thirds of both houses and two-thirds of the states to approve the proposed amendment. They note: "As Americans who have followed the plight of seemingly consensual, but ill-fated, amendments like the Equal Rights Amendment know, securing approval by three quarters of the states is a herculean task." (p. 102 Kindle edition) Francis Fukuyama (2014) acknowledged that the Madisonian version of democracy and its guarantee of the stability of institutions could not prevent the onset of "political decay"[14] in the US. He suggests major factors in creating the decline in quality of US government has been the usurpation of the proper functions of the executive by the courts and the legislature, as well as the spread of interest group influence. He argues that "[i]n many respects, the American System of checks and balances compares unfavorably with parliamentary systems when it comes to the ability to balance...strong state action with law and accountability" (p. 24). Earlier, he had noted the distinct advantage of the Westminster system, particularly in terms of budgeting and accountability, and the possibility of an unsatisfactory government being removed before its end of term with a vote of no confidence.[15] He suggests also that systems in the EU as a whole are beginning to resemble that of the US in terms both of growing numbers and sophistication of lobby groups "in depressing ways" (p. 25), and the addition of a European layer of decision-making.

For the US, Fukuyama's 2014 article concludes on a pessimistic note: "The depressing bottom line is that...the decay of American politics will probably continue until some external shock comes along to catalyze a true reform coalition and galvanize it into action." (p. 26). The election of Donald Trump in 2017 may indeed provide such a shock, not at all externally created, but with likely many global repercussions. But, at the end of his 2014 book on the same theme he balances the concept of political decay with that of political order, suggesting that the "demand for [high-quality democratic government] is large and growing day by day", and that there is a clear directionality to the process of political development (p. 548), reflecting an underlying belief on the general merits of liberal democracy that will somehow find a way forward.

Perhaps that will come to pass. But the increasingly urgent task to be faced squarely and immediately is to understand the major weaknesses in our present sets of rules and find ways to address these flaws more directly and effectively. We now have a wide experience of different forms of democracy and a range of social scientists are refining our concepts of democracy and developing clearer rules for accountability. Active consolidation of many of the themes that have been outlined earlier in this book and this chapter should be part of the way forward. As described, many agencies are working in these areas.

A great deal of this work must naturally be done in the US itself. Neither the nature of President Trump's electoral success, which derives from those very weaknesses, nor his election platform, however, suggest that his team will favour many of the objectives of the global community, such as managing climate change, reducing inequality or encouraging multilateral solutions to global growth, trade and security.[16] Trump's initial moves as President suggest that he aims to re-establish executive authority, in many ways quite contrary to the intentions of the Constitution; it remains to be seen how the other branches of government will react over the long term. Given the dominance of the Republican Party in all branches of government, however, business methodology and business interests seem likely to prevail over deep concerns with the broader public interest. Any serious progress towards global cooperation to address the major challenges that have been outlined in this book and by many others will depend heavily on the actual policies enacted under the Trump presidency and the reaction of other branches of government and the American people to his actual program, which in the initial stages is being enacted by executive order; budgetary measures will need Congressional support and will also be subject to the interests of individual congressional and senatorial representatives.

More broadly, institutional change in the US and globally remains extremely challenging precisely because it is path dependent—those in power must be persuaded to initiate the needed changes. Can this be done by ensuring that world leaders and their advisors are exposed to more high-level thinking and advice? Nicolas Berggruen and Nathan Gardels in their *Intelligent Governance for the 21st Century* have attempted to establish principles for fundamentally restructuring government institutions, including those of Western democracies, to balance what they term 'knowledgeable democracy' and 'accountable meritocracy'. It draws on the historical experience of 'institutional civilization' in China and the emergence (and internal tensions) of its current 'modern mandarinate', as well as reviewing development and dysfunction in Western democracies. The Berggruen Institute, established under the Chairmanship of Nicolas Berggruen, promotes these ideas in forums supporting the G20, the Council of Europe and governance in California, in areas covering key dimensions of the global governance problem.

The Institute has established high-level councils to advise world, national and state leaders. The 21st Century Council, a group of former world leaders, top global thinkers and social media founders and executives, aims to provide high-level thinking on such issues to national and international decision-makers and explore 'intelligent' reform of global governance systems, including a focus on the potential role of the G20. These initiatives aim at open multilateral discussion of the increasingly apparent weaknesses in national and global governance. However, the initiatives have shown little traction on the course of global policies or institutional change, despite the calibre of the Council members and the leaders who have attended.

Perhaps as Fukuyama suggests in the case of American political decay, a crisis is necessary to stimulate action. There is no shortage of crisis points in 2017: increasing tensions in the Middle East, including the failure of the so-called 'Arab Spring', the Syrian civil war, the rise of the Islamic State and its occupation of territory in Syria and Iraq, and the consequent flood of refugees from all affected territories, particularly to Europe, but also to the Asia-Pacific region—all should give grounds for unified international action to reduce conflict and provide humanitarian aid and safe passage and assistance to refugees. Much, however, depends on the openness of the competing hegemonic powers to such overtures and their internal decision-making dynamics. Instead, the major nations, with the notable exception of Germany, have largely emphasized protection of national boundaries and mainly emphasized national economic interests—particularly so in the case of Trump-led USA. The United

A Clash of Institutions: The Difficult Path to Multilateral... 233

Nations High Commission for Refugees (UNHCR) is grossly underfunded and lacks capacity to handle refugees properly at any time; the political and economic conditions that have developed since the GFC have greatly magnified its financial and management stress and the impact on the millions seeking sanctuary. Corruption in weaker nations surrounding conflict zones has created an environment for criminal gangs to take advantage of refugees and raise money to find ways to avoid border checks. International responses to this threat do little to address the weak governance that is the source of the problem.

As Michael Spence (2011) has observed, these problems are compounded by the need to spread growth beyond national boundaries and industrialized country horizons set by the G7/8[17] grouping of countries. Macroeconomic management, both nationally and globally, has been greatly complicated by increasing economic interdependence and the consequent growing role of emerging market countries and transnational operations of corporations. International cooperation to address cross-border issues of taxation and capital flows and to manage global balances in a 'multi-speed world' is becoming increasingly necessary. Many eminent thinkers have pointed to the practical imperative of finding common ground for tackling this interconnected mass of problems through multilateral action, with particular emphasis on the emerging role of the G20.[18]

In the initial years, however, G20 agendas were largely confined to its main remit of economic and financial reforms, though the issues of refugees and the Paris terrorist attack were taken up in the Communiqué of the 2015 summit under Turkey's presidency. While G20 summits now tackle a wider range of issues, concerns regarding the extent to which the G20 can help improve global cooperation have increased following the inauguration of President Trump. Brittaney Warren,[19] a researcher for G7/8, G20 and BRICS Groups, reports on a comparison between the 213 commitments (described as collective, politically binding, and future oriented) made in the G20 Leaders' commitments in Hangzhou on September 2016 and President Trump's inaugural priorities. These priorities were identified and compared with relevant G20 issue areas and assessed as fully matched (+1), partially matched (0) or not matched (−1) with the Hangzhou commitments. Strong mismatches were assessed on trade and financial stability, with the most strongly mismatched being on climate change and diversification of the energy mix. While three of the president's priorities *do* match specific G20 commitments—leveraging public-private partnerships, expanding vocational and technical training, and increasing infrastructure investment—his proposals are aimed specifically at America (and aim also to support fossil fuel production).

These assessments are of course very preliminary, and the actual direction of US policy will take some time to be fully clarified. First, actual policies will be shaped through the US Congress and judicial system of budget and regulatory approval. The likely long-term implications of the president's domestic and trade agendas and their international impact became more apparent after he met G7 World leaders in Taormina, Sicily in May, 2017, and then the G20 leaders in Hamburg, Germany in July.[20]

> **Global Security: The Ultimate Collective Good**
>
> The world in the twenty-first century is vastly different from that of the early twentieth, but the lessons from the last century have not been adapted sufficiently to address present realities or the possibility of creating more effective institutions to handle the all-too similar threats that are arising. We noted in Chap. 1 that while national security and defence constitutes a classical non-rival, non-exclusive public good, it is no longer so in a global context; rather, international competition to shore up national or regional defences and security arrangements often constitutes or is interpreted as a threat to those outside the national or regional arrangement. And, as Ferguson's description of the lead-up to WW1 described in Chap. 2 illustrates, diplomatic missteps leading to inter-nation military action may give rise to consequences bordering on global insanity.
>
> Richard Haas (2017) has introduced the valuable concept of 'sovereign obligations' that may in the long run help nations, particularly those with hegemonic or regional obligations, to recognize these obligations and take due regard of the national and global costs of ignoring such obligations. In many respects this concept parallels that of the need to recognize forms of capital beyond those of traditional financial and commercial transactions (Chap. 4); a similar recognition of global obligations applies even more strongly in the sphere of global security. Indeed, the question of climate change (see Chap. 6) is cited by Haas as one of the key dimensions of sovereign obligation.

(continued)

A Clash of Institutions: The Difficult Path to Multilateral... 235

Haas recognizes that it will take a great deal of time and consultation to define the full scope and nature of sovereign obligations. But it is also clear from his paper that many of the elements are already implicitly on the table through the UN processes concerning health, education, environment, refugees, SDGs and so on. Too many strategic issues that affect these areas of acknowledged international concern, however, are dominated by strategic moves and concerns of the main hegemonic and regional contenders for power; these quite clearly aim at short- to medium-term strategic or tactical gain with minimal recognition of sovereign responsibilities.

One of the newest, rapidly unfolding and most significant areas of conflict both internationally and between public and private interests is that of control over cyberspace, some key aspects of which were discussed in Chaps. 1 and 2. Haas suggests "international arrangements...[to] maintain a single integrated global network" (pp. 5–6). Many of his proposed controls would be extremely difficult to put in place, but the longer that action to address the issue of global cyber-control is delayed the greater will be both the current level of risks and potential long-term costs.

All of these areas of global concern and their vulnerabilities are readily identifiable, have high long-term risks, and need to be addressed as soon as possible. But who is going to take the initiative and lead the international community towards designing a more secure future?

The US itself is going through a critical series of regime and major policy changes that will continue to have a major impact on the world's security outlook. The failure of the Bush administration's attempts to impose regime change in the Middle East is now acknowledged as a major misstep. The subsequent attempts of the Obama administration to avoid deepening engagement in the Middle East, the disappointment of the Arab Spring, and US support for overthrow of Assad combined with uncertain support for various anti-Assad groups[21] in Syria are all situations that have allowed the Putin regime to establish a commercially and strategically advantageous position in the region. Continuation of these policies seemed unlikely either to lead to resolution of conflict or to establish the US as the natural leader of conflict resolution in any part of the world. Some degree of forceful confrontation will be unavoidable, but these confrontations must be contained as much as possible and long-term solutions sought through UN-sponsored mechanisms and negotiations. At some point, reform of the UN Security Council processes seems necessary.

The Trump administration's approach is not yet predictable. Acceptance of any form of sovereign responsibility towards global objectives is wholly absent from Trump's initial America-first stance. While there are some more moderate voices in the legislature and indeed in the Trump team, Republicans seem prepared to consolidate their position by removing as much of the Obama legacy as possible. Perhaps some of those actions will be mellowed by

(continued)

internal debate and public reaction or may have political consequences in the midterm elections. But there are also powerful conservative voices advocating a tough realpolitik stance towards foreign policy and national security. Niall Ferguson and Henry Kissinger are prominent advocates of America adopting a tough stance to withstand threats against the 'legitimacy of the postwar world order' as outlined in Ferguson's 2016 *Public Interest* article.[22] Their proposal purports to take advantage of Trump's supposed realism and deal-making abilities to use America's power to form strategic relationships, particularly with China and Russia, and return to a vision of the world ruled according to 'spheres of influence'. As a 'corollary', Ferguson suggests the three powers "might agree on the demotion of Europe from great power status".

Should Trump's presidency move too strongly in this direction it would make global governance and stability a distant dream for many. The global community needs to weigh in on these debates strongly and as soon as is politically practicable. Realpolitik as outlined in the Ferguson article represents a turn back to the politics of nineteenth-century Europe, the disastrous consequences of which Ferguson describes eloquently. The US is more than its current president and must begin, along with other nations, to acknowledge the very real benefits that the UN and BWI system has brought to the world and support its future development. They also need to begin examining the costs and benefits of foreign policy transactions through considering the relative global advantages of them, rather than as a continuation of spheres of uncertain influence by self-appointed major powers. Haas' notion of sovereign responsibility seems worth developing further along these lines.

Summary of Themes and Conclusions

The challenge that all governance reform proposals face is that change possibilities are determined by the existing institutions and those currently in power. The chapter has outlined how our present institutions, while broadly understood by most, have been inadequately defined and documented. They now present considerable barriers to reforms, ones that cannot happen unless these institutions change, as described in preceding chapters. The threats of market fundamentalism and the recent rise in populism and its potential for exploiting popular discontent make it urgent that we deepen our understanding of the nature of our present rules and their potential to change. These rules do not appear to be sufficiently developed to encourage the reforms needed to increase global well-being and avoid the conflicts and carnage that have plagued much of the twentieth century.

The rule of law is widely cited as being fundamental for efficient market operations, as well as being the basis for social justice, yet the precise nature of rule of law and its dynamics are not well defined or understood. Encouraging research is underway: the World Justice Project has compiled an index from key elements of the rule of law to help define its broad nature and as a basis for analysis of the relationship between these elements and progress across countries; the V-DEM project has established a database of more than 350 indicators of democracy across a wide range of countries. These important studies will help establish the key parameters that can help explain the nature of democracy and the dynamics of social progress.

Progress in behavioural theory has had a considerable impact on modern economics and in understanding political dynamics. But much of this work has yet to be fully absorbed in political theory or practice. The work of Kahneman and Tversky and other psychologists and neuroscientists has shown the fallibility of economic assumptions of rational behaviour by the individual and the group. Too many decisions in practice are governed by rules of thumb, and this empirical evidence puts in doubt the value of economic equilibrium theory taken in isolation. Institutionally, these findings suggest the need for deliberative political mechanisms to guide the operations of the market. Allied to these findings, the work of John Zaller on the formation of public opinion, which is founded in part on Walter Lippmann's views on public opinion and democracy, suggests a model of public opinion formation that helps explain recent electoral developments in the US and elsewhere.

The chapter advocates a continued steady move towards a system of deliberative democracy that can reconcile individual and national aspirations with broader cosmopolitan values that recognize each sovereign nation's obligations to foster global well-being. Thus far, the UN, despite being relatively neglected by the post-WW2 power nations (led by the US), has achieved a great deal in establishing universal principles of human rights, treatment of refugees, international justice, MDGs and SDGs, and many other areas of broad human concern. No single nation can establish these cosmopolitan values on which the future of humanity depends. Ultimately, hegemonic ambitions must become reconciled with the common global good.

Such aspirations, however, demand understanding of a much broader view of human potential and of the way deliberative governance can operate to achieve global well-being. These issues are taken up in the final chapter.

Notes

1. Antonin Scalia (1989) registered the case for a conservative approach to the interpretation of the US Constitution and its body of laws, arguing that "the Rule of Law and the law of rules...be extended as far as the nature of the question allows; and that...where [appellate judges]...have finally reached the point when we can do no more than consult the totality of the circumstances, we are acting more as fact-finders than as expositors of the law" (p. 1187). Many would argue for the law to be more open to change as society changes. President Trump, however, by his actions challenges this conservative interpretation of the Constitution as well as the right of litigants and lawmakers to verify the facts justifying his executive actions.
2. These comprise nine factors: Constraints on Government Powers; Absence of Corruption; Open Government; Fundamental Rights, Order and Security; Regulatory Enforcement; Civil Justice; Criminal Justice; and Informal Justice. Each factor has a series of dimensions that can be assessed to compile a composite index.
3. See for instance the discussion of the role of elites in WDR 2017, pp. 18–26, where interesting data on the role of elites is used to illustrate a discussion of how the thinking of elites can be formed to affect development policy change. This perspective also informs much of the philosophy underlying the MDG/SDG programs of the UN. There is little doubt that professional expertise is needed, but I argue that it should work by supporting country governance structures, not by supplanting them.
4. A substantial literature has grown on the topic of path dependency with an emphasis on including key variables of existing institutional states as variables helping to determine future states (see Kallberg and Lakomaa (2016) about a link between administrative inertia and implementation

of an EU directive by Sweden; such studies are useful but say little about changing the rules of the game).
5. He also briefly discusses the importance of the concept of parrhesia as a key element of democracy (p. 36).
6. See https://www.v-dem.net/media/filer_public/f9/08/f908eb53-c0e2-40f0-9294-e067537d8f0b/v-dem_policybrief_5_2016.pdf
7. Michael Lewis (2017) gives an excellent, and, as usual, highly readable overview of the relationship between Kahneman and Tversky and their work with a variety of behavioural and mathematical psychologists. His analysis gives a near-Kuhnian deconstruction of the process of paradigm change as well as an excellent biography of the intense intellectual relationship between Tversky and Kahneman.
8. To be fair, economists did not conceive of homo economicus as representing actual human decision-makers, but rather that the observed choice (revealed preference) represented considered choices and thus gave an authentic measure of utility value.
9. See Kahneman (Kindle Locations 371–375). Penguin UK. Kindle Edition.
10. Kindle Locations 297–298. Penguin UK. Kindle Edition. By 'inconsequential' he means information that doesn't materially affect the factual information but gives it from a different perspective. The point is illustrated by Kahneman as follows: "Different ways of presenting the same information often evoke different emotions. The statement that 'the odds of survival one month after surgery are 90%' is more reassuring than the equivalent statement that 'mortality within one month of surgery is 10%'. Similarly, cold cuts described as '90% fat-free' are more attractive than when they are described as '10% fat'. The equivalence of the alternative formulations is transparent, but an individual normally sees only one formulation, and what she sees is all there is." Kahneman, Kindle Locations 1592–1596. Penguin UK. Kindle Edition.
11. Kahneman (Kindle Locations 6792–6805). Penguin UK. Kindle Edition.
12. See https://hellenicnews.com/dumps-clinton-trump-professor-robert-zaller-special-hellenic-news-america/
13. The structure and history of the US Constitution is covered well in Wikipedia (see https://en.wikipedia.org/wiki/United_States_Constitution)

14. A term introduced by Samuel Huntington, as cited by Fukuyama, "to explain political instability in many newly independent countries after World War II" (p. 8).
15. In this context Mann and Ornstein (2012), writing just prior to the Obama second term election, concur with much of Fukuyama's diagnosis of institutional decay, but attribute much of the deterioration to the limited success of the Obama administration in achieving bipartisan support and consistent blocking of all initiatives in the Senate. They expressed the hope that Republicans would be more cooperative in Obama's second term. In the event, the loss of both House and Senate to the Republican Party hardened their resolve. The politics of the Obama era through to the ascension of Donald Trump is well presented in the PBS documentary *The Divided States of America* (January 2017).
16. Few major economists think that Trump's economic agenda will benefit the members of his electoral base. Nouriel Roubini (Project Syndicate, February 2, 2017) argues that his "undesirable mix of excessively loose fiscal policy and tight monetary policy will tighten financial conditions, hurting blue-collar workers' incomes and employment prospects". https://www.project-syndicate.org/commentary/trump-market-honeymoon-over-by-nouriel-roubini-2017-02?utm_source=Project+Syndicate+Newsletter&utm_campaign=c2b7198853-sunday_newsletter_us_subscribers_2_5_2017&utm_medium=email&utm_term=0_73bad5b7d8-c2b7198853-104959537
17. Since Russia's annexation of Crimea in 2014, the G8 grouping excluded Russia.
18. Both Spence (2011) and Berggruen and Gardels (2013) argue strongly for development of the G20 as a necessary forum to broaden the debate and as more likely than the G7/8 grouping to achieve cooperative agreements in the increasingly complex global economy. Spence makes many important points about the interdependence of developing country growth with that of the global economy (the 'great convergence') and argues that it is essential for OECD countries to have a basic knowledge of the evolution of these economies, which are becoming increasingly important systemically (pp. 6–7). Berggruen and Gardels emphasize the dysfunction that afflicts much of Western democracy and argue that failure to respond to the challenges of convergence "will result in a crisis of legitimacy for any governing system" (p. 13). Jeffrey Sachs (2008) also sees the need for

shaping new forms of government and improving intergovernmental processes and argues for the necessity of revitalizing the UN.
19. See http://www.g7g20.com/articles/brittaney-warren-from-trump-s-inauguration-to-the-g20-hamburg-summit
20. The first official encounter of Finance Ministers and Central Bank Governors at Baden Baden, on 17–18 March 2017, failed to clarify the US position, and the meeting resolved to avoid strong language on trade until the US position could be clarified. See http://www.reuters.com/article/us-g20-germany-trade-idUSKBN16P0FN. For a discussion of the Presidents G7 and G20 meetings, see Epilogue.
21. As Jeffrey Sachs notes, "funding an anti-government rebellion in another country...is completely prohibited under international law". https://www.project-syndicate.org/onpoint/navigating-the-new-abnormal-2017-02?utm_source=Project+Syndicate+Newsletter&utm_campaign=308bbd36ad-op_navigating_the_new_abnormal_2017_2_3&utm_medium=email&utm_term=0_73bad5b7d8-308bbd36ad-104959537
22. With respect to national security and foreign policy, supportive comments on Trump's early foreign policy moves have also been made by Matthew Kroenig (2017), a strong critic of Obama's policies with respect to Iran and Syria. He argues that the US must take a strong stand against both Russia and Iran, and that Trump, with some missteps has assembled a strong 'A-team' to put these policies in place.

From quite a different perspective, Rhoula Kalaf, in the *Financial Times* of April 26, 2017, has suggested that "there are important mitigating factors to the bluster from the White House. The first is that the president has little expertise but is willing to learn; the second is that he's a delegator-in-chief, taking the lead on the rhetorical front but leaving it to his lieutenants to devise and implement policy; and the third is that despite the influence of mavericks like Steve Bannon at the White House, foreign policy is being firmly led by two responsible and more mainstream-thinking grown-ups: James Mattis, the defence secretary, and Rex Tillerson, the secretary of state. The pair meet regularly and co-ordinate policy, the latter has good access to the president, and they are both buttressed by another sensible character—HR McMaster, the new national security adviser".

It's too early to say, but it's possible Trump may not turn out to be the 'destructive bozo' that Robert Mercer wished to place in the White

House (see earlier reference to Jane Mayer [2017]). So far, however, Trump policies on climate change appear to be fulfilling all negative expectations.

References

Berggruen, Nicolas, and Nathan Gardels. 2013. *Intelligent Governance for the 21st Century: A Middle Way Between West and East*. Cambridge/Malden: Polity Press.
Coase, Ronald. 1960. The Problem of Social Cost. *Journal of Law and Economics* 3: 1–44.
Coppedge, Michael, John Gerring, and others. 2011. Conceptualizing and Measuring Democracy: A New Approach. *Perspectives on Politics* 9 (2): 247–267.
Coppedge, Michael, Staffan Lindberg, Svend-Erik Skaaning, and Jan Teorell. 2016. Measuring High Level Democratic Principles Using the V-Dem Data. *International Political Science Review* 37 (5): 580–593.
Dunn, John. 2005. *Setting the People Free: The Story of Democracy*. London: Atlantic Books.
Elkins, Zachary, Tom Ginsburg, and James Melton. 2009. *The Endurance of National Constitutions (2009)*. Kindle ed. New York: Cambridge University Press.
Ferguson, Niall. 2016. Donald Trump's New World Order: What a Kissinger-Inspired Strategy Might Look Like. *The American Interest* 12 (4).
Fukuyama, Francis. 2014. America in Decay: The Sources of Political Dysfunction. *Foreign Affairs* 93 (5): 5–26.
Haas, Richard N. 2017. The Case for Sovereign Obligations. *Foreign Affairs* 96 (1): 2–9.
Kahneman, Daniel. 2011. *Fast and Slow Thinking*. London: Allen Lane.
Kallberg, Jan, and Erik Lakomaa. 2016. Institutional Maximization and Path Dependency: The Delay of Implementation of the European Union Public Sector Information Directive in Sweden. *JeDEM* 8 (1): 84–101. (ISSN 2075-9517) PDF.
Keane, John. 2009. *The Life and Death of Democracy*. New York/London: W.W. Norton.
Kroenig, Matthew. 2017. The Case for Trump's Foreign Policy: The Right People, the Right Positions. *Foreign Affairs*, Comment: May/June.

Lewis, Michael. 2017. *The Undoing Project: A Friendship That Changed Our Minds*. New York: W.W. Norton & Co.

Mann, Thomas E., and Norman J. Ornstein. 2012. *It's Even Worse Than It Looks: How the American Constitutional System Collided with the New Politics of Extremism*. Kindle ed. New York: Basic Books.

Markus, Gregory. 1994. The Nature and Origin of Mass Opinion. By John Zaller, Review. *The Public Opinion Quarterly* 58 (4): 633–636. Published by Oxford University Press on Behalf of the American Association for Public Opinion Research.

North, Douglass C. 1992. *Transaction Costs, Institutions, and Economic Performance*. San Francisco: International Center for Economic Growth Publication/ICS Press.

Sachs, Jeffrey D. 2008. *Common Wealth: Economics for a Crowded Planet*. New York: The Penguin Press.

———. 2012. Government, Geography and Growth: The True Drivers of Economic Development. *Foreign Affairs* 91 (5), September/October 2012 (see also http://jeffsachs.org/2012/12/reply-to-acemoglu-and-robinsons-response-to-my-book-review/).

Scalia, Antonin. 1989. The Rule of Law as a Law of Rules. *The University of Chicago Law Review* 56 (4): 1175–1188.

Spence, Michael. 2011. *The Next Convergence: The Future of Economic Growth in a Multispeed World*. New York: Picador/Farrar, Strauss and Giroux.

8

Ideas, Power and Social Progress

Foucault and modern social and philosophical investigation have in many ways rearranged the nature of humanity's philosophical project. Foucault frequently denied being a philosopher, and I certainly lay much less claim to that discipline. No thinker, however, can avoid being confronted by the vast literature of philosophy and its diverse heritage of exploration of the meaning of existence and of our physical surroundings. Foucault's major contribution to investigating these issues with respect to individual and societal truth was his formulation of the transformations of social experience as epistemes, as described in Chap. 1. This concept captures the main elements of the way that society reaches new appreciation of advances in social understanding, or 'truth', through the ever evolving contest between ideas (spanning many 'structural' disciplines) and power at all levels.

Foucault identified the key biological forces that need to be controlled and the necessity for understanding how interactions among competing disciplines and separate structuralist areas of thought could lead to disastrous outcomes. His work provides a powerful benchmark from which to challenge the main ideological strands that continue to compete for power over the direction of families, tribes, nations, and ultimately the global community. We are all tackling the same set of philosophical and life problems, and whatever the professional starting point, recorded knowledge has expanded enormously and is now almost universally accessible. Barriers between disciplines need to be broken down further, particularly between economics, political science and behavioural theory—and, one surmises, even within philosophy itself.

From Plato to Kant, the metaphysical (or ontological) element of classical philosophy aimed to establish fundamental explanations of the nature of being that are arguably accessible through the exercise of reason alone. Kant argued that categories of knowledge exist that are only accessible by reason and are independent of experience. His elaboration of the nature of fundamental (or *a priori*) knowledge aimed in part to counter Hume's propositions that all knowledge is based on sensory experience and that a clear explanation of causal relationships is not self-evident. His *Critique of Pure Reason* elaborated the categories of knowledge that precede sensory experience and others, such as space and time that are intuitive. While these concepts have long been accepted as among the most significant contribution to the philosophical agenda, modern developments in science, ontology and epistemology suggest that Kantian categories and intuitive knowledge are themselves subject to doubt, revision and improvement; space, time and the nature of logic and mathematics are open to further thought, even experiment, and deeper understanding.

The classical distinction between ontology and epistemology thus, though intellectually and historically vital, has become less relevant—a past episteme. All types of knowledge should now be appreciated as open to new understanding and experience through exchange of ideas, our understanding at any time being acknowledged as limited, though growing—possibly exponentially. This is broadly the case made by Deutsch in *The Beginning of Infinity*. He applies Popperian principles of conjectures and refutations to all forms of knowledge, the physical and biological sciences, social sciences, ethics and aesthetics, to achieve progressively better explanations. As we have discussed, however, important distinctions need to be drawn between these different areas of science and philosophy when we are pursuing self-knowledge, but the general principle of seeking open debate and better explanation across all disciplines seems incontestable. In this final chapter we look at ways in which the variety of disciplines discussed throughout the book can be coordinated more effectively in a socio-philosophical model of epistemic development and social progress towards truth.

A Model of Episteme Formation and Testing

Twentieth-century advances in the physical and biological sciences have transformed not only technology and life prospects but our whole concept of the possible nature of being. Life's possibilities in the seventeenth century were appreciated mainly from the point of view of individual cognition tempered with visions of perfect knowledge arising either from religious faith or transcendental knowledge of first principles. The Cartesian *cogito* and supposed ontological proofs of the existence of a deity were major themes of the philosophical debates of that time, but though several strands remain relevant today, most of the old arguments have been largely laid to rest.

The ever-increasing likelihood of humanity being able to explain the nature of its *biological sentience, salience* and *sapience* is now at the centre of modern philosophical and scientific explanations. The salient dimension of intelligence was undoubtedly critical from an early stage, when perception and understanding of what was essential for species survival was needed; our modern developed sapience is even more in need of these instincts in a much more complex world. The nature of evolution and of the emergence of biological sentience and consequent sapience has been explored sufficiently to suggest that we will (because of our acquired knowledge-seeking abilities, but undoubtedly over a very long time) be able to understand reasonably well how the laws of physics and biological developments have led to the progression of our self-awareness to the point where humanity will understand the basic mechanics of development of its own sapience.[1] The unity of body and mind is now largely accepted in science and philosophy. The essential unity of life and the evolution of human self-understanding are miracles that need to be understood as clearly as possible to diagnose how that understanding can best be used to avoid tribal and civilizational clash and take us beyond a Darwinian struggle for survival.[2] In the very long term, the development of non-biological sentience, salience and sapience seems likely to be a necessary step for long term-survival of human-gained knowledge in this galaxy and beyond.

The change towards interdisciplinary coordination is underway. The breakthrough work done by Kahneman and Tversky to introduce empirical psychological investigation to modify the basic assumption of utility maximization applied by economics to explain human behaviour was described earlier. These ideas have introduced a valuable new theoretical dimension to economics, which so far has challenged conservative neoclassical economics in a relatively modest way. As discussed earlier, Kahneman argues for state intervention at least to the extent that individuals should be protected against the consequences of system 1-dominated (fast-thinking) choices, such as ensuring that contracts provide full and clear information and do not hide details in pages of fine print, or by requiring opt-out rather than opt-in clauses in company savings schemes for employees. He also argues for careful *framing* of choices to ensure that individuals are protected from manipulation of the way in which choice questions are put forward—for instance, whether gains or losses are emphasized. But this interpretation of behavioural theory is two-edged; it informs both social protective impulses and social manipulation. The latter form of engagement seems most attractive to commercial and ideological interests—both the advertising industry and those seeking political power can and do take advantage of the persuasive opportunities opened by knowledge of system 1 thinking. The question of which use of these theoretical developments should dominate is ultimately a moral one. That question should be addressed by good government—seeking social truth—rather than by commercially oriented enterprises or political manipulators.

The implications of Kahneman/Tversky's theories and related developments in neuroscience thus go well beyond marginal improvements to economics. The phenomenon of fast-thinking helps to explain public support of ideologies that are not well supported by fact-based evidence and the difficulties of encouraging political debate over complex social policies, such as humane policies toward refugees and asylum seekers, or care of the environment and climate change. John Zaller's model of

A Model of Episteme Formation and Testing 249

interaction between elite discourse (system 2 thinking) and the public—tiered into 'informed minorities' and the broad public—primarily operating under system 1 thinking, seems to describe current public behaviour fairly and in a way that is open to testing. Government, in principle, has the authority and can apply system 2 processes to develop its policies, which should extend to ensuring that public policies are framed accountably. A well-articulated policy of establishing (or in many cases, restoring) Zaller-type elite knowledge-based (system 2-type) structures that are accountable both to the sovereign state and to the broad public could help overcome the present widespread breakdown between governments and the people they govern.[3] The term 'elite' is often used pejoratively because expert power like any other power is open to abuse; stronger accountability for performance by both elites and government will be critical to establish effective system-2 governance. A populist alternative to shape social media into a deliberative force for more direct rule by the people seems much less likely and more dangerous.

Figure 8.1 below brings these interlocking sets of ideas together. The diagram illustrates the contest of forces that could operate within social discursive frameworks along the lines of Foucauldian epistemes but incorporating Popperian principles of empirical methodology and Kahneman's portrayal of rival heuristic and analytical systems of decision-making. The top half of the diagram shows the main elements of society's slow-thinking, system 2 processes; the bottom characterizes the main elements of fast-thinking in day-to-day exchanges—including social media. The upper half shows the central driving forces of ideas and power generating both better explanations of individual and social experience and developing social institutions. The overall driving mechanism for validating ideas is the Popper/Deutsch infinite process of evidence-based conjecture and refutation. Conjectures give rise to a degree of belief, perhaps particularly by the initiator, but inevitably questions and doubt arise and may lead to reformulation or complete refutation, in turn giving rise to fresh conjectures.

The elements of doubt and refutation would apply with most force in the system 2 sphere. The system 1 domain, however, would tend to be driven very much by entrenched/traditional beliefs—except to the extent that elite communication to the broad public is effective. Common

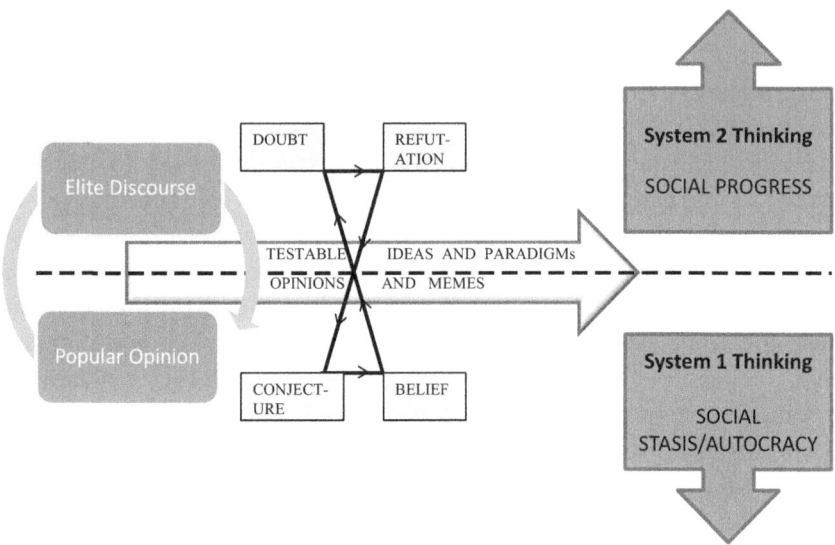

Fig. 8.1 Ideas, power and social progress (Source: Author)

experience in less developed governance structures, however, suggests that politico-social decisions are not governed by a systematic objective contest of ideas; power and influence over heuristic decision-making is often the dominant influence in this domain. System 1 thinking and power dynamics can drive public support to ideas that may be easily open to objective refutation; conjecture leads to belief buttressed by power.

Good governance processes should therefore ensure that the nature of the choices is presented in a way that is most likely to develop the best explanations of likely consequences, and moral as well as economic dimensions. A good civil service and independent media and civil society have generally been regarded as essential supports to government and to effective social discourse. Good government should enshrine these requirements in the design of its institutions. Democracy has long been seen in the West as a sufficient guarantee of good government, but as argued in Chap. 7, these assumptions need increasingly to be questioned—not by rejecting democracy, but by looking critically at the detailed nature of these institutions.

The model of social discourse presented in the diagram also suggests a nuanced view of both the philosophical approaches to ethical and moral questions and the divide between judgements of fact and value. Morality[4] is concerned with social valuation of good versus bad or evil and is therefore subject to community or religiously defined beliefs and standards; ethics on the other hand aims to establish standards of good social based on reasoned examination of the effects of individual or community actions on self and others. Morality is very much a product of system 1 thinking and often subject to stasis; ethics emerges from a system 2 approach—and it, like science, is open to doubt and progressive improvement.[5]

On the fact/value divide, our conception of 'fact' is based substantially on observation of physical events that can be confirmed by other observers; judgement of value, however, stems from subjective assessment, but that too can be recorded and its merits debated by others. Economic data, as discussed in Chap. 4, primarily represents observations of the value of commercial transactions rather than the physical empirical evidence central to the physical sciences. This point does not invalidate the application of the scientific method to social science; it does, however, open the door to a wider range of methodology and to strong methodological disagreement.

These characteristics offer a radically fresh starting point for social theory; in terms of improving government they point to the need for a thorough reappraisal of the whole range of governmental institutions, democratic or otherwise. Kahneman's concept of system 1 thinking is thus much more than a mere addendum to standard economic theory; rather the overall model of scientific and social interaction opens new avenues to help generate a much broader social explanation of the role of government and how to address its present weaknesses.

A key element of the model is that continuous opening of ideas to questioning is the most important tool that society possesses to guarantee social progress and to avoid the socially inhibiting effects of the raw exercise of power. Logically, the two systems of individual and social deliberation could be firmly linked by observing the rule that *no belief*[6] *is immune to doubt and possible refutation*—the line in the diagram linking system 1 belief to system 2 doubt. Over time, as ideas, science and social progress are progressively improved by better explanations, the process of conjecture and refutation itself will be strengthened. Design of appropriate measures toward this end, however, depend crucially on system 2 operations—and these operations depend in turn on a form of government to encourage and harness spontaneous individual initiative. Good government will face many difficult and highly contested social issues, but in order to address any of them its institutional framework must be robust enough to manage all competing interests; all beliefs and vested interest should be regulated even-handedly.

Bad government can and has taken many forms. The worst have been characterized by autocratic rulers who believe that they have access to the knowledge and power to command all state activities. Louis XIV, who declared "l'état, c'est moi" is a prominent example, though his reign helped set the scene for the excesses of the regime, for the French Revolution, and ultimately the development of representative democracy in the West. Hitler and Stalin set much worse examples led by 'incontestable' ideological belief, leading ultimately to massive armed conflict in the former case and overpowering military build-up and Western economic victory in the latter.

Neoliberalism has not been incontestable but the alliance between ideologically committed politicians and selected economic theory has tilted the balance of public opinion away from reliance on expert theory and debate towards heuristic political judgements and simple slogans. Arguably, this phase of political development, which led to the GFC and the faltering recovery from it, has set the stage for populist power and diminution of the authority of professional (elitist) debate over alternative theories and policies. Even more troubling is the rise of terrorism as a weapon directly aimed at suppressing debate or allowing co-existence of belief systems other than Salafi-jihadism.[7] While terrorist activities represent a relatively small risk to much of the world, they are a critical part of Middle Eastern politics, as well as a potentially significant impact on other countries with large Muslim populations—and suppression of 'terror' in some countries may be used simply to oppress legitimate protest. Terror and counter-terror also pose wider dangers for the world through the growing populist reaction in non-Muslim countries. Our only protection from the various forms of bad government is to develop (or rather redevelop) institutions for critical, evidence-based examination of policies and their basis of belief at all levels of society. While our modern institutions may suffer from decay from time to time, civil society, encouraged by international organizations and institutions, should eventually force a re-examination of the issues and a regeneration of the formal structures necessary for continuing and more equitable social development.

The degree of enlightenment of a modern state should thus be gauged by the extent to which professional, evidence-based, governmental discussion and regulation has been developed—or diminished. It is evident, however, that even in the most advanced present societies political and social structures are still very much dominated by System 1 thinking, and completely free thinking discouraged or prohibited in many social groups within all countries. There is no rapid way forward. System 2 thinking does not favour radical change through rapid adoption of untested new ideas; armed revolution, generally relying on rudimentary ideas and poorly defined alternative institutions, has proved an unreliable pathway. And on the conservative side, and part of the pivotal catch-22 we have highlighted several times, major changes must in any case be introduced by presently constituted governments who will almost invariably wish to preserve their existing power base. Nonetheless, awareness of such dilemmas and the possibility of better processes are a necessary start towards moving judiciously toward better explanations and better ways of tackling social problems.

> **It's Not Just Science or Economics**
>
> Many groups are engaged in interpretation of public policy, and not necessarily in direct deliberative discourse. The complexity of governance institutions, the fluid relationship between 'elite' discourse and the broad public, and the trajectory of recent political development, however, all indicate that neither elites nor groups formed within the broad public consistently apply system 2 methods in determining their social policy stance. Elites historically have tended to claim, and generally establish, the high ground in terms of

(continued)

science-based discourse. But discourse both within the elites and at the level of the broad public is not and never can be wholly based on scientific verification: social veridiction, as we have discussed, relies on a variety of competing mechanisms of social discourse and power relationships.

All thinkers are informed by multiple perceptions of physical and social reality. Foucault was keenly aware of the limitations of rationality and scientific explanation to aid our understanding of our own existence and environment. In *Madness and Civilization*, among others, he invoked references to Shakespeare's *King Lear*, Goya's *The Madhouse* and to Hieronymus Bosch's *The Ship of Fools* to illustrate the limits of conventionally understood Cartesian rationality as a sufficient explanation of our being. Bosch's painting he interpreted as representing the way in which lepers and other outcasts were treated by society—a graphic illustration of our incapacity to deal with those falling outside the norms of social health and rationality. More recent interpretations of Bosch suggest that this painting reflected not so much horror at the fate of the ship's passengers as a warning against irreligious behaviour.[8] But this shift does not negate the value of the reference. Literary or artistic expression conveys the importance of such experiences to both elites and ordinary people; their reinterpretation confirms the possibility of objective discussion of their significance.

David Deutsch too has made a case for recognizing the importance of aesthetic and cultural knowledge to our infinite search for truth; he argues also that we can objectively understand the nature and evolution of truth in these fields. His propositions, however, are more narrowly focused than Foucault's and dependent on meme rather than epistemic theory. In his *Why Are Flowers Beautiful?* (Chap. 14), he argues first, that beauty serves a practical purpose in terms of attracting helpful insects, but second, through millennia of experience humanity has developed a more general and objectively challengeable body of aesthetic and cultural knowledge. This knowledge is as much a part of human development as is objectively testable scientific knowledge of the physical world. It remains true that the mode of explanation and its verifiability differ appreciably when comparisons are made of scientific, mathematically more precise language to the freer, evolving forms of literature, poetry, art and music. Nonetheless most would agree that aesthetic and cultural knowledge: (a) is tangible and objectively describable; and (b) forms an essential part of the body of human knowledge. But how can these modes of perception and debate work together in promoting system 2 discourse at all levels of society?

This question echoes somewhat C.P. Snow's concern with the civilizational clash between science and the humanities in his 1959 book, *The Two Cultures*. Much has changed since then. Even before the 1960s, interchange between Snow's two cultures was on the increase. Science and 'scientism' had certainly invaded the social sciences, particularly economics. As discussed in Chap. 4,

(continued)

Keynes' economic theories were strongly oriented towards broad social and geopolitical goals, but social themes were submerged by mathematical models that focused on commercial activity, developing the System of National Accounts, and with GDP as its principle measure and target of economic progress and equilibrium. Hopes such as Keynes had for his grandchildren have gradually diminished in the neo-Keynesian world—and have not featured in either neoliberal or current populist visions of the future.

Such visions continue to be prominent in literature and art. Foucault, as we describe, chose the anarchic satire of Jarry in his choice of the Ubu metaphor to represent conflict among social disciplines. Orwell's *1984* certainly reflected similar concerns to Foucault's use of the panopticon metaphor for governments' social disciplinary mechanisms. Heller's *Catch-22*, first published in 1962, captures important tragi-comic dimensions of hierarchical rule-setting that contributes to ineffectual bureaucratic policy-making. More recently, Gary Shteyngart's *Super Sad True Love Story* draws Orwellian control and collapse of language and relationships forward to a deeply depressing vision of the twenty-first century. Artists such as William Kentridge and Ai Weiwei show many dimensions of response to their political and social environment. Viet Thanh Nguyen's stories in *Refugees* and his novel *The Sympathizer* tell compelling stories of the complex relationships that develop in civil war and in relocation to a new culture that expects only assimilation. These emotional responses contribute to broader social understanding and convey important meanings beyond structuralist models; they lead both scientists and citizens to think more deeply.

Quite likely, social theory conjectures derive in the first place from broader cultural appreciation of key social relations. Whether or not this is the case, more abstract mathematical theoretical constructs should be regularly checked against cultural understanding. Deutsch makes the important point that an abstract mathematical attribute should not be confused with a physical one with the same name.[9] This cautionary note seems particularly relevant to the social sciences, where we've argued among other things that basic measurements of production, and modelling based on such measures, can be misleading as a guide to increasing well-being.

No less an eminent theoretician than Thomas Schelling (2010) distanced himself from both economic equilibrium and game theory. Of the latter, for which he received his Nobel Prize, he considered himself a practitioner rather than a theorist, arguing that "the great contribution of game theory is probably the pay-off matrix, an accounting device comparable to the equals sign in algebra" (p. 27). His central point was that mathematical game formulations help to identify situations rather than predict solutions.

Often, it can be added, while game situations can be identified it requires a great deal of negotiation among the actual players to achieve a socially beneficial outcome. Elinor Ostrom (1990), a sociologist, undertook a series of

(continued)

studies of the institutional environment in various common pool resource (CPR) management situations (often characterized as 'tragedy of the commons', following Hardin and Olson). Like Olson, she characterized these as being examples of 'prisoner's dilemma' games, but was critical of the tendency to use game theory formulations as metaphors representing the participants being caught in 'a grim trap'. She concluded that model-based solutions were inadequate and deeper institutional reform was necessary, but "'getting the institutions right' is a difficult, time-consuming, conflict-invoking process. It is a process that requires quires reliable information about time and place variables as well as a broad repertoire of culturally acceptable rules".[10] She recommended a 'self-financed contract-enforcement game' as an alternative to the enclosed 'prisoner's dilemma; its rules were designed to give the common pool participants greater control over decisions about who could exercise fishing or grazing rights. She did not, however, see this as a panacea. Economic theory and game formulations of situations can help point to solutions, but joint efforts by public officials and participants in CPR arrangements will almost invariably be necessary to achieve a practicable and sustainable solution. Her work, which earned her Nobel laurels, points to the need for much wider engagement between disciplines and between social theory and direct involvement of public groups directly impacted by the resulting policies.

This aim can only be achieved through conscious design of discursive institutional structures at all levels of global society. No single nation is likely to achieve the knowledge and power needed to establish and control the rest of the world. Such a task will be impossible for a nation that is closed to artistic vision and critical examination of its own institutions and policies.

Where to Next?

This chapter has discussed the marvel of humanity and its extraordinary capacity to understand the nature of ourselves and the world we live in. But part of that understanding is that we have inbuilt instincts and mechanisms for defence, survival and acquisition. Our experience, particularly in recent years, is also, however, that we have an enormous capacity for destruction via WMDs and massive production of smaller lethal weaponry and organized capacity to use these weapons. Ian Morris (2014) made a case for the contribution of war to civilization over the centuries, which he summarizes as follows: First, "by fighting wars, people have created larger, more organized societies that have reduced the risk that their members will die violently (Kindle Locations 282–283)".

Second, "governments have made us safer and... war is pretty much the only way we have discovered to make governments" (Kindle Locations 318–319). Third, "the larger societies created by war have also—again, over the long run—made us richer. Peace created the conditions for economic growth and rising living standards... [although this] process too has been messy and uneven: the winners of wars regularly go on rampages of rape and plunder (Kindle Locations 319–321). Fourth, "humanity has gotten so good at fighting—our weapons so destructive, our organizations so efficient—that war is beginning to make further war of this kind impossible" (Kindle Locations 331–332).

One can readily concede that these virtues have emerged alongside violent conflict, and that perhaps, even likely, conflict was part of our initial learning process. But surely as part of that process of learning technical and industrial skills we should also have learned that governments collectively need to take every step possible to achieve global security, to address the major global threats of climate change, growing inequality and its repercussions, and achieve global economic stability. These goals cannot be achieved without developing good governance standards and good government for every major population group—ultimately for all. Morris' final point is not reassuring: war is not impossible even though mutually assured destruction (MAD) has technically been achieved.

It is essential that the world's leading nations recognize first that their bargains with other nations should acknowledge sovereign responsibility for impacts beyond the countries involved directly in limited inter-country agreements. Nation-states will remain the main centre of governance for the foreseeable future, but it is vital that all states recognize the rights of their neighbours and, over time, adopt cosmopolitan values as they evolve. However imperfect, the UN represents the best institutional development so far to achieve these goals. As stated several times, its efforts on climate change, human rights, protection of civilians and refugees are both wholly admirable and disgracefully underfunded. The latter result comes in part from neoliberal distrust of government, but also because of the complexity of its operations and weak accountability mechanisms. A new world order should embrace refinement and development of the UN/BWI system. Present proposals from the Trump administration threaten a radically different direction. If put in practice the costs may be extremely high.

Summary of Themes and Conclusions

This concluding chapter is both more and less than the sum of the themes developed throughout the book. Here we returned to the Foucault/Nietzschean thesis of humanity's capacity to establish a will to power and knowledge, but while we can establish a model of how this challenge is being addressed, we cannot establish any certainty of success, nor can we predict the future course of events. We have moved well beyond structural theories of social progress; uncertainty prevails as it always has.

Earlier chapters have nonetheless attempted to set out basic principles and measures that should be put in place to improve global well-being in all dimensions judged to be significant. While all principles and measures proposed are contestable, all were supported by evidence and argument. Chapter 7 particularly emphasized the importance of critical assessment of the institutions that permit changes in currently agreed principles and measures. All, it is argued, is possible if our institutional frameworks are also open to critical review and change. This chapter has outlined the social dynamics that could encourage progressive change. But activation of these dynamics is itself dependent on humanity's capacity to recognize its current limitations and find the will to create a set of institutions leading to a future directed by our growing intelligence rather than primitive biopolitics. The choice is ours; that choice should be based on evidence and reason.

Current trends to base policies on strongly worded but unsubstantiated assertions on critical areas of national and global public policy endanger the foundations of governance that have been established over the past two millennia. We must defend these foundations.

Notes

1. Cox and Cohen (2013; an imprint of a BBC television series—one of a sequence showing the linkage between laws of physics, cosmology and life) give an excellent and accessible overview of the linkage between the basic laws of physics and chemistry and the emergence of biological processes, from single-celled prokaryotes capable of photosynthesis through to the evolution of eukaryotes and separation of non-photosynthetic mobile life forms that, driven by sentient development found increasingly diverse ways of surviving and acquiring food and protection. Carlo Rovelli's *Reality Is Not What It Seems* (2017) *almost* provides a non-mathematician an understanding of where fundamental physics has come from and is going to! Thomas Suddendorf's *The Gap: The Science of What Separates Us from Other Animals* (2013, Basic Books/NY) gives a good evolutionary overview of the relation of human sentience to that of other animals. While he does so from the perspective of emphasizing the large differences between human and other animal sentience, it nonetheless points to the likelihood of these evolutionary trends and the nature of human sentience being explained in terms of the laws and concepts of physics. Wohlleben (2015) provides a range of evidence that mechanisms of survival and communication have evolved over time in the plant world and that these mechanisms need to be recognized in humankind's intervention and commercial exploitation of natural forest ecosystems.
2. This mode of discovery neither proves nor disproves the existence of a deity or 'designer'. The evidence that the phenomenon appears to be knowable does point to the possibility of perfect knowledge, but parallel to the dismissal of the ontological proof this possibility does not show that perfect knowledge exists now or that a supreme designer does or does not exist. Somewhat beyond the present purpose, the notion of biological sentience also raises the possibility of non-biological sentience and sapience or some grand unity of human and machine mechanisms of finding and verifying knowledge. Many, notably Kurzweill (2005) and Bostrom (2014), suggest that technological advances will enable the creation of non-biological intelligence in the not-too-distant future, leading to what Kurzweill has termed the 'singularity' where human intelligence is replaced by (or merged with) machine intelligence. Bostrom in particular sees the necessity for humans to prepare for what he describes as a series of

possible existential threats to humanity when its intelligence is superseded. The singularity concept also features in Ian Morris' (2010, *Why the West Rules for Now: The Patterns of History and What They Reveal About the Future*, Profile Books, London) writing on the evolution of economic and political systems over the past 15,000 years,) emerging from the exponential increase in scientific and technological knowledge predicted for the twenty-first century. The exponential progress of technology by humanity does not of itself guarantee that a 'singularity' is a necessary outcome. But the long-term survival of sentience would seem to require the emergence of a less vulnerable physical form for it to survive beyond the life of this planet and this solar system. Notions of human spirituality and ethics, however, would be significantly different in a non-biological entity, and the transitional issues of the emergence of non- or quasi-biological sentience would be formidable.
3. Proposals made by Berggruen and Gardels (2013) are consistent with this proposal; they argue for a middle way between West and East, whereas the present book aims to apply principles of governance that are equally applicable to all forms of government.
4. Frans de Waal (2013) provides a summary of evidence establishing an evolutionary basis for morality and emergence of basic moral behaviour among primates that is similar in a number of respects to human empathetic morality, and demonstrates (pp. 162–165) the interdependence between 'is' and 'ought' statements· ·as he notes David Hume originally intended (*The Bonobo and the Atheist: In Search of Humanism Among the Primates*, WW Norton: NY/London).
5. Simon Blackburn's *Being Good: A Short introduction to Ethics*, OUP: Oxford UK (2001) gives a clear summary overview of the philosophy of ethics. Part I: Seven Threats to Ethics, could all be discussed comfortably in terms of the fast- and slow-thinking processes illustrated in Fig. 8.1.
6. A coda, however, is that individual belief, however open to doubt, is of no consequence unless others are coerced into subscribing to it; in large part a question of power relationships.
7. The development of Islamic State thinking and ideology is well-described in Robert Manne's book *The Mind of the Islamic State* (2017), from which the term 'Salafi-jihadism' is taken.
8. A reinterpretation of Bosch's work given in the film *The Curious World of Hieronymus Bosch*, prepared for the Noordbrabants Museum for the 500th anniversary of the painter's death, emphasizes that Bosch was

deeply religious and the purpose of his paintings was primarily a moral one to show the dire consequences of sinful behaviour. At the time few were literate, so painting was a major medium for communicating moral messages.
9. He says "the mistake is to confuse an abstract attribute with a physical one of the same name. Since it is possible to prove theorems about the mathematical attribute, which have the status of absolutely necessary truths, one is then misled into assuming that one possesses a priori knowledge about what the laws of physics must say about the physical attribute" (p. 183). Penguin Books Ltd. Kindle Edition.
10. Elinor Ostrom. *Governing the Commons: The Evolution of Institutions for Collective Action* (Kindle Locations 307–308). Kindle Edition. See also Kindle Location 340.

References

Berggruen, Nicolas, and Nathan Gardels. 2013. *Intelligent Governance for the 21st Century: A Middle Way Between West and East.* Cambridge/Malden: Polity Press.
Bostrom, Nick. 2014. *Superintelligence: Paths, Dangers, Strategies.* Oxford: Oxford University Press.
Cox, Brian, and Andrew Cohen. 2013. *Wonders of Life: Exploring the Most Extraordinary Force in the Universe.* London: Harper Collins Publishers, by arrangement, with the BBC.
De Waal, Frans. 2013. *The Bonobo and the Atheist: In Search of Humanism Among the Primates.* New York/London: W.W. Norton.
Kurzweill, Ray. 2005. *The Singularity Is Near: When Humans Transcend Biology.* London: Duckworth Overlook.
Morris, Ian. 2010. *Why the West Rules – For Now: The Patterns of History, and What They Reveal About the Future.* Kindle ed. London: Profile Books.
———. 2014. *War: What Is It Good For? The Role of Conflict in Civilisation, from Primates to Robots.* Kindle ed. London: Profile Books.
Ostrom, Elinor. 1990. *Governing the Commons: The Evolution of Institutions for Collective Action.* Cambridge/New York: Cambridge University Press.
Rovelli, Carlo. 2017. *Reality Is Not What It Seems: The Journey to Quantum Gravity.* New York: Riverhead Books.

Schelling, T.C. 2010. Game Theory: A Practitioner's Approach. *Economics and Philosophy* 26: 27–46.

Wohlleben, Peter. 2015. *The Hidden Life of Trees: What They Feel, How They Communicate*. Carlton: Black Inc., an imprint of Schwartz Publishing Pty Ltd.

Epilogue

Three influences led me to write this book. First, experience advising on public financial management and good governance practices in developing countries revealed many of the limitations of international development efforts to promote governance reform programs. Second, economic and social science literature is increasingly showing that the discipline of economics cannot, by itself, provide guiding principles to improve global well-being in its broadest sense. Third, Foucault's interpretation of the way society advances through interaction among social rules and disciplines provided vital insights to the ever-evolving biopolitical contests that shape the world and its governance.

This vision, linked to recent social science explanations, pointed the way towards my final chapter's idealized model of deliberative social processes that could harness well-established methods of science in the service of rational and accountable societal ends. National and global government must seek all relevant explanations and evidence for any increase or diminution of well-being in order to create truthful and just social relationships over time. Alternative explanations, dominated by poorly contested ideological belief, seem certain to lead to societal conflict. The proposed model, however, has no predictive aspirations, instead offering a logical and evidence-supported method of political deliberation that can lead to broad and fair social progress; it does not aim to define the major variables and processes determining social progress or to predict future equilibrium or collapse.

But one way or another we must grapple with society's current set of problems. Are our current institutions and leaders inclined or capable of aspiring to a truth-seeking mode of governance? If so, what can be done to help them achieve that goal? If not, what practices seem likely to emerge to guide the global future? Answers to these questions require an intensive evaluation of current social and political trends and possibilities, a task that could only be partially explored in this book. Global society is becoming increasingly complex. The global financial crisis has become a watershed for our times and, as argued in the book, that event combined with the longer-term impact of globalization and the ICT revolution has already contributed to political decay even among the more advanced countries. The notion that market forces will or can resolve these issues without competent government intervention is untenable. However, signs of a workable regrouping of political and professional talent to tackle the existential threats to global well-being are not yet reassuring.

On the contrary, the events in the first half of 2017 suggest that evidence-based policy analysis and decision-making are under severe threat. The recent dominance of neoliberal ideology and its degeneration into what has been labelled 'populism', particularly in the US, seem now to threaten our global future, potentially as deeply as did the tragedies of the twentieth century. The ascendancy of Donald Trump to the United States presidency and his blatant lack of concern for evidence-based arguments to justify policy are deeply troubling for the US and the world. The election result itself revealed significant flaws in the United States' system of democracy; several have been highlighted in the book. President Trump's subsequent behaviour, bordering on the 'ubuesque', threatens to test the strength of US governance institutions even more. His modus operandi of using Twitter to project unsubstantiated policy ideas and Facebook to build popular support may realize a temporary popular groundswell, but ultimately he and the US will be judged by the long-term consequences.

Thus far his performance appears to have greatly damaged the credibility of US domestic and foreign policies, and most analysts, including the IMF,[1] expect the policies being proposed will fail to meet the expectations of his supporters and damage the US and world economy.

Equally worrying for the US (and the world) is that Republican majorities in both houses of Congress appear willing to support these presidential postures and tactics to retain power and support for their embedded belief that the size of government must be reduced; it is regarded as self-evident, needing no deeper debate. The long-established view of US institutions is that the elaborate system of checks and balances between federal executive, legislative and judicial branches, and between federal and state governments, ensures that policies will always be carefully evaluated and those directed for the common good will prevail. But modern political developments in the US cast considerable doubt on that comfortable understanding. The adversarial nature of the system and its successful gaming, particularly, but not exclusively, by the Republicans strongly suggests the need for deep institutional review.

That may come, but likely not with the urgency that appears warranted. And institutional economics reminds us that, while the 'rules of the game' determine what can be done, institutional change, particularly at the constitutional level, is path-dependent and fundamentally difficult. It was good news that in June 2017 the United States Supreme Court took up the case to examine the constitutionality of 'partisan' gerrymandering for the Wisconsin State Assembly.[2] It is less good that the Supreme Court itself divides on judicial ideological grounds—not unconnected to political ideology. Its composition depends on a partisan strategy over appointments, which party has the presidency, and the timing of departure of incumbents, who are appointed for life. At least the need to reduce partisanship in setting electoral boundaries is gaining the attention of the Court and a variety of ways of tackling the issue are being considered—including the possibility of measuring the 'efficiency gap' of boundary settings to assist judicial decisions.

The term 'populism' is now widely used to describe the latest direction of political ideological development. The 2016 November/December edition of *Foreign Affairs*, issued just before the presidential election, was headlined "The Power of Populism". The contributing essays and an interview with Marine Le Pen gave divergent views on what the term means; clearly, its significance varies among countries and regions and over time. Two important dimensions of the emergence of 'populism' in Europe and the US are clear: first, there has been an increasing level of discontent among lower-income sectors of the population, very often combined with hostility to competing groups because of ethnicity, religion or immigrant status. The second dimension is one of political opportunism: 'populist' politicians, such as Le Pen in France, espouse many of the views of the discontented, particularly anti-immigrant and anti-Muslim sentiments; their campaigns are built around these themes and the failure of the party in power to address the problems. The problems are real, but, for the many reasons covered in this book, they are often inadequately addressed. But no populist politicians seem able or feel any pressure to offer defensible, socially viable solutions. The Trump campaign certainly felt little such obligation, and the candidate added his own brand of high disregard for the verifiability of his claims and the practical consequences of his extreme proposals for border security, reversal of Obamacare (the Affordable Care Act) or action to limit global warming. It is not possible to gauge either the extent to which he shares the beliefs of his populist supporters or whether he will eventually give explanations showing clearly and accountably how his policies will directly benefit the country, global growth and his supporters. The US under Trump threatens to take us a very long way away from deliberative democracy—or indeed customary political and administrative practice. Is this a temporary aberration that will be corrected by the United States' constitutional strengths, or does it represent a fundamental institutional shift?

Evidence suggests that the Trump campaign was not built simply on his flamboyant show business style; it was backed by billionaire supporters and apparently substantial research on voter behaviour. As noted in the book, the particular kind of research carried out on behalf of Trump and financed by Robert Mercer and the Koch brothers, paralleled (and likely drew upon) the work on decision-making and polling carried out by Kahneman, Zaller and other behavioural and political scientists to investigate and counter the weaknesses of 'rational' decision-makers and voter behaviour. As the book observes, behavioural research has both a good and a dark side: socially constructive government can 'nudge' groups towards supporting achievement of just policies; ruthless politicians can build on these weaknesses and apply behavioural and voter research to gain political support through dog whistle slogans and promises with no intention of meeting supporters' needs. Trump's actual policies seem likely to be modified, and the administration, in its present form, seems likely to fail. The real and possibly lasting costs, however, are ineffective public policies and a badly damaged policy development processes.

Ideological conflict remains a staple force in determining the direction of national and global governance. As Martin Wolf has observed,[3] much of the so-called populist surge is a direct result of neoliberal dominance and its failure, combined with the failure of austerity measures to address the needs of economic recovery post-GFC. That case has been made broadly in Chapter 2 of this book, drawing on the analysis of Wolf, Summers, Stiglitz, Krugman and others.

The Trump administration and its Republican support, quite predictably, show no signs of recognizing the evident failures of neoliberalism. Little in their proposed policies are even superficially designed to benefit the groups drawn into the Trump camp; claims of returning job growth through automobile manufacture and coal mining are unlikely to meet the needs of unemployed workers, investors or the public good. In the long cycle of democracy, such failures of policy and political calculation should rebound on the governing party. But populism and the weaknesses already revealed in the US system give no assurance that this result will be either certain or timely.

Martin Wolf and several others[4] have described what is being put in place in the US as 'pluto-populism'. Market fundamentalists in the GOP, particularly the 'Tea Party' contingent, and powerful business interests like Mercer and the Kochs, have cobbled together a policy package that appeals to the underprivileged and disenfranchised through dog whistle messages like 'draining the (Washington) swamp', but their proposed tax reductions will benefit the already rich directly and generate few, if any, extra jobs for their gullible supporters. The IMF, Wolf and many others argue that the fiscal policy proposals issued so far (perhaps other than the proposed infrastructure boost) are inappropriate to the current state of the US economy and unlikely to deliver benefits to anyone other than the very rich. These policies, when combined with anti-Muslim and anti-Latino language, appear to be moving in the same direction as fascism in the lead up to WW2. Sherri Berman in the *Foreign Affairs* issue mentioned above prefers the label of 'right-wing populism' to 'fascism' on the grounds of the strength of US democracy (obviously so in comparison with Weimar Germany). She also warns of the need for mainstream politicians to reach out to all citizens and to avoid extremism. That conclusion may be fair, but restoration of the quality of the relatively open, policy-oriented debate of past administrations seems critical to achieve the moderation she seeks.

The political divide in the US, which has deep historical roots, adds greatly to the difficulty of determining how to or who can restore reason and evidence-based political debate. Neoliberal domination of US politics over the past 30 years, including Republican suppression of Obama reforms, has set the stage for Trumpian populism. The task of setting a new and constructive course for domestic and US-led global policy-making will test the abilities of the present crop of US politicians and professionals to the extreme. But that test must be met. Letting the present impulsive policy-making continue poses enormous dangers not just for the US but for the world. America has many talented and visionary leaders and potential leaders. They must organize more effectively and work towards institutional reform to stop the present drift to plutocracy and deeper social injustice. Fast thinking, as Kahneman has pointed out, poses grave dangers at any level of society, but these become much more extreme when impulse rules at the very highest levels of policy-making.

It is not only up to the United States; other countries, including hegemonic contenders, should play an increasingly important role—as envisaged in establishing the G20 configuration for global summitry. Richard Haas, as discussed in this book, argued that all countries should accept a sovereign responsibility for global issues. That aim, however, runs into the free-rider problem familiar to economists: countries with limited power and influence are willing to accept the benefits of hegemonic-led world order but not to pay for it. The hegemon, on the other hand, welcomes the privileges that accrue from its dominance but is generally unwilling to cover all the dangers that threaten outside its own borders. The US has undoubtedly accepted much of the burden of maintaining world order since the end of WW2, in large part because of sincere belief in democracy and American values and a deep-rooted rejection of communism as represented by the totalitarian USSR and China. The present ideological turn taken by the US signifies a much more isolationist approach. Haas (2017) argues strongly for maintenance of the earlier traditions of US-led world order. Achieving this goal will require both a significant shift from its present isolationist policy direction and a more cooperative approach to global problems by all nations. Active US encouragement of such an approach would be essential, but it will depend on maintaining—or better, increasing—the strength of the professional administration as well as longer term institutional reform through electoral change and restoration of stable policy processes.

Still, the self-centred outlook of the Trump administration is balanced by more promising developments within the US at state and city level and in other democracies, as well as in China's growing role (though the latter fuels nationalist/populist concerns within the US). Anatole Kaletsky's concept of Capitalism 4.0, discussed in this book, maintains that both democratic capitalism and directed capitalism largely accept the importance of market mechanisms, though to differing degrees. He implies that this widespread acceptance of the legitimate role of markets in the latter group will allow them to work in the interests of global progress and prosperity. For Kaletsky's vision to materialize, however, the concept of capitalism in both groups must go beyond commercial growth and take account of not just financial capital but also environmental and human capital assets. The elements of such a vision are embodied in the IIRC's recognition of six capitals outlined in Chapter 4 of this book. All entities, whether in Western democracies or planned economies, private or government, should be aware of their impact on value creation and diminution through use (or misuse) of environmental and human capital. Acceptance by all entities of responsibility for all forms of capital use and measurement and accountability for value creation or diminution in these realms is essential for Capitalism 4.0 to succeed.

Beyond these ideas, however, I have come to the view that the idea of six capitals may not define adequately all constraints and opportunities that will rule future Capitalism 4.0 societies. A seventh capital, that of access to data and management of its use by ICT-based enterprises and their algorithms, has already become a dominant commercial influence. Its management for commercial and public purposes, including global security, may be the most important challenge of this and future centuries. This issue has certainly been recognized as important in the book, but its potentially central role in creating wealth and power for its owners as well as benefits and dangers for society was not linked to the overall issue of managing the global economy and society. The reform agenda that needs to be constructed for twenty-first century society should encompass measurement, reporting and control of all seven capitals. The book acknowledges that this level of reform will only be established over the long term, but efforts need to be made in the very near future to consolidate and deepen the <IR> initiative.

The growing role that corporate finance is playing in elections in the Western world plays a major role in sustaining neoliberal power over national governance. Oligarchs in the directed capitalist economies play a similar, but likely more direct, role in the hierarchy of power in these countries. This problem is by no means new, but as politicians come more directly under the influence of corporate/oligarchic power, it becomes increasingly difficult to create pressure for reform through the ballot box. Taking firm action against corporate financing of political parties is an area of progressive political strategy that could provide a stronger basis for the more detailed and technical reforms of measurement and accountability proposed in Chapter 4 of this book.

Climate change policy, as highlighted in Chapter 6, is a vital strategic area of reform in terms of recognition of and commitment to evidence-based national and global policy-making and outcome accountability. The case for all nations to recognize the global costs of greenhouse gas emissions by use of fossil fuels for industrial and domestic energy production is overwhelming; it is opposed by narrowly focused commercial and political interests who feel no obligation to mount testable counterarguments. Despite global recognition of this mechanism in the 2015 Paris agreement, progress in tackling the strongly evidence-supported likelihood of anthropogenic climate disruption remains slow and uncertain. If anything, centrally planned economies, particularly China, have shown a much stronger commitment both to recognize the evidence and act to reduce GHG emissions. Trump's dismissal of climate change as 'a

Chinese hoax' and his decision to withdraw the US from the accord are emblematic of his lack of concern with evidence-based policy-making as well as his contempt for conventions of the past US-led world order.

These flagrant anti-science reactions have been widely criticized[5] and have encouraged counter-movements in the US and in other Western democracies. The US itself is becoming increasingly divided over social and environmental issues, partly on red/blue state lines and partly in the cities versus towns and rural dwellers dichotomy. Europe generally supports both of environmental action and social justice, but is more divided on the latter issue because of the influx of refugees from Africa and the Middle-East.[6] Australia, despite continuing public support, remains politically divided on both sets of issues; so far, too little has changed from the political impasse described in Chapter 6. But climate change action enjoys broad support by the G20, as well as at local and state level within G20 and a wider range of countries. The G20 meeting in Hamburg on July 7–8 put the sustainable use of natural resources on the agenda for the first time. As expected, particularly after the Taormina G7 meeting in June visibly displayed a rift between President Trump and other G7 leaders, the US' formal position on climate disruption changed little, even though a unanimous communiqué was issued. The communiqué took note of the US' planned exit from the Paris agreement but included words to the effect that the US would support lower emissions while supporting economic growth and energy security. Trump's performance was declared 'alarming' by Lawrence Summers.[7] The fact that most other G20 countries, other affected regions and internal state and city interests maintain strong pressure on climate change action is encouraging for the eventual acknowledgement of evidence-based policy-making. Advancing technology and the ever-increasing evidence of the impact of climate change, including vulnerable parts of the US—and in Australia on its Great Barrier Reef— should continue to build internal and global support for achieving and exceeding the Paris targets.

Support for evidence-based policy-making in the directed capitalist countries seems, at least to Westerners, less assured than in the democratic West. Centralized and oligarchic controls pay much less heed to populist discontent, and party administrations are much more inclined to allow only party-favoured candidates to enter parliament or its equivalent (such as the National People's Congress of China). But centralized-country institutions are also evolving. China is responding vigorously to the threat of climate change and environmental pollution. Interactions and policy debate bilaterally and through the UN combined with the inevitable growth of public education and awareness of alternatives appears to be leading most emerging-market countries towards policy formulation that is based on a systematic examination of evidence for and against proposed climate policies.

More generally, most of these countries are actively encouraging PFM and accounting practices based on OECD practice, and most receive extensive technical assistance and advice from the IMF, the World Bank, other multilateral development banks and the OECD.

China's establishment of the Asian Infrastructure Investment Bank (AIIB) as a means of financing global infrastructure and particularly its 'Belt and Road' (B&R) initiative demonstrates its interest in playing a strong development role. It aims to invigorate trade flows between China and the rest of the world by building better land infrastructure through Central Asia over the old silk road route (the 'Belt') and sea trade centred on Shanghai (the 'Road'), and it will offer potentially greatly extended opportunities to Central Asian countries. Of these, Kazakhstan, where I've recently worked, supported by the World Bank, OECD and IMF, is embarking on modernization policies[8] that include the adoption of fiscal management practices based on OECD standards, infrastructure investment and restructuring economy and state administration—including giving greater powers to the parliament.

China itself, through the B&R and its assertive territorial claims in the South China Sea, appears to be building claims as the new leader of the world order and the dominant power in the Asia-Pacific region. It is important, however, not to conclude too hastily that we are witnessing the ambitions of the new hegemon replacing the old. As Berggruen and Gardels suggested, it is more a matter of civilizations learning from one another and from past mistakes. They submit that Chinese 'institutional civilization' has much to teach modern democracies about accommodating different ideas to achieve a socially viable solution. Perhaps so, but all institutions need review in this rapidly changing modern world. The mandarinate in China functioned well to maintain popular well-being in the face of changing imperial fortunes. But civil services in Britain, Europe and the US have, in recent past years, served similar functions. These structures have been weakened in recent decades in the West mainly because of market fundamentalist hubris and its targeting of bureaucratic red tape more to favour business than to improve social efficiency. Party and oligarchic power have had a similar impact in centrally planned states. In the present ideologically uncertain environment, rebuilding a deliberative civil service structure with cooperative national and international arms to ensure protection of the collective good seems increasingly necessary. To this end, the Berggruen Institute continues to support high-level council support to flagship policy areas like the G20, Europe and California, although more emphasis now seems to be given to a generic search for governance ideas through the Institute's Los Angeles-based Governance Center.[9]

As this book emphasizes, a range of reforms is already underway and others are being proposed. More attention needs to be paid to strengthening and coordinating these initiatives. Radical improvement in measurement of social well-being is crucial for establishing evidence-based principles of governance. Environmental and equity concerns must be given due weight relative to the present dominance of commercial activity in present GDP-based measures. Many of the elements to improve measurement and accountability for results in these areas are already being initiated, and a wide array of international and bilateral agencies are involved in implementing aspects of the needed program. The best way to counter plutocratic and oligarchic influence on government is for governments to focus on key social issues–communicating the results and building community and national support based on measured achievements rather than dog whistle slogans. It is true that the sprawling development bureaucracy must be reformed and strengthened, but that will best be achieved by recognizing responsibility, accountability and communication focusing on improvement of social well-being rather than commercial success.

Some suggest that Chinese leadership considers that the time has come for its earlier promise to lead the world to be restored. Certainly, by force of population and engagement with modern technology and productive capacity China must take its place at the forefront of the modern world.

But, as Elizabeth Economy's recent *Foreign Affairs* review[10] of new books by Howard French and John Pomfret argues, we should not be overwhelmed by claims that China is reclaiming its rightful place in the global order. The world is much more complex and interdependent than in the days of China's eminence in Asia; global governance beyond the twentieth century must be carefully negotiated by people to ensure human survival and progress, not by imperial contenders competing for 'rightful' leadership roles. Citing French and Pomfret, Economy argues that engagement between the US and China represents the best way forward—a 'better version' of the US' efforts in the past when it had sought to 'pull China into the World'. Such a solution, however, is not well served either by the 'America First' stance adopted by the Trump administration or, as Economy notes, by China's resistance to the inward flow of foreign ideas and capital and its assertion of political, economic and military influence abroad.

Aside from the aberration of the recent US election, the factors in favour of the major nations of the world adopting more cooperative modes of national and global governance seem likely to prevail over the long term. Informed opinion generally rejects the Trump administration's approach to policy-making and populist influences on elections. Political change will not be easy, however. Lessons of history are not easily assimilated—either from long-past or recent experience. The deep experiences of racism and religious intolerance remain as part of common belief in many countries, and outside military intervention is rarely based on a deep understanding of the nature of the problems. The notion that democratic countries can enforce or give military support to regime change in tyrannies should by now have been dispelled by the 1979–89 Soviet intervention in Afghanistan, the 2003 US-led intervention in Iraq, the false hope of the 'Arab Spring' and US-led intervention in Syria. Democracy, as we've discussed, is a complex concept—not well understood even in democracies. Constructive intervention, while led by cosmopolitan principles of human rights, must rely heavily on understanding the capacity of regime opponents and should aim to establish internal governance reform capacity as the first and fundamental objective of reform support.

Institutions, as we've frequently noted, are often trapped by the past and are not well-designed to handle either the present or the future. Much of our high-level institutional legacy derives from the design of the victors, post-WW2. The UN Security Council relies heavily on the authority given to the WW2 victors and too often simply results in deadlock, thwarting constructive reform proposals. As discussed at several points in this book, neither the present hegemonic contenders nor the private sector have developed adequate answers to control and develop cyberspace for the good of humanity. Rather, this topic has become a contentious area for potential cyberwarfare as well as for competitive commercial exploitation of the Internet. The book has argued the need to understand and control the six capitals identified by the IIRC; I've suggested adding the seventh and likely pre-eminent capital, that of data and management of cyberspace. Along with many others, I've emphasized the need for stronger action to tackle the longstanding problem of corporate finance and its influence on politics. Commercial and military success followed by neoliberalism, pluto-populism and oligarchy have so far been able to set rules of the game based on the beliefs of the commercially rich and powerful. If all the evidence is properly assessed and both governments and enterprises are held accountable for how they manage the seven capitals, these ideological beliefs may be successfully challenged and imperial rule progressively replaced by deliberative democracy. Those who believe that reason and accountability of both government and commercial enterprise are an essential basis for human progress, and indeed survival, must continue to build the case against currently ascendant neoliberal and populist ideologies. A strong and unified coalition for governance reform is essential to ensure socially efficient use of the planet's resources and justice for the weak and poor.

Notes

1. http://www.imf.org/en/News/Articles/2017/06/27/ms062717-2017-article-iv-consultation-with-the-united-states-of-america.
2. https://www.washingtonpost.com/politics/courts_law/supreme-court-to-hear-potentially-landmark-case-on-partisan-gerrymandering/2017/06/19/

d525237e-5435-11e7-b38e-35fd8e0c288f_story.html?utm_term=. 6ce4d597ce03; and https://www.nytimes.com/2017/05/15/us/politics/when-does-political-gerrymandering-cross-a-constitutional-line.html. The practice in the US of legislatures setting their own federal and state electoral boundaries for partisan advantage was used as early as 1789, but the term 'gerrymander' and its practice became more established in 1812 after the governor of Massachusetts, Elbridge Gerry, signed a law that defined a salamander-shaped voting district designed to help his own party. See https://en.wikipedia.org/wiki/Gerrymandering.
3. https://www.ft.com/content/5557f806-5a75-11e7-9bc8-8055f264aa8b.
4. See https://www.ft.com/content/69fe4862-2f20-11e7-9555-23ef563ecf9a?mhq5j=e1; and https://www.ft.com/content/76def9b0-d481-11da-a357-0000779e2340.
5. See https://www.ft.com/content/5de9e360-5d15-11e7-9bc8-8055f264aa8b?segmentId=778a3b31-0eac-c57a-a529-d296f5da8125; a clear rebuttal of Trump is given in https://www.project-syndicate.org/commentary/trump-climate-change-fairness-argument-by-joseph-e--stiglitz-2017-07.
6. See Tony Barber in the FT regarding need for shifts in EU policy in this regard, https://www.ft.com/content/efa57ef4-5cbb-11e7-b553-e2df1b0c3220?desktop=true&conceptId=423f0857-e5b5-3256-a8b8-857e2378f433&segmentId=7c8f09b9-9b61-4fbb-9430-9208a9e233c8#myft:notification:daily-email:content:headline:html.
7. https://www.ft.com/content/ea2849ea-6335-11e7-8814-0ac7eb84e5f1?segmentId=7d033110-c776-45bf-e9f2-7c3a03d2dd26.
8. See http://www.akorda.kz/en/speeches/internal_political_affairs/in_speeches_and_addresses/address-of-the-president-of-the-republic-of-kazakhstan-on-the-issues-of-reauthorization-of-governmental-departments.
9. See http://philosophyandculture.berggruen.org/ideas/41.
10. See https://www.foreignaffairs.com/reviews/review-essay/2017-06-13/history-chinese-characteristics.

Reference

Haas, Richard. 2017. *A World in Disarray: American Foreign Policy and the Crisis of the Old Order*. New York: Penguin Press Random House.

References

Acemoglu, Daron, and James A. Robinson. 2012. *Why Nations Fail: The Origins of Power, Prosperity, and Poverty*. New York: Crown Business, Random House.

Allan, William. 2013. Managing Foreign Aid Through Country Systems, Chapter 25. In *The International Handbook of Public Financial Management*, ed. Richard Allen, Richard Hemming, and Barry H. Potter, 540–554. New York: Palgrave Macmillan.

Allan, William, and Keith Hinchliffe. 1982. *Planning, Policy Analysis, and Public Spending: Theory and the Papua New Guinea Practice*. Aldershot: Gower.

Allen, Danielle. 2016. Equality and American Democracy: Why Politics Trumps Economics. *Foreign Affairs* 95 (1): 23–28.

Ashendon, Samantha, and David Owen. 1999. *Foucault Contra Habermas*. London/California/New Delhi: Sage Publications.

Assange, Julian. 2015. *The WikiLeaks Files: The World According to US Empire*. London/Brooklyn: Verso.

Becker, Garry S. 1992. *The Economic Way of Looking at Life,* Nobel Lecture, December 9.

Berggruen, Nicolas, and Nathan Gardels. 2013. *Intelligent Governance for the 21st Century: A Middle Way Between West and East*. Cambridge/Malden: Polity Press.

Betley, Mary, Andrew Bird, and Adom Ghartey. 2012. *Evaluation of Public Financial Management Reform in Ghana 2001–2010*, Final Country Case Study Report, Joint Evaluation 2012.

Betts, Richard K. 2010. Conflict or Cooperation? Three Visions Revisited. *Foreign Affairs* 89 (6): 186–194.

Bhojani, Fatima. 2016. How ISIS Makes IEDs: The Supply Chain of Terrorism. *Foreign Affairs*, Web March 2.

Blackmore, Susan. 1999. *The Meme Machine*. Oxford: Oxford University Press.

Blackwill, Robert D., and Jennifer M. Harris. 2016. The Lost Art of Economic Statecraft: Restoring an Economic Tradition. *Foreign Affairs* 95 (2): 99–110.

Blyth, Mark. 2016. Capitalism in Crisis: What Went Wrong and What Comes Next. *Foreign Affairs* 95 (4): 172–179.

Brewer, John. 1989. *The Sinews of Power: War Money and the English State*. New York: Alfred A Knopf.

Bostrom, Nick. 2014. *Superintelligence: Paths, Dangers, Strategies*. Oxford: Oxford University Press.

Burchell, Graham, Colin Gordon, and Peter Miller, eds. 1991. *The Foucault Effect: Studies in Governmentality*. Chicago: University of Chicago Press.

Canning, David, Sangeeta Raja, and Abdo S. Yazbeck, eds. 2015. *Africa's Demographic Transition: Dividend or Disaster?* Africa Development Forum Series. Washington, DC: World Bank.

Chomsky, Noam, and Michel Foucault. 1971. *Human Nature: Justice Versus Power*, Noam Chomsky debates with Michel Foucault (https://chomsky.info/1971xxxx/).

CIPFA (Chartered Institute of Public Finance and Accounting). 2016. *Public Financial Management – A Whole System Approach*, Volumes 1 and 2 (http://www.cipfa.org/policy-and-guidance/reports/whole-system-approach-volume-1).

CIPFA and World Bank Group. 2016. *Integrated Thinking and Reporting <IR> Focusing on Value Creation in the Public Sector: An Introduction for Leaders*. Washington, DC: World Bank Group.

Coase, Ronald. 1960. The Problem of Social Cost. *Journal of Law and Economics* 3: 1–44.

Coppedge, Michael, John Gerring, and others. 2011. Conceptualizing and Measuring Democracy: A New Approach. *Perspectives on Politics* 9 (2): 247–267.

Coppedge, Michael, Staffan Lindberg, Svend-Erik Skaaning, and Jan Teorell. 2016. Measuring High Level Democratic Principles Using the V-Dem Data. *International Political Science Review* 37 (5): 580–593.

Cowen, Tyler. 2014. Capital Punishment: Why a Global Tax on Wealth Won't End Inequality. *Foreign Affairs* 93 (3): 158–164.

Cox, Brian, and Andrew Cohen. 2013. *Wonders of Life: Exploring the Most Extraordinary Force in the Universe.* London: Harper Collins Publishers, by arrangement, with the BBC.

Darwin, John. 2006. *After Tamerlane: The Global History of Empire.* New York: Bloomsbury Press.

———. 2012. *Unfinished Empire: The Global Expansion of Britain.* Kindle ed, xiv. London: Penguin.

Dawkins, Richard. 2006. *The God Delusion.* London: Bantam Press.

De Waal, Frans. 2013. *The Bonobo and the Atheist: In Search of Humanism Among the Primates.* New York/London: W.W. Norton.

Dean, Mitchell. 1999a. Normalizing Democracy: Foucault and Habermas on Democracy, Liberalism, and Law, Chapter 6. In *Foucault Contra Habermas: Recasting the Dialogue Between Genealogy and Critical Theory,* ed. Samantha Ashendon and David Owen. London/Thousand Oaks/New Delhi: Sage Publications.

———. 1999b. *Governmentality: Power and Rule in Modern Society.* London Thousand Oaks/New Delhi: SAGE.

Deutsch, David. 2011. *The Beginning of Infinity: Explanations That Transform the World.* London: Penguin.

Dobson, Jerome E., and Peter E. Fisher. 2007. The Panopticon's Changing Geography. *The Geographical Review* 97 (3): 307–323.

Dornbusch, Rudiger. 1996. Euro Fantasies: Common Currency as Panacea. *Foreign Affairs* 75 (5): 110–124.

Dorotinsky, William, and Joanna Watkins. 2013. Government Financial Management Systems, Chapter 36. In *The International Handbook of Public Financial Management,* ed. Richard Allen, Richard Hemming, and Barry H. Potter, 797–816. Basingstoke/New York: Palgrave Macmillan.

Dunn, John. 2005. *Setting the People Free: The Story of Democracy.* London: Atlantic Books.

Elkins, Zachary, Tom Ginsburg, and James Melton. 2009. *The Endurance of National Constitutions (2009).* Kindle ed. New York: Cambridge University Press.

Engelman, Robert. 2016. Six Billion in Africa. *Scientific American* 314 (2)

Ferguson, Niall. 2006. *The War of the World: Twentieth-Century Conflict and the Descent of the West.* New York: Penguin Group USA, Hudson Street.

———. 2016. Donald Trump's New World Order: What a Kissinger-Inspired Strategy Might Look Like. *The American Interest* 12 (4).
Flannery, Tim. 2015. *Atmosphere of Hope: Searching for Solutions to the Climate Crisis*. Melbourne: The Text Publishing Company.
Foucault, Michel. 1965. *Madness and Civilization: A History of Insanity in the Age of Reason*. Trans. R. Howard. London: Tavistock.
———. 1966. *The Order of Things: An Archaeology of the Human Sciences*. Trans. Tavistock 1970. London/New York: Routledge Classics.
———. 1969. *The Archaeology of Knowledge*. Trans. A.M Sheridan Smith 1972. London/New York: Routledge Classics.
———. 1977. *Discipline and Punish: The Birth of the Prison*. Trans. A. Sheridan. London: Penguin Books 1991.
———. 1980. *Power/Knowledge: Selected Interviews and Other Writings 1972–1977*, ed. Colin Gordon. New York: Vintage.
———. 1997a. *Society Must Be Defended: Lectures at the Collège de France (1975–76)*. English ed. Arnold I. Davidson; Trans. David Macey. New York: Picador
Foucault, Michel/Paul Rabinow. 1997b–2000. *Essential Works of Foucault, 1954–1984*, Paul Rabinow, Series Editor: Vol. 1, *Ethics Subjectivity and Truth*, (1997), Paul Rabinow, Editor: Vol. 2, *Aesthetics, Method, and Epistemology*, (1998), James D. Faubion, Editor: Vol. 3 *Power*, (2000), James D. Faubion, Editor. New York: New Press.
Foucault, Michel. 2003. *Abnormal: Lectures at the Collège de France (1974–75)*. Trans. Graham Burchell. New York: Picador/Palgrave Macmillan.
———. 2004. *Security, Territory, Population: Lectures at the Collège de France (1977–78)*. Trans. Graham Burchell; English ed. Arnold I Davidson. New York: Picador/Palgrave Macmillan)
———. 2008. *The Birth of Biopolitics: Lectures at the Collège de France (1978–79)*. Trans. Graham Burchell. New York: Picador/Palgrave Macmillan.
———. 2011a. *The Government of Self and Others : Lectures at the Collège de France, 1982–1983*. New York: Picador/Palgrave Macmillan.
———. 2011b. *The Courage of Truth (The Government of Self and Others II): Lectures at the Collège de France, 1983–1984*. New York: Palgrave Macmillan: Picador.
Friedman, Milton. 1962. *Capitalism and Freedom*, 40th Anniversary ed., 2002. Chicago/London: University of Chicago Press.

Fukuyama, Francis. 1992. *The End of History and the Last Man*. New York: Free Press.
———. 2012. The Future of History. *Foreign Affairs* 91 (1): 53–61.
———. 2014a. America in Decay: The Sources of Political Dysfunction. *Foreign Affairs* 93 (5): 5–26.
———. 2014b. *Political Order and Political Decay: From the Industrial Revolution to the Globalization of Democracy*. New York: Farrar, Strauss, and Giroux.
Garnaut, Ross. 2008. *The Garnaut Climate Change Review: Final Report*, Commonwealth of Australia. Port Melbourne: Cambridge University Press.
———. 2009. *The Great Crash of 2008*. Victoria: Melbourne University Press.
———. 2011. *The Garnaut Review 2011: Australia in the Global Response to Climate Change* (PDF http://www.garnautreview.org.au/update-2011/garnaut-review-2011/garnaut-review-2011.pdf).
———. 2013. *Dog Days: Australia After the Boom*. Collingwood: Redback.
Garton Ash, Timothy. 2012. The Crisis of Europe: How the Union Came Together and Why It's Falling Apart. *Foreign Affairs* 91 (5): 2–15.
Gleeson-White, Jane. 2014. *Six Capitals: The Revolution Capitalism Has to Have – Or Can Accountants Save the Planet*. Sydney/Melbourne/Auckland/London: Allen & Unwin.
Glennerster, R., and Y. Shin. 2008. Does Transparency Pay? *IMF Staff Papers* 55 (1): 183–209.
Greenspan, Alan. 2007. *The Age of Turbulence: Adventures in a New World*. New York: Penguin Press.
———. 2013. Never Saw It Coming: Why the Financial Crisis Took Economists by Surprise. *Foreign Affairs* 92 (6): 88–96.
Haas, Richard N. 2017. The Case for Sovereign Obligations. *Foreign Affairs* 96 (1): 2–9.
Habermas, Jürgen. 1979. *Communication and the Evolution of Society*. London: Heinemann, (German text 1976).
———. 2012. *The Crisis of the European Union: A Response*. Trans. Ciaran Cronin. Cambridge : Polity Press.
Hacker, Jacob S., and Paul Pierson. 2016. Making America Great Again: The Case for the Mixed Economy. *Foreign Affairs* 95 (3): 69–90.
Hameed, Farhan. 2005. Fiscal Transparency and Economic Outcomes, IMF Working Paper, WP/05/225, December 2005.
Hashim, Ali, and Moritz Piatti. 2016. A Diagnostic Framework to Assess the Capacity of a Government's Financial Management Information System as a Budget Management Tool, IEG Working Paper 2016/No.1.

Hayek, Friedrich August. 1944. *The Road to Serfdom*. London/New York: Routledge.
Heald, David. 2013. Strengthening Fiscal Transparency, Chapter 33. In *The International Handbook of Public Financial Management*, ed. Richard Allen, Richard Hemming, and Barry H. Potter, 711–741. New York: Palgrave Macmillan.
Heller, Joseph. 1962. *Catch-22*. Corgi. Random House/Corgi: London, UK.
Heller, Peter S. 2003. *Who Will Pay: Coping with Aging Societies, Climate Change, and Other Long-Term Fiscal Challenges*. International Monetary Fund: Washington DC.
Henshall, Nicholas. 2010. *The Zenith of European Monarchy and Its Elites: The Politics of Culture, 1650–1750*. Houndmills, Basingstoke, Hampshire: Palgrave Macmillan.
Herman, Arthur. 2013. *The Cave and the Light: Plato Versus Aristotle, and the Struggle for the Soul of Western Civilization*. New York: Random House.
Herman, Edward S., and Noam Chomsky. 1988. *Manufacturing Consent: The Political Economy of the Mass Media*. New York/Toronto: Pantheon Books of Random House. (reprinted with a new Introduction, 2002).
Huntington, Samuel P. 1993. The Clash of Civilizations? *Foreign Affairs* 72 (3): 22–49.
ICAP. 2016. *Emissions Trading Worldwide: Status Report 2016*. Berlin: ICAP.
IEO. 2014. *IMF Response to the Financial and Economic Crisis: An IEO Assessment*, Independent Evaluation Office of the IMF, November, 2014. Washington, DC: IEO.
———. 2016. *Behind the Scenes with Data at the IMF: An IEO Evaluation*, Independent Evaluation Office of the IMF, February, 2016. Washington, DC: IEO.
IMF. 2014. New Fiscal Transparency Code (http://www.imf.org/external/np/fad/trans/).
———. 2015. *Government Finance Statistics Manual 2014*. Washington, DC: IMF.
———. 2016. *Analyzing and Managing Fiscal Risks: Best Practices*. Washington, DC: IMF (PDF http://www.imf.org/external/np/pp/eng/2016/050416.pdf).
Kahneman, Daniel. 2011. *Fast and Slow Thinking*. London: Allen Lane.
Kaletsky, Anatole. 2010. *Capitalism 4.0: The Birth of a New Economy*. London/New York/Berlin/Sydney: Bloomsbury.
Kallberg, Jan, and Erik Lakomaa. 2016. Institutional Maximization and Path Dependency: The Delay of Implementation of the European Union Public

Sector Information Directive in Sweden. *JeDEM* 8 (1): 84–101. (ISSN 2075-9517) PDF.

Kausikan, Bilahari. 2017. Asia in the Trump Era: From Pivot to Peril? *Foreign Affairs*, Review Essay, May/June (online version).

Keane, John. 2009. *The Life and Death of Democracy*. New York/London: W.W. Norton.

Kelly, Mark. 2010. International Biopolitics: Foucault, Globalisation and Imperialism. *Theoria* 57 (123): 1–26.

Kenny, Anthony. 2007. *Philosophy in the Modern World: A New History of Western Philosophy*. Vol. 4. Oxford: Clarendon Press.

Kopits, George, and Jon Craig. 1998. *Transparency in Government Operations*, IMF Occasional Paper No. 158. Washington, DC: International Monetary Fund.

Kroenig, Matthew. 2017. The Case for Trump's Foreign Policy: The Right People, the Right Positions. *Foreign Affairs*, Comment: May/June.

Krugman, Paul. 2007. *The Conscience of a Liberal: Reclaiming America from the Right*. London: Allen Lane/Penguin.

Kuhn, Thomas. 1962. *The Structure of Scientific Revolutions*. Chicago: University of Chicago Press.

Kurzweill, Ray. 2005. *The Singularity Is Near: When Humans Transcend Biology*. London: Duckworth Overlook.

Lakner, Christoph. 2016. *Global Inequality: The Implications of Thomas Piketty's Capital in the 21st Century*, Policy Research Working Paper 7776. Washington, DC: World Bank Group (PDF http://documents.worldbank.org/curated/en/323831470153290439/pdf/WPS7776.pdf).

Lanchester, John. 2016. Money Trap: Can Europe Survive the Euro. *The New Yorker*, October 24, pp. 73–76.

Lemke, Thomas. 2011. *Bio-politics: An Advanced Introduction*. New York/London: New York University Press.

Lewis, Michael. 2010. *The Big Short: Inside the Doomsday Machine*. New York: W.W. Norton & Co.

———. 2017. *The Undoing Project: A Friendship That Changed Our Minds*. New York: W.W. Norton & Co.

Lieber, Keir E., and Daryl G. Press. 2009. The Nukes We Need. *Foreign Affairs* 88 (6): 39–51.

Lippman, Walter. 1922. *Public Opinion*. New York: Free Press Paperbacks; published 1997.

Lo, Stephanie, and Kenneth Rogoff. 2015. *Secular Stagnation, Debt Overhang and Other Rationales for Sluggish Growth, Six Years On*, BIS Working Papers No 482.

Majone, Giandomenico. 2012. *Rethinking European Integration After the Debt Crisis*, Working Paper No. 3. European Institute.

Mallaby, Sebastian. 2016. *The Man Who Knew: The Life and Times of Alan Greenspan*. London/New York: Bloomsbury Publishing.

Mann, Thomas E., and Norman J. Ornstein. 2012. *It's Even Worse Than It Looks: How the American Constitutional System Collided with the New Politics of Extremism*. Kindle ed. New York: Basic Books.

Manne, Robert. 2008. What Is Rudd's Agenda? *The Monthly, Long Read*, November (https://www.themonthly.com.au/issue/2008/november/1277253191/robert-manne/what-rudd-s-agenda).

———. 2016. *The Mind of the Islamic State*. Carlton: Redback Quarterly.

Martin, John P., and Michael Förster. 2013. Inequality in OECD Countries: The Facts and Policies to Curb It (PDF http://insights.unimelb.edu.au/vol15/pdf/Martin.pdf).

Masood, Ehsan. 2016. *The Great Invention: The Story of GDP and the Kaing and Unmaking of the Modern World*. New York/London: Pegasus Books.

Mayer, Jane. 2016. *Dark Money: The Hidden History of the Billionaires Behind the Rise of the Radical Right*. New York/Toronto: Doubleday/Random House.

———. 2017. The Reclusive Hedge-Fund Tycoon Behind the Trump Presidency: How Robert Mercer Exploited America's Populist Insurgency. *New Yorker*, March 27.

Mazower, Mark. 2009. *No Enchanted Palace: The End of Empire and the Ideological Origins of the United Nations*. Kindle ed. Princeton: Princeton University Press.

———. 2012. *Governing the World: the History of an Idea*. London/New York/Melbourne: Allen Lane/Penguin.

McKnight, David. 2012. *Rupert Murdoch: An Investigation of Political Power*. Sydney/Melbourne/Auckland/London: Allen & Unwin.

McPhee, Peter. 2016. *Liberty or Death: The French Revolution*. New Haven/London: Yale University Press.

Milanovic, Branko. 2016. *Global Inequality: A New Approach for the Age of Globalization*. Cambridge, MA: Harvard University Press.

Morris, Ian. 2010. *Why the West Rules – For Now: The Patterns of History, and What They Reveal About the Future*. Kindle ed. London: Profile Books.

———. 2014. *War: What Is It Good For? The Role of Conflict in Civilisation, from Primates to Robots*. Kindle ed. London: Profile Books.
Nathan, Andrew J., and Andrew Scobell. 2012. How China Sees America. *Foreign Affairs* 91 (5): 32–47.
Nietzsche, Friedrich Wilhelm. 1887. *The Genealogy of Morals*. Trans. Horace B. Samuel. Nabu Public Domain Reprints.
———. 1954. *The Portable Nietzsche*. Trans. and Ed. Walter Kaufman. New York: Viking Portable Library/Penguin.
Nguyen, Viet Thanh. 2017. *The Refugees*. New York: Grove Atlantic.
North, Douglass C. 1992. *Transaction Costs, Institutions, and Economic Performance*. San Francisco: International Center for Economic Growth Publication/ICS Press.
OECD. 2010. Growth-Oriented Tax Policy Reform Recommendations, Chapter 1. In *Tax Policy Reform and Economic Growth*, (OECD PDF). Paris: OECD.
———. 2016. *Accruals Practices and Reform Experiences: Results of the OECD 2016 Accruals Survey*, Handout for 16th Annual OECD Public Sector Accruals Symposium, 21–22 March.
Olson, Mancur. 1965. *The Logic of Collective Action: Public Goods and the Theory of Groups*. Cambridge MA/London: Harvard University Press.
———. 2000. *Power and Prosperity: Outgrowing Communist and Capitalist Dictatorships*. New York: Basic Books.
Orphanides, Athanasios. 2015. What Caused the Crash? The Political Roots of the Financial Crisis. *Foreign Affairs*, June 16; a review of Wolf (2015).
Ostrom, Elinor. 1990. *Governing the Commons: The Evolution of Institutions for Collective Action*. Cambridge/New York: Cambridge University Press.
Ostry, Jonathan D., Andrew Berg, and Charalambos G. Tsangarides. 2014. *Redistribution, Inequality and Growth*, IMF, SDN/14/02X. Washington, DC: International Monetary Fund.
Ostry, D., Prakash Loungani, and David Furceri. 2016. Neoliberalism: Oversold. *Finance and Development* 53 (2): 38–41.
Otto, Friederike E.L., and others. 2015. Attribution of Extreme Weather Events in Africa: A Preliminary Exploration of the Science and Policy Implications. *Climatic Change* 132 (4): 531–543.
Parkinson, Martin. 2016. Economics of Power: Stepping Towards a New Global Order. *Griffith Review* 51: 59–173, South Bank Campus, Griffith University, Queensland.
PEFA. 2016. The PEFA Framework (https://pefa.org/content/pefa-framework).

Petrie, Murray. 2013a. Managing Fiscal Risk, Chapter 28. In *The International Handbook of Public Financial Management*, ed. Richard Allen, Richard Hemming, and Barry H. Potter, 590–618. New York: Palgrave Macmillan.

———. 2013b. *The Current State of Fiscal Transparency: Norms, Assessment, and Country Practices*, PREM Notes, September 2013, No. 4. Washington, DC: World Bank.

Piketty, Thomas. 2014. *Capital in the Twenty First Century*. Cambridge, MA/-London: The Belknap Press of HUP.

Plehwe, Dieter. 2009. Introduction. In *The Road from Mont Pèlerin: The Making of the Neoliberal Thought Collective*, ed. Philip Mirowski and Dieter Plehw, 1–42 (http://uberty.org/wp-content/uploads/2015/10/mt-pelerin.pdf).

Poole, Emily. 2015. The IMF's 'Surveillance': How Has It Changed Since the Global Financial Crisis, Reserve Bank of Australia. *Bulletin*, March Quarter.

Robinson, David J. 2014. *The IMF Response to the Global Crisis: Assessing Risks and Vulnerabilities in IMF Surveillance*. BP/14/09 Independent Evaluation Office of the International Monetary Fund.

Rossanvallon, Pierre. 2016. How to Create a Society of Equals: Overcoming Today's Crisis of Inequality. *Foreign Affairs* 95 (1): 16–22.

Rovelli, Carlo. 2017. *Reality Is Not What It Seems: The Journey to Quantum Gravity*. New York: Riverhead Books.

Sachs, Jeffrey D. 2005. *The End of Poverty: How We Can Make It Happen in Our Lifetime*. London/New York: Penguin.

———. 2008. *Common Wealth: Economics for a Crowded Planet*. New York: The Penguin Press.

———. 2012a. From Millennium Development Goals to Sustainable Development Goals. *Lancet* 379: 2206–2211.

———. 2012b. Government, Geography and Growth: The True Drivers of Economic Development. *Foreign Affairs* 91 (5), September/October 2012 (see also http://jeffsachs.org/2012/12/reply-to-acemoglu-and-robinsons-response-to-my-book-review/).

Sandel, Michael J. 2012. *What Money Can't Buy: The Moral Limits of Markets*. New York: Farrar Strauss, and Giroux.

Sandler, T. 2004. *Global Collective Action*. Cambridge: Cambridge University Press.

Sardar, Ziauddin. 2000. *Thomas Kuhn and the Science Wars*. London: Icon Books.

Scalia, Antonin. 1989. The Rule of Law as a Law of Rules. *The University of Chicago Law Review* 56 (4): 1175–1188.

Schelling, T.C. 2010. Game Theory: A Practitioner's Approach. *Economics and Philosophy* 26: 27–46.

Schrift, Alan D. 2006. *Twentieth Century French Philosophy: Key Themes and Thinkers*. Blackwell Publishing.

Scull, Andrew. 2015. *Madness in Civilization: A Cultural History of Insanity, from the Bible to Freud, from the Madhouse to Modern Medicine*. Princeton: Princeton University Press.

Scullion, Rosemarie. 1995. Michel Foucault the Orientalist: On Revolutionary Iran and the "Spirit of Islam". *South Central Review* 12 (2): 16–40.

Sembene, Daouda. 2015. *Poverty, Growth, and Inequality in Sub-Saharan Africa: Did the Walk Match the Talk Under the PRSP Approach*, IMF Working Paper WP/15/122. Washington, DC: IMF.

Sen, Amartya. 2009. *The Idea of Justice*. Cambridge, MA: The Belknap Press of HUP.

Shteyngart, Gary. 2010. *Super Sad True Love Story*. New York: Random House.

Skidelsky, Robert, and Edward Skidelsky. 2012. *How Much Is Enough? Money and the Good Life*. Kindle ed. New York: Other Press.

Smith, Gordon S. 2011. *G7 to G8 to G20: Evolution in Global Governance*, Centre for International Government Innovation (CIGI) G20 Papers, No 6, May.

Stiglitz, Joseph E. 2012. *The Price of Inequality: How Today's Divided Society Endangers Our Future*. New York/London: W.W. Norton & Company.

———. 2016. *Rewriting the Rules of the American Economy: An Agenda for Growth and Shared Prosperity*. New York/London: W.W. Norton.

Stiglitz, Joseph E., Amartya K. Sen, and Jean-Paul Fitoussi. 2009. *Report by the Commission on the Measurement of Economic Performance and Social Progress* (http://library.bsl.org.au/jspui/bitstream/1/1267/1/Measurement_of_economic_performance_and_social_progress.pdf).

Summers, Laurence H. 2016. The Age of Secular Stagnation: What It Is and What to Do About It. *Foreign Affairs* 95 (2): 2–9.

Tampke, Jürgen. 2017. *A Perfidious Distortion of History: The Versailles Peace Treaty and the Success of the Nazis*. Melbourne/London: Scribe.

Tett, Gillian. 2015. *The Silo Effect: Why Putting Everything in Its Place Isn't Such a Bright Idea*. Kindle ed. Little, Brown Book Group

Tinbergen, Jan. 1966. International Economic Planning. *Daedalus* 95 (2), Conditions of World Order (Spring): 530–557 (http://www.jstor.org/stable/20026983).

UNDESA (Department of Economic and Social Affairs). 2015a. *Partnerships for Sustainable Development Goals*, October 2015 (https://sustainabledevelopment. un.org/partnerships/unsummit2015).

UNDESA (Department of Economic and Social Affairs). 2015b. *Transitioning from the MDGs to the SDGs: Accountability for the Post-2015 Era*, CDP Background Paper No. 25 (ST/ESA/2015/CDP/25). New York: United Nations.

UNHCR. 2016. Global Report on Internal Displacement, UNHCR, Internal Displacement Monitoring Centre.

United Nations. 2016. *The Sustainable Development Goals Report*. New York: UN (https://unstats.un.org/sdgs/report/2016/The%20Sustainable%20Development%20Goals%20Report%202016.pdf).

Wapshott, Nicholas. 2011. *Keynes/Hayek: The Clash that Defined Modern Economics*. Brunswick: Scribe Publications.

Wilkins, Roger. 2008. *Strategic Review of Australian Government Climate Change Programs*. Canberra: Department of Finance and Deregulation Financial Management Group.

Wohlleben, Peter. 2015. *The Hidden Life of Trees: What They Feel, How They Communicate*. Carlton: Black Inc., an imprint of Schwartz Publishing Pty Ltd.

Wolf, Martin. 2014. *The Shifts and the Shocks: What We've Learned – And Have Still to Learn from the Financial Crisis*. New York: Penguin Press.

World Bank and Ecofys. 2016. *Carbon Pricing Watch 2016* (May). Washington, DC: World Bank and Ecofys.

———. 2017. *World Development Report 2017: Development and the Law*. Washington, DC: World Bank and Ecofys.

World Justice Project, Rule of Law Index. 2016. http://worldjusticeproject.org/sites/default/files/media/wjp_rule_of_law_index_2016.pdf

Zaller, John R. 1992. *The Nature and Origins of Mass Opinion*. Cambridge: Cambridge University Press.

———. 2016. In the Dumps with Clinton and Trump. Posted by *Hellenic News*, September 13 (https://hellenicnews.com/dumps-clinton-trump-professor-robert-zaller-special-hellenic-news-america/).

Index

A
Accountability
  and democracy, xx, 15, 220, 222, 223, 231
  and framework, xxi, 15, 81
  and MDGs/SDGs, 164, 165
  and measurement of value, 92–96
  and transparency, xx, 96, 110, 113, 131, 132, 134, 138, 164, 218, 220, 222, 223
  and WikiLeaks, 15, 52
Accrual basis accounting
  and PFM reform, 135
  and risk management, 115–118, 135

B
Balance Sheet Approach (BSA), 117, 128–131
  and whole of government/risk management, 109, 114, 136
Behavioural science, viii, xx
Biopolitics
  and Gary Becker/Mont Pelerin Society (MPS), ix
  and neoliberalism, ix, 49
Brewer, John
  and Britain's fiscal processes, 43
  and the fiscal military state, 43

C
Capabilities, 67, 72n8, 151, 177
  and distribution (Sen), 149
Capital, *see* Integrated reporting
  <IR> and International Integrated Reporting Council (IIRC)

Note: Page numbers followed by "n" refers to note.

© The Author(s) 2017
W. Allan, *The Last Empires*, https://doi.org/10.1007/978-3-319-59960-1

Climate change action
  and Australia, 195–203, 208n16
  and emissions trading/carbon pricing, 120–122, 191, 192, 197–201
  and UNFCCC, 186, 187, 190, 191, 196
Coase, Ronald, 215
  and Olson's 'free-riders' refutation, 188, 189
Conjecture and refutation
  and episteme, 9
  and Karl Popper/David Deutsche, xxi, 249
  and modern social science, 252

D
Darwin, John, 43, 44, 46, 71n4, 71n6, 72n7
  and the fiscal military state, 43
Democracy
  and autocracy, 148, 193, 222, 223
  and ideology, 49, 50, 52
  and parrhesia, 21–23, 239n5
Demographics
  and demographic dividend, 169, 171, 178
  sub-Saharan Africa, 68, 160, 178
Deutsch, David, xxi, xxii, 9, 10, 25n3, 25n5, 29n15, 29n17, 29n18, 246, 254, 255

E
European Union
  and Brexit, 23, 54, 55, 57, 70
  and Greece, 54, 85

F
Ferguson, Niall, 17, 32n31, 39–42, 45–47, 234, 236
Fiscal risk
  analysis and management, 109, 111, 115, 118
  fiscal risk statements, 117
Foucault, Michel
  archaeology and genealogy, 5–8
  and episteme and modern social science, xiv, 7–11, 24, 28n12, 28n14, 29n16, 245, 246
  ideas and power, 6, 8, 24
  and memes and paradigms, xxii, xxiv, 10, 30n20
  social truth, ix, xiv, xxi, xxii, 4, 8–11, 13–15, 20, 29n16, 30n20, 32n29, 32n30, 50, 248
  structuralism, 6, 8
Friedman, Milton, 3, 20, 82, 83, 91, 98n4, 98n6
  and Keynes, 88
  and neoliberalism, 18
Fukuyama, Francis, vi, 33n33, 49, 65, 97n1, 230, 232, 240n15

G
Games and game theory, 13, 30n23, 63, 94, 95, 102n21, 188–191, 213, 255, 256
  and Schelling, Thomas, 255
Garnaut, Ross, 100n10, 197, 198, 207n9, 207n12
  and climate change action in Australia, 198, 199
Global financial crisis (GFC)
  and Bush-Cheney Administration, 73n10
  response to, 84

Global Initiative on Fiscal
  Transparency (GIFT), 134, 135
Global security
  and the classical collective good, 48
  and control of cyberspace, 235
  and hegemony, 62, 63
  and the modern panopticon, 51
Greenspan, Alan, 83, 99n7, 100n10
Gross Domestic Product (GDP)
  and <IR>, xiv, xvii, 109, 110,
    118, 121, 125–127
  and Measurement of Economic
    Performance and Social Progress,
    39, 105, 110, 126, 127
  and UN SNA, 126

H
Habermas, Jürgen, xv, 25–26n5, 56,
  57, 147–150
Hayek, Freidrich, 25n3, 55, 73n12,
  81–83, 98n3, 98n6, 101n15
Hegemony
  and European imperialism, 46
  and US hegemony and
    development policy, 60

I
Ideology
  and market fundamentalism,
    72n10, 80, 96, 185
  and marxism, 6, 50
  religion, 50
  and social discipline, 4, 9, 24, 50
Information and communications
  technology (ICT)
  and GIFMIS, 167, 175, 176
  national security, 15

Institutions
  and rules of the game, vii, xiv, xix,
    107, 206, 213–238
  rule of law, xvii, xix, 102–113,
    133, 136, 138, 138n5, 139n8,
    150, 159, 202, 214, 220
Integrated reporting <IR>, xvii,
  xxvii, 95, 109–113, 118–129,
  133, 136, 138, 138n5, 139n8,
  139n9, 139n12, 150, 159,
  202
International Budget Partnership
  (IBP), 133
International Integrated Reporting
  Council (IIRC), xvii, 95, 109,
  118, 119, 123, 125, 128, 129,
  139n9, 139n11, 195
International Monetary Fund (IMF)
  and public financial management
    (PFM), v, 132
  and risk assessment, 118, 129
  and Standards and Codes and
    World Bank, 95, 131
  surveillance, 130–134, 136,
    141n18, 163, 181n23

K
Kahneman, Daniel, viii, xx, xxii,
  101n17, 224–228, 237, 239n7,
  239n9, 239n10, 239n11, 248,
  249, 251
Kaletsky, Anatole, xv, 49, 73n10, 84,
  89, 91, 92
Keane, John, xx, 34n37, 219, 220,
  222, 223
Keynes, John Maynard, 3, 33n32, 70,
  81, 82, 88, 90, 99n7, 140n13,
  145, 178n1, 178n2, 255

292   Index

Krugman, Paul, xv, xvii, 3, 29n19, 72n10, 86, 88, 89, 100n12
Kuhn, Thomas, 10, 27n11, 29n16, 158

L

Lippmann, Walter, 19, 86, 87, 101n15, 101n16, 226, 227, 237

M

Mazower, Mark, 58–62, 73n15, 74n17, 74n19
Millennial Development Goals (MDGs), 161–165, 167, 174, 177, 180n12, 180n16, 218, 237, 238n3

N

National and global politics, xv, xvi, 34n36, 195, 204
Neoliberalism
  and Foucault, 4, 5, 18, 24, 101n16
  global financial crisis (GFC), xvi, 3, 4, 73n10, 79, 83, 96, 252
  and Mont Pèlerin Society (MPS), xin2, 11n2, 19, 20, 101n15
  and populism, 23, 24, 80, 173, 186
  and Reagan/Thatcher administrations, viii, 85, 98n6

O

Olson, Mancur, 3, 94, 188, 189, 216, 256
Organization for Economic Cooperation and Development (OECD)
  and accrual basis accounting, 109, 124, 201
  and balancesheet approach (BSA), 109
  and PFM, 118, 125, 131

P

Paris Declaration on Aid Effectiveness, 164, 180n19
Piketty, Thomas, xvii, 154–156
Politics and the press
  and modern media, 4, 228
  and Rupert Murdoch, 85, 101n15, 227
Populism, vii, 23, 24, 69, 80, 173, 185, 186, 236
Public Expenditure and Financial Accountability Assessment (PEFA), 133, 134, 141n23
Public Financial Management (PFM) Code of Good Practices, 115
  and sustainable development, xviii, 167

R

Rule of law
  and institutional economics, 214
  and neoliberalism, 19

S

Sachs, Jeffrey, 162, 163, 172, 217, 240n18, 241n21
  and Ghana, 167, 218
Sandler, Todd, 102n21, 188, 190, 206n5
  and climate change and Montreal Protocol, 189, 190
Sen, Amartya, xvii, 34n37, 105, 126, 127, 140n13, 147–150, 179n4

income and capability distribution, 149
Stiglitz, Joseph
and GDP measurement, 105
and inequality, xv, xvii, 155–159
Summers, Lawrence, 89, 90, 102n19
Sustainability
and fiscal and debt policies, 93, 114, 130
and MDG/SDGs, 162, 165, 166, 178
Sustainable development goals (SDGs), 96, 161–169, 172–174, 177, 178, 180n16, 235, 237, 238n3

T

Thatcher, Margaret, viii, xin2, 3, 11n2, 80, 83, 85, 98n3, 98n6
Transparency, xiv, xx, 52, 110, 113, 132–134, 138, 164, 202, 203, 218, 220, 222, 223
and IMF standards and codes, 115
Trickle-down theory, 160
and Pareto principle, 146

U

United Nations (UN)
and climate change, xxi, 96, 257
and cosmopolitan values, xxi, 56, 237, 257
and US international development policies, 60
United States Administrations
Bush, George W., 67, 97n1, 235
Clinton, William, 73n10, 80, 100n12
Obama, Barack, 64, 67, 85, 87, 192, 235, 240n15
Reagan, Ronald, xin2, 11n2, 83, 85, 98n6
Trump, Donald, 52, 61, 67, 68, 70, 98n5, 157, 159, 214, 235, 257

V

Verification and veridiction, xiv, xxi, 6, 9, 10, 19, 21, 24, 94, 189, 254

W

Will to knowledge and power, x, xiv, xxiii, 258
World Bank
and Government Integrated Financial Management Information System (GIFMIS), 111, 167, 168, 174–176, 180n18, 181n20
and public financial management (PFM), v, vii, xvii, xxi, 105, 111, 113–119, 125, 127, 129, 131–136, 138n5, 141–145, 141n22, 142n27, 162, 164, 165, 167–169, 174, 175, 177, 179n11, 180n14, 180n18, 180n19, 181n20, 181n21, 201–203, 218, 222, 223
and Standards and Codes (S&C), 95, 131, 132, 136

Z

Zaller, John, xx, xxii, 17, 101n17, 207n8, 226–228, 237, 248

The manufacturer's authorised representative in the EU is Springer Nature Customer Service Centre GmbH, Europaplatz 3, 69115 Heidelberg, Germany. If you have any concerns regarding our products, please contact ProductSafety@springernature.com

Printed and bound by CPI Group (UK) Ltd, Croydon, CR0 4YY

23/03/2026

02076739-0007